CITIZEN SCHOLAR

CITIZEN SCHOLAR

PUBLIC ENGAGEMENT
FOR SOCIAL SCIENTISTS

PHILIP N. COHEN

Columbia University Press   *New York*

Columbia University Press
Publishers Since 1893
New York   Chichester, West Sussex

Library of Congress Cataloging-in-Publication Data
Names: Cohen, Philip N., author.
Title: Citizen scholar : public engagement for social scientists /
Philip N. Cohen.
Description: New York : Columbia University Press, [2025] |
Includes bibliographical references and index.
Identifiers: LCCN 2024024404 | ISBN 9780231204187 (hardback) |
ISBN 9780231204194 (trade paperback) |
ISBN 9780231555418 (ebook)
Subjects: LCSH: Social sciences. | Citizenship.
Classification: LCC H61 .C5125 2025 | DDC 300.1—dc23/
eng/20241007

Cover design: Noah Arlow

CONTENTS

CITIZEN
SCHOLAR

INTRODUCTION

Scholars today face both personal and institutional imperatives to make our work engaging and influential, to connect with communities beyond our disciplines and institutions. These imperatives were present before multiple escalating social crises drove many social scientists to question our own professional and political priorities and our relevance, resolve, and efficacy. Indeed, I've been writing and talking to people about this subject for years, but it's no accident that the confluence of the COVID-19 pandemic, the conflagration of the (first) Trump presidency, the racial justice reckoning, and the burgeoning catastrophe of climate change have pushed me to escalate the issue to a book-level project. What you hold in your hands is that book. It's about why—and how—to pursue the career goal of "engagement" and the personal goal of contributing intellectually to civic life, together.

I place the citizen scholar in the flow of these seismic social events, which dramatically intervened in both my public and scholarly life (and yours, too). I want to help us move beyond the model of public work as broadcasting our scholarship, beyond the laudable efforts to get more readers or help them understand our work better. The citizen scholar model I develop here is one of reciprocity and openness, reflexivity and accountability. It changes our research workflow and our interventions as citizens, and it enables them to better reinforce each other.

In many social quarters, *intellectual* is an epithet and *academic* is a pejorative synonym for "trivial." And that usage seems to produce no cognitive dissonance among many people whose lives (like all of ours) depend on the work of intellectuals and academics. This goes beyond the ignorance of the uninformed voter who says, "Get your government hands off my Medicare" or "I don't know anyone who's died from measles." It's a deeply felt conviction among many of our fellow citizens that modern life is livable despite, rather than because of, the efforts of nerdy, probably liberal scientists and writers and doctors and philosophers—people often derided as "experts," with quotation marks.[1] And that the good parts of progress, like year-round avocados or Wikipedia or elections, are the result of natural or automatic processes that real, living professional intellectuals mostly just obstruct or corrupt.

This reminds me of the famous "cerulean sweater" monologue in *The Devil Wears Prada*, in which the fictionalized Miranda Priestly, played by Meryl Streep, scolds her assistant for snickering at a choice between two very similar belts for a fashion spread. "It's sort of comical," the empress of high fashion sneers, "how you think that you've made a choice [to wear her cheap cerulean sweater] that exempts you from the fashion industry, when in fact, you're wearing a sweater that was selected for you by the people in this room." Sometimes it seems the people all around us just don't appreciate all the intellectual work—our work, our underappreciated work—that goes into making the daily choices in their lives not just possible, but seemingly effortless.

To overcome these attitudes, Miranda Priestly's response will not suffice. We intellectuals need to make an argument with passionate reason *and* produce facts on the ground with demon-strably valuable deeds. We have to make our case, but we also have to earn our place. Where the social utility of medical researchers or engineers is often proven tangibly, the position of the social scientist is more tenuous. Our work, from social surveys and pandemic trends to cultural analysis, is often useful, but many of us also garner approval (or opprobrium) from the implications of our conclusions rather than from their scientific merit. In particular, we tend to get accolades (or scorn) for reinforcing (or opposing) what people (especially powerful people) already believe, rather than for producing original discoveries or analysis. If some people decide whether they like our work based on whether they agree with our assumptions and conclusions, that is a blessing and a curse, a source of encouragement and success as well as a temptation that threatens to corrupt our scholarship (even when we're right).

Some mainstream social scientists join with conservatives who blame highly visible scholars for the lack of social trust our disciplines engender. One such critic, Neil Hall, assailed those scholars who are "renowned for being renowned . . . people who have high-profile scientific blogs or twitter feeds but have not actually published many peer-reviewed papers of significance," and he developed a measure, the Kardashian Index, to identify such unweighty academic celebrities.[2] The "K Index" was basically a ratio of Twitter followers to academic citations. In a high-profile application of the tool, John Ioannidis took issue with the perception that he and a group of scientists who opposed pandemic lockdowns in favor of a herd immunity strategy were "fringe, arrogant, and wrong"—a view he believed was "created by social media."[3] To prove his point, Ioannidis showed that critics from a rival group had much higher K Index scores and that their "massive superiority . . . in terms of Twitter firepower may have helped shape the narrative." Rather than simply claim that social media reach itself was evidence his critics are wrong, Ioannidis argued that it was the ratio of social media to scholarly influence that undermined their credibility. As ridiculous as Ioannidis's argument may have been, it highlights the important issue of the relationship—good and bad—between different kinds of influence, impact, and engagement.

Ivory tower scolds use the visibility of academic activism to denigrate the work of those perceived as *too* engaged, too driven by social purpose to be trustworthy in their scholarly work (especially when they are members of marginalized groups). Their paragon of science is the disinterested pose. When right-wing trolls roll their eyes and say, "Of course you're a *sociologist!*", the moderate, above-the-fray social scientists blame the victim—the, to their minds naïve, sociologists who entered rather than remain above the fray. But social improvement was the original purpose of social science, and pursuing that goal need not undermine our science. This counterargument goes back at least to W. E. B. Du Bois and Jane Addams. My mission in this book is to promote social engagement and to help make our purpose-driven work more credible and effective. That means a scholarly approach that doesn't shy away from reporting bad news or criticizing perceived allies or from the task of understanding and accounting for the repercussions of such work.

Journalism has wrestled with these issues forever. The *NPR Ethics Handbook* says, for instance, "We're not advocates. We may not run for office, endorse candidates or otherwise engage in politics in a participatory or activist manner."[4] Academics do not have this code. Many of us participate in campus politics (such as the faculty senate or a union), but also in off-campus politics through activism, political contributions, and advocacy—and these two arenas may not be separable. As anthropologist Susan Greenhalgh reflected about her long efforts against China's notorious one-child policy, "I have always been forthcoming about the politics of my own scholarly practice. For nearly 30 years I sought to use every ounce of scientific creativity I possessed to educate the public and research community."[5] When this political participation is within mainstream bounds, it is rarely questioned. But we shouldn't only debate the role of our advocacy when it's radical; we're responsible for our public behavior regardless of its purpose. We don't give up our citizenship (or its public expression) when we become scholars—professional intellectuals—and we don't give up our scholarly perspective when we work to fulfill our obligations as citizens.

A scholar's level of social influence beyond academia is not an indicator of the veracity of their scholarship. But influence is one metric of quality. Work that is well conceived, well written, and well translated for different audiences is more valuable than opaque, obscure work—if it's true (and more damaging if it's not). Good scholarship contributes to good citizenship, and vice versa. This book argues that we should embrace the reciprocal relationship between these social roles and perspectives, which will enhance our public and scholarly contributions to society as well as to our careers. In our lives, this is a way to align two primary identities, one personal and one vocational, that are implicated in each other. I want to give straightforward advice—which acknowledges professional risks as well as rewards—and inspiration for a model of professional and civic life that can be more fulfilling in all ways.

CITIZEN SCHOLAR

The word *citizen* has largely been captured by a narrow definition of legal citizenship within a nation-state. That's helped make the word a hub for toxic dehumanization, that place where

"America First" is a self-evident value and the majority accepts policies that exclude noncitizens from civic and social life, including from basic benefits for survival, such as social welfare programs and even coronavirus vaccination. We should free *citizen* from this constraint and restore its meaning as a sense of active belonging to a community, however delineated. When we speak of someone as a "good citizen," we evaluate them in terms of their "duties and responsibilities of a member of society," specifically as a nongovernmental, civilian actor. That opens up an aspirational sense, as in "global citizen" (someone who seeks to act in affirmation of universal human purpose).[6] I hope to revive that here as *citizen scholar*.

When I first considered hanging this book on the concept of the citizen scholar, it seemed simply pretentious. Who besides the ivory tower elitist calls themselves a scholar? But the concept should not have such a rarefied air. In our knowledge-based, education-driven economy, an increasing share of the U.S. population is employed to work in and around ideas (not just the 750,000 PhDs who work in academia or the three million who don't). The conception of scholars here refers to people who are expert in a particular area of knowledge but who also continuously study and learn. A scholar is not a broadcaster of knowledge, but someone who generates knowledge, which requires communicating—listening as well as speaking, reading as well as writing. A citizen scholar is a person who accepts and fulfills the duties and responsibilities of a scholar in society, to generate and deploy knowledge in the practice of citizenship.

The concept of citizen scholar evokes other terms, which I should clarify. I do not pair it with *citizen science*, which is when citizens who are not professional scientists pool their efforts to do scientific work, such as collecting and categorizing data for projects like the awesome Cornell eBird project or iNaturalist.

My concern, and the intended audience for this book, is the professional scholar or student training to become one. In that, I have a similar target as Max Weber did in his 1917 lecture, "Wissenschaft als Beruf." This is usually rendered in English as "Science as a Vocation," but translator Rodney Livingstone suggests the title could have been "Scholarship as a Profession." He writes, "*Wissenschaft* means 'science' but can refer to any academic discipline or body of knowledge," and "*Beruf,*" although it has a "workaday meaning of 'profession' . . . has strong overtones of 'vocation' or 'calling.'"[7] That alternative title, "Scholarship as a Profession," would apply more directly to this book, though I take a wider view of the scholar with respect to subject and method but a less sacred perspective on the job than "vocation" may imply. You might treat your scholarly career as a vocation, or even a calling, but that's not necessary to engage with the content of this book.

Many social scientists do work with little direct social implication. They are developing research methods or conducting research on a more basic level of discovery, solving puzzles. If this describes your work, or the work you aspire to do, I hope to convince you of two things: first, that all of our work is *within* politics and society in the sense that the allocation of resources (including education) and the identification of problems to be solved are outcomes of socially contested processes; and second, that your work is also part of a system that needs public support and trust, which it earns by demonstrating not just its usefulness, but also its openness, transparency, and accountability. The engagement of any one research career with the public may be indirect, but it is systemic in the aggregate—through our funding, the governance of our institutions, our teaching, and our norms and standards. The responsible citizen scholar has duties and responsibilities beyond the workaday conduct of research, even if they don't involve protest or social media. Those research-ers who see themselves outside the political fray nonetheless owe the scholarly community their allegiance and support in build-ing a knowledge system the public can get behind.

Some say a scholar's politics and public work must be sepa-rate from their research. Others (especially in academic sociol-ogy) insist research is inherently political and refuse to accept the division between the two. In this book, I show how these types of work may best be seen as distinguishable practices that transparently inform each other, making both more valuable. Social and political concerns make the research more relevant and better informed; grounding one's contributions as a citizen in scholarship makes that engagement as a citizen more legiti-mate. I return to this debate in chapter 6. Successfully integrat-ing these elements of our work and lives requires mastering the skills and norms of communicating in multiple overlapping social arenas. In short, the book is part advocacy and part how-to for the engaged and engaging social scientist. In the process, it also emerges as part testimonial.

TRUTH, TRUST, AND SCIENCE

Truth is complicated. There are no "alternative facts," but there are different levels of veracity. Some things are simply true, and some things are true at higher levels of complexity. Neither is truth unidimensional, as in a fundamentalist sense of Biblical inerrancy. Scholars who produce and disseminate truth claims have an opportunity and a responsibility to do so at a high level of veracity, which means demonstrating the basis for the claim, offering the evidence to support it and the transparency to verify it, and having the accountability to admit our uncertainty. You can sometimes force truth down to a pure essence, but in the more probing sense—what I mean by *veracity*—it connotes an underlying trustworthiness, a trait of an extended character rather than a single datum. Veracity is achieved at the level of the whole scholar over a body of work, or across the units of a research organization, or even at the system level over time—the government, the market, the university.

We all had the importance of system-level truth pounded into us with every blow of Donald Trump's Twitter hammer, which, rather than merely dispensing discrete lies, set out to demolish truth's very foundation, to reduce the veracity of all public discourse to rubble. This point has been made by early antiauthoritarian critics of Trumpism, such as Michiko Kakutani,[8] Jason Stanley,[9] and Timothy Snyder,[10] who showed how Trump—like Hitler and others more recent—attacked not particular truths so much as truth itself. By torching public confidence in knowledge, expertise, and the rational evaluation of information, authoritarians scorch the earth to make way for a new scaffolding of nationalism dressed in a cult of personality.

Science, on the other hand—especially in the shadow of authoritarianism—emerges as the embodiment of modern rationality, a core institutional component of the liberal project, which makes the scientific enterprise central to the ideal of a democratic society.[11] That is partly because democracy rests on foundations of knowledge and trust—and not just any trust. Liberal democracy needs institutional trust of the kind that was supposed to have replaced religious faith but that has, in reality, grown up alongside it, each continuously denigrating the other. We need to trust that our votes will count, our search engine will be there when we need it, and our vaccines will not carry gene-altering microchips. In short, we need trust in *disembedded systems*: systems that are opaque or invisible, peopled by individual and corporate actors distanced from us by time and space.

For Anthony Giddens, who developed this idea, trust is "confidence in the reliability of a person or system, regarding a given set of outcomes or events."[12] That may adhere at an interpersonal level (as with marital fidelity), but more to the point here, it involves confidence in "the correctness of abstract principles (technical knowledge)." This goes beyond the interpersonal trust that your lover will come back from going out to buy smokes. It's a deeper, more complicit, systemic trust that permeates our modern existence to produce a sense of security in an uncertain world. It goes beyond individual situations and calculations and evolves into a "continuous state" of trust in people or systems that are "distanciated"—those whom we cannot trust by direct observation. "*All* trust is in a certain sense blind trust!" says Giddens.

Giddens, not by accident, is echoing Weber, who situated systemic trust in the scientific endeavor as well. "Unless we happen to be physicists," Weber wrote in "Science as a Vocation," "those of us who travel by streetcar have not the faintest idea how that streetcar works. Nor have we any need to know it. It is enough for us to know that we can 'count on' the behavior of the streetcar."[13] The explosion of scientific discovery doesn't mean modern people have a greater understanding than premodern people did of the "conditions under which we live," he argued. Rather, modern society has given us the understanding that "if *only we wished* to understand [those conditions] we *could* do so at any time. It means that we are not ruled by mysterious, unpredictable forces." This is what he called "the disenchantment of the world." In modern society, understanding of immediate circumstances has been replaced by trust in the process of systemic knowledge.

From here, and at the risk of offending people who study political theories and structures systematically, I want to situate

TABLE 0.1 TWO CONFLICTS OF MODERNITY

	Rational, scientific	Nonrational, nonscientific
Democracy, inclusion	Secular democracy	←Trumpism ↓
Monarchy, oligarchy, authoritarianism	↑ Scientism→	Theocracy, authoritarianism, fascism

the trust issue in the much grander scheme. This truth, science, and democracy relationship is a core struggle of the modern era. On one dimension, modernity pits science and rationality against nonrational knowledge systems (tradition, religion, cults, and so on). On the other dimension, democracy and participatory inclusion oppose monarchy, oligarchy, or authoritarianism (table 0.1). These tendencies can be flexibly blended at the individual level, such as with egalitarian religious scientists.[14] But when elevated to the level of political or social systems, their alignment or misalignment is crucial.

The clear opposition—the key diagonal of the table—presents the conflict between authoritarianism or fascism and secular democracy. The top left spot is home base for the modern social scientist: science and inclusion, generating knowledge in a democratic social system in which truth-seekers and truth-tellers are free to be active political participants and are also held accountable through legitimate mechanisms, such as state funding and regulation by democratic governments. Its opposite, against the alliance of science and democracy, is the modern authoritarian, theocracy, or fascist system, in which neither science nor democracy can thrive.

The other two cells on the table—off the diagonal—are unstable and vulnerable to scientific or democratic encroachment. In one, the rational authoritarian or scientistic system (of which contemporary China is the most powerful archetype), science functions, but in tension with democratic impulses that threaten the system of authority. We saw this clearly in the tragic case of Li Wenliang, the Wuhan doctor reprimanded for sounding the alarm about COVID-19, before succumbing to the disease.[15] In the other, the antiscience movements of formally democratic societies, such as that represented by Trumpism (especially during the pandemic) and the contemporary conservative movement (with its White Evangelical contingent), science and knowledge represent dire regime threats. In short, both science and democracy can pose threats to the stability of these off-diagonal systems.

The reason I stress the centrality of this conflict to the modern era specifically is to combat the nihilistic conclusion that truth itself has died in our era, that truth-based modernity has been replaced by a postmodernity without narrative or direction. In other words, George Packer was only half right when he wrote, "Trump's lies were different. They belonged to the postmodern era. They were assaults against not this or that fact, but reality itself."[16] We don't live in a postmodern era. Trump's authoritarianism was of a piece with Hitler and Viktor Orban's (themselves inbred creatures of modernity). And thus, truth remains a viable weapon in our society, perhaps the most important weapon we have. If we don't believe this, our mission as citizen scholars becomes very different (which doesn't mean it's true; it just means I hope it's true).

One important role of the citizen scholar in this battle of the era is to make the turn from disembedding to reembedding. If "disembedding is the 'lifting out' of social relations from local contexts of interaction and their restructuring across indefinite spans of time-space," then reembedding is accomplished in part by the representatives of expert systems bringing their impact into human relief.[17] Science is part of the disembedding process of expert systems, which "remove social relations from the immediacies of context." You can't see how a streetcar or a vaccine works, even as you're living in a world made possible by electricity and immunology. But science is not just a system, an anonymous "they" to trust (or not). One feature of the social media–science interface is the personal, if virtual, appearance of actual scientists, scholars, historians, and journalists. That engagement of the scholar in human form can play the role that Giddens described as reembedding. The citizen scholar can be a reembedded representative of the system of legitimate knowledge (scientific and otherwise), partly through their presence in the mass-intimate sphere of social media.

The discussion of truth and science in modern society leaves some academic social scientists cold, or at least uncomfortable. Some people experience a disciplinary version of impostor syndrome, doubting our capacity as scholars or whether our subject matter—agentic humanity—is a proper subject of study with the tools of real science. (For assurance that we are not real scientists, just go on a social media platform and shout, "Sociology is science!" and watch the reaction.) Others are simply not interested in playing a scientific legitimacy game, either because science itself is suspect in their eyes (because it's patriarchal, racist, and Western) or because they don't believe their goals (teaching liberation or pursuing social justice, for example) are best achieved through its mechanisms.

The history of this debate is long and important, and it's worth wrestling with for its origins as well as implications.[18] It matters that when we call the social sciences *sciences*, not everyone so labeled abides. My own perspective on the science question may be clouded by my location in academic sociology. At our faculty meetings (and even more in the graduate student lounge), we have strong adherents to both science and antiscience identities. Perhaps because of that diversity within the field and the need to maintain a working peace, the line is often left murky and uncontested. We have shared seminars, panels, journals, and individual collaborations across this divide, usually without stating or debating it. Our students get science in their statistics classes and antiscience in (some) theoretical seminars. Some of us believe this diversity makes us stronger. I can't prove they're wrong, but I can say that the failure to rigorously grapple with the science (or scientism or positivism) question is not a strength of our discipline, especially in our training.

We don't have to resolve these complex issues all at once, though. The science question is relevant to my introduction because of its implications for the standards of practice of openness, transparency, and reproducibility, the focus of chapter 3. Research transparency is a core element of science that depends on replication for validity. However, even for scholars who don't mine the science vein, transparency is vital for "understandability and persuasiveness. . . . Hence, research openness is a broader ideal, and one from which scholars can benefit regardless of which viewpoint they take on replication."[19]

Beyond openness, transparency, and reproducibility—all essential to the workings of science—*social* science in particular requires scholarly principles that emerge from our interactions with our individual research subjects and the communities they represent. One sociologist I interviewed told me, "We don't have the luxury of studying rocks, where no one has feelings. I mean, people *have* feelings about rocks, but people have feelings about *all* the stuff that we study." It is not just that our subjects read our research and feel its implications, but that the conduct of the research itself is fertilized by sentient soil. For such a practice to be both ethical and efficacious requires principles that include reciprocity, reflexivity, and accountability.[20] And I will argue here that we can't show fidelity to these principles unless we also embrace those we get from science—science as the practice of pursuing knowledge. Openness in our research (within the appropriate ethical bounds) is what allows us to implement reflexivity in our communications outside of academia, to be accountable to our communities, and to engage in reciprocal knowledge development. When a geologist shares their mineral data publicly, most people outside the discipline can't use it. That is less true with a sociologist's raw survey data, but in both cases, the messages sent to the public by that practice are similar.

That is how I use the science question: to launch the accountability principle. But critics of the hegemonic science establishment should embrace these issues as well.[21] That is, whether or not social science is science, we should have transparency, accountability, and a sharing culture in our work; because we're social, we also need reflexivity. Whether our work is survey research, ethnography, literary analysis, or particle physics, championing these principles makes that work better and increases our public legitimacy.

REFLEXIVITY

We can and should be critical of science (in theory or practice) from a political perspective, but that need not include an epistemological evisceration. My thinking on this was influenced many years ago by the feminist Donna Haraway, whose pitch for feminist science helped motivate my own career transition into social science. "Feminists have stakes in a successor science project that offers a more adequate, richer, better account of a world," she wrote, "in order to live in it well and in critical, reflexive relation to our own as well as others' practices of domination and the unequal parts of privilege and oppression that make up all positions."[22] Reflexivity is the quality needed to make social science emancipatory instead of a tool of domination, and engagement is the necessary precursor to reflexivity. Haraway continued:

> Above all, rational knowledge does not pretend to disengagement: to be from everywhere and so nowhere, to be free from interpretation, from being represented, to be fully self-contained or fully formalizable. Rational knowledge is a process of ongoing critical interpretation among "fields" of interpreters and decoders. Rational knowledge is power-sensitive conversation. Decoding and transcoding plus translation and criticism; all are necessary. So science becomes the paradigmatic model, not of closure, but of that which is contestable and contested. Science becomes the myth, not of what escapes human agency and responsibility in a realm above the fray, but, rather, of accountability and responsibility for translations and solidarities linking the cacophonous visions and visionary voices that characterize the knowledges of the subjugated. . . . Situated knowledges are about communities, not about isolated individuals. The only way to find a larger vision is to be somewhere in particular.

Drawing from this perspective, which has echoes in Pierre Bourdieu[23] and others, my position in *Citizen Scholar* is a middleground stance: we can do both science and politics. Being a social scientist doesn't have to ruin your politics by contaminating it with Western, positivist, masculinist, or other oppressive perspectives; nor does politics have to ruin your science by undermining its veracity or corrupting its motives. We have to get work done in our science *and* in our politics. Neither can be sacrificed.

The training and practice of social science are wellsprings of social and civic virtue, which means eating your vegetables.

Emerson wrote, "No picture of life can have any veracity that does not admit the odious facts."[24] Weber made this more concrete in the case of higher education: "The first task for a competent teacher is to teach his students to acknowledge . . . facts that are *inconvenient* for their own personal political views." Leading students to "accustom themselves to such facts" is an "ethical achievement," in Weber's view.[25] That sentiment helps illustrate one of the great strengths a social scientist can develop and then bring to public discourse: a verified dedication to integrity and transparency—traits that are rightfully considered precious in the political arena. To be truthful implies a willingness to confront hard truths and to make judgments about complex ones. And our ethical practice is to publish detailed instructions for anyone who wants to prove us wrong.

From the thousands of graduate applications I've reviewed, it's clear that many, maybe a majority, of students enter professional sociology because they are looking for a way to attack social problems and move society in a direction determined by their moral and political values. And obviously they usually lean left. That doesn't always lead to a successful academic career, but there are a lot of ways it can turn out well. Throughout their training, they will have the opportunity to learn a lot of facts and theories and research methods. And they might also learn to avoid some common intellectual problems. Some things students learn—or learn to appreciate further—include: things do not always automatically get worse for oppressed people; not all state institutions are harmful to subordinate groups; some facts undermine our prior understandings and political views, and it's okay to discuss them; and, no matter how oppressed your people are, if you're in an American university graduate program, chances are there are people somewhere who are even more oppressed. And in the research that follows, which may last a lifetime, we can take those lessons into "the field," bring them into contact with the subjects of our study, and together (maybe) work something out.

OUTLINE

Having sketched out the principles behind my approach and the purposes of this book, here's what's to come. Next, in chapter 1, I will place the project in the context of the COVID-19 pandemic, which changed everything—including how we research, write, teach, and learn about and communicate with society. The pandemic upended the practice of scholarly communication and the interaction of scientists with the news media, the public, and each other; it exacerbated but also revealed the depth of our disinformation problems and their structural underpinnings; it disrupted our professional lives and led many scholars to reconceptualize their roles and redirect their efforts; and *through catastrophic loss and untold human suffering, it exposed an opening for changes to our careers and our institutions* that will have long-term consequences we can only just (but must) imagine.

The chapters that follow include principles and persuasion as well as how-to advice and guidelines for best (or at least better) practices. Chapter 2 picks up the entreaty for social scientists to do descriptive work in our fields. This is important both for understanding our subject matter and for communicating about it with people who are not specialists in our areas of work. If we want to grow the circle of trust around our scholarship, to teach and learn beyond our immediate professional settings, *we need to devote time and resources to the production and dissemination of descriptive work*—timely statistics, graphics, writing, speaking— that can help shape the wider discussion.

In chapter 3, I make the case that *the principles and practices of open science are central to the quality of our research, our public communication, and our accountability.* I do this in light of the pandemic and in consideration of the history of intellectuals in the public arena. Many of our readers will not be expert enough to check our work processes and products for reliability and scientific soundness. However, the relative few who have that competence may play an outsize role in evaluating and communicating our credibility. And making ourselves open to such evaluation is a key signal to everyone else, including journalists, funders, and politicians. By increasing open access to our research outputs and materials, we also promote equity and diversity in the research community by providing more points of entry into the research process.

In chapter 4, I argue that *the participation of citizen scholars in the daily public discourse about science and research represents the contemporary embodiment of the principles of scientific peer review.* Rather than undermining the staid standards of peer review, that incisive social media post on a newly published paper takes peer review to a new and necessary level. We can use the weight of our skills and knowledge, and our scholarly reputations, to help everyone assess and employ the flow of research. We saw this operating at high speed during the pandemic, when epidemiologists' Twitter threads became must-read, real-time commentary on breaking-news research, statistical models, and public health advice. It was rapid and chaotic, and mistakes were made, but it showed the essential value of scholars deploying their expertise to address urgent public needs. In the process, we saw something like the demystification of the peer review process, which is not— and should not be—wholly owned by academic journal editors.

Having put the cart of public peer review before the horse of communication platforms, in chapter 5, I double back to discuss the social media elephant in the faculty lounge. *These platforms are vital to the work of active citizen scholars, because of their reach, efficiency, and capacity to bring disparate populations together in omnidirectional communication.* The tools of social media allow us to meet and interact with scholars we know and those we don't, including those who work in adjacent areas of research, as well as journalists, activists, and all manner of other unexpected, international interlocutors (from vicious trolls to kindly awards committee members). With their embedded one-click language translation affordances, we can now even carry on reasonable, real-time conversations beyond language barriers. Social media are widely misused, or at least underused and misunderstood, by academics who treat them as broadcast devices. The platforms themselves are also deeply problematic. This is part of why the appearance of trolls and mob attacks can be surprising as well as awful—because it reflects the uncomfortable reality that communicating in public makes us vulnerable.

I conducted a survey of social scientists about their uses of social media, then interviewed a strategic subsample of them to make sure my view of the experience wasn't too limited by my own perspective. They appear here and there, but mostly in chapter 5. That's where I address the concrete issues of wasting time and falling victim to distraction, but also the risks and costs experienced by scholars exposed to online attacks. The consequences are not just personal, in terms of psychological tolls and squandered time, but also systemic, as trauma and fear drive good people out of the online public square. This problem is vastly inequitably distributed, falling in grotesque disproportion on the vocal members of marginalized groups who contribute their efforts to enhancing the public good in both scholarship and citizenship. So our solutions must not be limited to the personal and individual; we must apply our efforts to the betterment of these environments, which will require structural interventions as well as personal good behavior.

In chapter 6, I turn to the issue of politics and activism, which sharply divides social scientists and challenges the legitimacy of citizen scholars working in public. The simple prospect of stating moral value propositions strikes fear in the hearts of some academics. For people who hope to get tenure, annoying or undermining people higher up in the professional hierarchy can jeopardize a lifetime ambition and career path. For those who have tenure, if they keep their heads down, not much can threaten their jobs for life—but a social media scandal just might. And beyond personal concerns, many people fear that being "political" in public will undermine trust in our work and institutions. All these are reasonable concerns, but we need to get past them. In chapter 6, I draw on my experience as a member of the anti-Trump resistance, which led to successfully suing the president for blocking me on Twitter, to reflect on the pros and cons of public activism for citizen scholars and offer some advice. *Rather than being a virtue, I argue that withholding our opinions from the public square is an abdication of the citizen scholar's responsibility*—even though, and maybe especially because, being held accountable for them is uncomfortable and difficult. That's a price we should be willing to pay for the privilege of an intellectual professional life. Chapter 7 concludes with a nuts-and-bolts discussion of tools and strategies for the citizen scholar's career as a professional intellectual.

1

RIDE THE WAVE

On January 23, 2020, Chinese authorities were shutting down the city of Wuhan, a city I love and have visited twice.[1] With hospitals filling and the Chinese New Year celebration upon them, 11 million people were going into what would become the greatest epidemic lockdown in world history.[2] In a place with the tourism slogan "Wuhan, Different Everyday!"[3] things were, indeed, changing by the day—for the worse. Sharing some old photos, I tweeted that the city is "massive and overwhelming and made me think how big humanity is and how fast it changes. . . . Sad for all the people who can't be with their families this year."[4] The personal is sociological.

How big humanity is and how fast it changes. A week later, the sociologist Andrew Noymer, an expert on historical epidemiology who was reliably ahead of the curve, tweeted, "Duck tape your underpants. 2020 is going to be a wild ride."[5] By July, he had updated his faculty profile page to read, "my current scholarly focus is nearly exclusively on COVID-19."[6] That would become true for many of us academics.

To take the temperature of my own bubble at the start of March, I conducted a Twitter poll, asking what percentage of Americans my followers thought would end up infected with COVID-19. The most common response was 1–10 percent.[7]

Philip N Cohen ✔
@familyunequal

···

Evidence for undetected spread in Washington for weeks, per @washingtonpost. Also here's the west coast plane traffic right now
washingtonpost.com/health/coronav...

12:03 AM · Mar 2, 2020 · Twitter for iPhone

FIGURE 1.1 Nothing would be the same.

(In fact, the estimated infection rate reached 58 percent within two years.[8]) The next day, as the first reported evidence of uncontrolled spread of the virus in the state of Washington emerged,[9] I tweeted out a screenshot of a live flight tracker showing the western third of the United States.[10] There were, of course, thousands of planes in the air. It was too late; nothing would be the same. (We still held my daughter's birthday party in Maryland that week, but I washed my hands a lot.)

On March 2, I was called on, for the first of many times, to interpret science that was outside my expertise. A group of fifty undergraduate students in my Social Problems class needed help getting a grip on the worrying flow of information. I set aside the day's lesson plan and, using knowledge I had acquired in the previous few days, explained to them how asymptomatic spread meant we didn't have a good estimate of the epidemic's prevalence, but that the infection fatality rate would be lower than it looked. (I said probably below 1 percent, which was close to the true rate before vaccines were introduced.[11]) I summarized what was known about the origins of the virus. I said it was possible our university would close and that they wouldn't be able to take trips to Europe for spring break. I showed them the brand-new Johns Hopkins University epidemic dashboard (a web design that would become ubiquitous) and explained how exponential growth drives epidemics. I gave some advice: "Wash your hands. Don't touch your face. If you have a fever, stay home." Then, for some quick public feedback (and "to see how I look on this in a month or two"), I shared my advice on Twitter, joining a rolling discussion among sociologists with similar experiences.[12]

A week later, with the announcement that the university would not reopen after spring break, and now working from home (in a guest room with a cobbled-together desk), I was making and tweeting graphs of daily case counts by state, complaining about the pace of CDC data updates, urging the *New York Times* to make their county-level data download-friendly, sharing code and borrowing graphic techniques from people I'd never met, and discussing the best metrics for understanding the epidemic.

Meanwhile, in Berkeley, as the University of California suddenly shut down its campus and local schools closed, biochemist Jennifer Doudna decided, "We need to make our expertise relevant to whatever is happening right now."[13] The Innovative Genomics Institute, of which she was the director, set aside much of its work and transformed into a COVID-19 testing lab, running thousands of tests per week for the campus community and eventually deploying a new cadre of liquid-handling robots. Doudna, who happened to win a Nobel Prize in chemistry that year for her earlier research developing the gene-editing platform CRISPR, obviously does work that is much more important than mine.[14] But from Doudna all the way down to me, many of us felt, in the gravity of that moment, a strong identity with the scientific endeavor and our human place within it.

Although I contributed some minor research of my own to the world of pandemic studies, I mostly played a role in the development of other people's research: peer reviewing articles on how the pandemic affected families,[15] screening dozens of submissions about fertility trends for the annual demography conference, advising graduate students, and commenting about the pandemic "baby bust" in the news media. Eventually, that included writing the "textbook version" of how COVID-19 affected families,[16] analyzing the effects of the crisis on the system of scholarly communication,[17] and promoting the use of SocArXiv to researchers. I learned new things and met new people, experiencing an accelerated version of career development and change, ironically at the maddeningly stilted pace of endless Zoom meetings under home confinement.

Millions of people similarly rethought their life priorities in ways large and small—giving up formal work clothes, moving out of the city, quitting their jobs.[18] Down the street from my house, a neighbor, who already had a practice of sharing her dumpster-diving remnants in a bin outside her apartment, converted her yard into a full-time food pantry, dispensing thousands of dollars' worth of food per week to people in need. When the county threatened to crack down on her operation, she successfully mobilized fellow citizens to oppose an order to clear her yard. She changed, and her work changed the community and institutions around her.[19]

DOORS OPENED

Like a seismologist whose volcano erupts in the middle of an experiment or an entomologist lucky enough to be bombarded by periodic cicadas during their field research, social scientists woke up to an event that was life changing as well as disruptive to our research agendas. Through catastrophic loss and untold human suffering, the pandemic exposed an opening for changes—in our careers and our institutions. Many of us were already scholars seeking both *scholarly impact* and *society impact*, in the words of Sascha Friesike and colleagues,[20] but history fanned the flames.

When events intervene in the plans of researchers, we can only respond with the tools and skills we have at the moment, developed in response to previous adaptation. In the military metaphor, this means we're always fighting the *last* war. And we do so in institutional environments not of our own making. If the social context shapes our research careers directly with regard to our personal experiences, interests, and motivations, it does so indirectly through more institutional mechanisms and resources such as available grants, opportunities to publish, media inquiries, consulting engagements, and course enrollments—and those institutional elements create cascading effects through the careers and investments they shape. For those of us who study contemporary society as it evolves, trying to ride waves like this was not unprecedented, but it was an extreme case. It offered the chance to learn how to make the process of integrating our work with the really happening social world more explicit and purposeful in the short and long term—the chance to gain new ways of scholarly doing and being that would prepare us to, as it were, fight the next war.

Consider the COVID-19 pandemic in comparison with a few relatively recent American crises: the September 11 attacks, Hurricane Katrina, and the rising tide of antiracist social protest associated with Black Lives Matter. In each of the years 2021 and 2022, the Web of Science database listed more than 24,000 papers with the word "pandemic(s)" in the Social Science Citation Index. Compared with only 154 such papers in 2019, this was a tremendous response—representing thousands of people changing their research plans. For historical comparison, papers referencing terrorism increased about fivefold between 2000 and 2002. Figure 1.2 shows these trends, as well as those for research on racism and hurricanes, with much smaller but still discernible spikes after Hurricane Katrina in 2005 and Black Lives Matter in 2013. Note that, in 2022, there were almost ten times as many papers on the pandemic as there were mentioning racism. The pandemic radically reoriented research priorities, echoing trends surrounding other crises (albeit on a much larger scale).

One reason for this spike was the academic impulse to try to get work out faster. Maybe that reflected a new commitment to the public good (in time to influence an extremely uncertain policy environment), a sense of desperation, or a desire to share in the pandemic clicks and grant money; probably, it was all of these. An analysis of more than 30,000 papers about COVID-19 posted on the servers of bioRxiv (life sciences) and medRxiv (medical

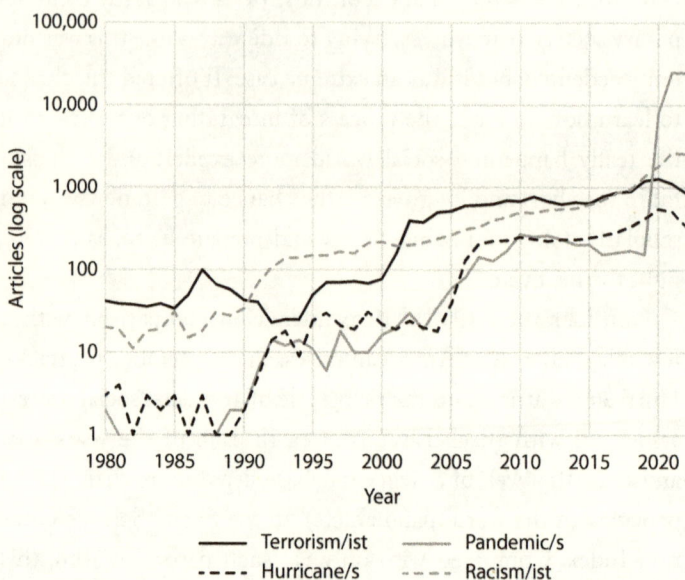

FIGURE 1.2 Articles in the Social Science Citation Index with selected keywords: 1980–2022 (log scale).

sciences) during the first ten months of the pandemic found they were, on average, shorter than non-COVID papers during the same period, suggesting an accelerated timeline.[21] And communication protocols changed as well: 85 percent of COVID-19 papers were by authors using the emerging preprint mechanism to share their work for the first time, compared with 69 percent of non-COVID papers. The supply of research was rising to meet a voracious demand, as COVID-19 papers were downloaded, cited, tweeted about, and mentioned in news articles much more frequently than others, on average.

In journal publishing, too, there were formal as well as informal incentives to respond in print. Journals reviewed and published

COVID-19 papers faster. To meet the demand for a public inter-est orientation, many academic journals (like many mainstream news publications) lifted their paywalls, at least those surround-ing information about the pandemic. Hundreds of journals across the disciplines announced special issues related to the pandemic almost immediately, from the *Archives of Sexual Behavior* and the *Journal of Homosexuality* to *Sociology of Religion*, *Urban Geography*, and *Organization Science*. Maybe their editorial boards were hop-ing to attract submissions from people working on the topic any-way, or they hoped to steer people in their fields to direct more attention to the crisis. But the massive, uncoordinated interven-tion of many journals effectively incentivized researchers to con-sider redirecting their efforts to pandemic topics, if for no other reason than to take advantage of publishing opportunities.

When I shared a list of one hundred journals with special COVID-19 issues on Twitter, Nate Breznau, then a postdoc studying public opinion at the University of Bremen, responded, "[the] pandemic inspired me to research Covid-19, [the] special issue was selected because it would be published faster and maybe carry a higher likelihood of acceptance." The paper he wrote was an international comparison of risk perceptions, published in a special issue of the journal *European Societies* just five weeks after he submitted it.[22] (And by sharing his data and code, he helped other researchers move in the same direction.)

Examples from my own work illustrate the point as well. Before these were widely available, in early 2020, I invested some effort in building a database of COVID-19 cases and deaths, which allowed me to pore over (and share) the trends each day and look for patterns across counties, states, and countries. I didn't have a specific research project in mind, but I wanted to have the capacity to investigate and respond to events for my own understanding and so I could help explain them to others.

(I may not be a pandemic expert, I reasoned, but I had a scientist's numerical literacy and skills to offer.) And I hoped my dataset and code would be helpful to others. I noticed that there was a set of rural U.S. counties with very high infection rates, where there were outbreaks in and around meat processing plants, prisons, and nursing homes. Despite news reporting, I didn't see systematic analysis of the epidemic in rural counties. Thus, I wrote a short paper describing the pattern, posted it on SocArXiv, and submitted it to the *European Journal of Environment and Public Health*, a minor open-access journal with no publication fee, where it was quickly accepted and published.[23] I knew the paper's value would be ephemeral at best, but I wanted to raise the issue, provide a source for people to cite with reference to the problems in rural areas, get my database on the record, and have a COVID-19 paper published under my name to help establish my credibility in the future. In the next six months, the paper was downloaded 1,000 times (from the journal and from SocArXiv) and cited a few times in academic journals, so I considered it a success.

If new opportunities were pulling researchers toward the pandemic, there were also institutional forces pushing people away from *non*-pandemic research. At the extreme, there were explicit limits on non-COVID research. At my university, the administration put a stop to all nonessential research requiring an on-campus presence, but there was an exception for COVID-19–related research. And anyone who published work on non-pandemic topics during the pandemic experienced the diminished attention for the entire world of "other" research as the crisis ate up not just the news cycle and academic journal pages but also lab space and grant money. Not surprisingly, perhaps, a survey of business and economics researchers found that 40 percent agreed the pandemic had led them to shift their research focus away from other topics.[24]

The same wave swept through journalism. The writer Ed Yong had fewer than 2,000 Twitter followers in May 2020,[25] when he took a break from writing another book on the wonders of wildlife to cover the pandemic for the *Atlantic*. After becoming one of the most trusted journalists on the subject and winning a Pulitzer Prize for his reporting, he finally finished that book, and (now with about 400,000 followers) it debuted at number two on the *New York Times* nonfiction bestseller list in 2022.[26] At the same time, the pandemic created a devastating wave of financial collapses in the news media, especially in local news, as local newspaper and local TV ad revenue tanked,[27] and corporate media imposed massive layoffs and cutbacks.[28]

In short, the information ecosystem was upended. The COVID-19 pandemic was not a stress test—it was what stress tests are for. The responses of our many institutions and individual lives demonstrated all manner of success and failure, redirection and repurposing, silver linings, and bottomless pits. The very pace of life exhibited a disjointed gear-slipping, with some experiences bewilderingly accelerated while others maddeningly ground to a halt. Researchers who were stuck at home so much that they lost track of time—the days and weeks melting together—were desperately trying to focus on analyzing and responding to a novel disease outbreak that roared around the world at the speed of passenger jets. People who couldn't keep their households stocked with toilet paper were engaged in massive international scientific collaborations to sequence the virus, learn its diabolical ways, and develop and implement an unprecedented medical and public health response.

WORK, LIFE

We have to decide how to integrate world events, politics, and whatnot into our research and other work. You may not be able to predict the future, but you can be mindful and purposeful about its direction and your orientation toward the social world. You can invest in an approach to be prepared. Some researchers are attuned to the next foreseeable crisis—studying epidemics, recessions, democratic crises, or climate change. Others of us can think in terms of more generic technological or social infrastructure, such as community networks, data hubs, publishing platforms, journalism connections, or specific writing skills.

The decision to orient one's work and career around anticipated or potential social events entails compromises. Among the many legendary scholars with whom I like to compare myself, consider Noam Chomsky, one of the great linguists of the last century, who devoted much of his life to political pursuits because he judged that they were more important than the linguistics work he would have preferred to do. He told the *New Yorker* in 2020, at age ninety-one: "The kind of work I really like is the professional work. I mean, *if the world would go away*, I would be perfectly happy to just work on the problems of real intellectual interest [emphasis added]. They are exciting. I think there's been real insight into the fundamentals of language, mind, human thought, how it's constructed, its nature, its origins, and so on. That's really exciting work and much more engaging to the mind than [the politics] we've been talking about—which is very important but pretty much on the surface." He said he spent time on politics, "but not much brain space. I mean to tell you the truth: while I'm giving interviews and talking about things, one part of my mind is working on technical problems, which are much more interesting. . . . [Politics] has to do with the most urgent things you can imagine—human survival, the fate of my grandchildren, all sorts of things."[29]

If you want to engage the most challenging intellectual project possible at all times, the role of public intellectual might not appeal to you—that's a choice, even a sacrifice, you might make. As a scholar of social inequality, I long ago decided that the work of teaching, communicating, and responding to inequality was more pressing to me than the basic research of exploring and unearthing its more complex mechanisms—even if that research strikes me as more intrinsically interesting. (We already know enough to do much more than we currently are about the inequalities we face.) The opportunity the pandemic gave us was to ask (and answer) big questions about the purposes of our work, about our relation to our publics and our colleagues, about the institutions that employ us and the civil societies within which we interact.

In that *New Yorker* interview, Chomsky went on to cite favorably Bertrand Russell, who also sacrificed his "purely intellectual" pursuits to devote his energies to the pressing social issues of the day. Russell's work in philosophy and mathematics was interrupted—permanently, in the end—by world wars and then the threat of nuclear war. In the course of comparing myself to more important White men, I found this illuminating exchange in a 1967 interview, when Russell was ninety-five years old.[30]

Q: And when *Principia Mathematica* was finished [in 1913], did you at that time have the feeling that you express in retrospect, that you had passed the purely intellectual highpoint of your life, that you were done with your purely intellectual work?

BR: Well, I couldn't think about that, because the War was going on, and I thought only about the War, and things connected to the War. And it seemed to me that all this abstract work was just fiddle-faddle.

Q: Really.

BR: Yes.

Q: Do you think of it now as fiddle-faddle?

BR: No, I don't. But I couldn't bring myself to do it now. I mean, if I was to try to devote myself to it now, I should fear I was twiddling while Rome burned.

NEW DIRECTIONS

When Matthew Yglesias, a self-described "generalist political pundit," complained about "college professors doing hot takes outside their domain of specialization," the demographer Leslie Root asked, "How come when you do it it's 'being a generalist' but when we do it it's 'having hot takes.'"[31] We citizen scholars don't owe anyone an explanation for our interests, but we do have a reputation to maintain, and there are trade-offs to consider professionally, politically, and personally. Abdicating the responsibility to respond to the news of the day might mean losing out on a certain currency, sacrificing opportunities for attention, and risking alienation and isolation. Yet undertaking "engagement" is not without risks. If you have an academic career, you might face an institutional environment in which public engagement is (selectively) celebrated while academic work is what's actually evaluated. In my own College of Behavior and Social Sciences (BSOS) at the University of Maryland, for example, we are told that, "While pursuing dramatically different projects and areas of research, each individual in BSOS seeks to *Be the Solution* to the world's great challenges." Unfortunately, "being the solution" is not on the list of criteria for tenure.

In a recent review, the aforementioned Sascha Friesike and colleagues consider five useful questions geared toward the concerns of early career researchers with regard to "impact work" in the field of management and organizations.[32] These questions concern (1) whether addressing issues of public concern detracts from time spent on academic publications (it doesn't have to); (2) the pitfalls of working toward crude quantified metrics of public engagement; (3) the reality that much of academic research is too incremental to be immediately useful in a crisis (but it can be combined with others' work to make a real difference); (4) the dearth of actionable results in much of our work (and the caveat that our research doesn't have to yield "plug and play" results to be useful); and (5), the fear of saying something wrong in public. Their concluding suggestion threads a middle ground between "heroic" and "non-heroic" approaches to impact work, offering a "post-heroic" perspective, in which "impact emerges as a result of many small but directed activities."

My own suggestions below follow the middle-ground spirit of Friesike et al., without, I hope, precluding more ambitious undertakings or denigrating any well-founded decisions to keep your distance from the news. If my advice seems prosaic to some readers and unrealistic or idealistic to others, I may have struck the right balance.

So, if you are thinking about a turn toward publicly engaged work in your career, consider this to-do list for the citizen scholar:

1. *Study*

We know how to do this. Despite the academic imperative to specialize, the first turn in the work of citizen scholarship is reading more widely. Those of us who mentor graduate students know the thrill of seeing a young scholar integrate knowledge from diverse fields and subjects into a new approach to the challenging questions of the day. We can all aspire to that spirit. By a certain age, there may be no escaping the growing sense that what we know now is greater than what we will yet learn and there is no hope of keeping up with all that's new. But, hey, as the old saying goes, old age and treachery will still at least sometimes overcome youth and skill. Don't give up.

One way to put your specialized knowledge to good use is to deploy it by launching into adjacent areas of study. Our training taught us how to learn, and we should reject any view of a scholarly career that constrains our expertise to the range of fields we mastered in grad school. If you know the demography of one region, you can learn about another. If you've read a lot about a pandemic, you can read about other public health crises. If you work with odds ratios, you can read public health studies; if you analyze survey data, you can learn new survey research methods. Reducing your research "productivity" (measured in lines on your CV) to read deeply in such nonpressing works may be the key to your next big breakthrough, indispensable collaboration, or political intervention. And it might make your life more interesting. If you're one of those well-organized scholars who makes and follows a plan of work, you can do this by allocating a mind-expansion time budget. If (like me) you're more impressionable and distractible, you might need a time limit instead. Either way, learn things you don't need to learn.

2. *Listen*

I will discuss social media in greater depth in chapter 5, but for now, the trick is to get a handle on the platforms as aides to listening and learning rather than speaking and broadcasting. You have to wrangle with the affordances of the platforms to make them work for you, but they all provide tools that permit customizing information flows—using lists or hashtags, identifying key influencers, search tools, selective muting and blocking.

Edward, an academic sociologist I interviewed, is a tenured professor at a small college, and at the time, he checked in on

Twitter once a day. He described one way he made the other-wise overwhelming platform work for him: muting words. As he put it, "My Twitter sucked until I started muting words," because "I really wanted to just stick to sociology." Now, "my Twitter is fantastic. . . . I wouldn't want everybody to know this, but I don't really want to hear about people's kids as much. And so there are a few words related to kids' stuff that I muted."

With his timeline thus cleansed, Edward became free to use Twitter to keep up with new research, learning new things and finding new potential sources "all the time": "I mean, there's some very practical stuff like data visualization Twitter or just people sharing code or new packages. I learn things all the time from that. . . . But also one of the things that I love a lot is—I don't do this, I wish I did—the people who read things and then share their notes or reactions to it. . . . I love it because it gives me things to add to my reading list."

Many academics share lists of handles or accounts by subject speciality. (I left a list of a few thousand sociologists on Twitter that you can peruse at the time of this writing: https://x.com/i/lists/54978486.) If a war or epidemic breaks out and you want to study up, you could read a two-year-old review piece in an academic journal to get deep background. But you should also consider starting with what the leading public figures in the rel-evant disciplines are sharing right now.

The key to making yourself useful in troubled times is listening and learning. Doing this well takes practice and effort, but you needn't invest much before you start gaining important benefits.

3. *Identify your contribution*

You don't want to be the person who jumps into the middle of a social media thread among experts to self-importantly divert their attention toward your work—or worse, explain their jobs (or their lives) to them. Michelle, a Hispanic woman working as a postdoc in a research university, said: "Because I do stuff a lot about racial ethnic inequality, and as, like, a white-presenting person, I also feel like it's not always—it's a hard balance to think about: Well, okay, should I speak on things because of that privilege, or should I also let other voices who have not been amplified? And so it's also like a balance for me thinking about: Okay, well, moving forward, too, how am I going to kind of navigate that, being kind of open and speaking out, but also not dominating the conversation?"

One point of entry may be to reflect on one aspect of a pressing issue from your standpoint of expertise and knowledge. I share Michelle's concern about not trying to dominate discussion about race. However, once I noticed a racist meme gaining traction, which linked to table from a Bureau of Justice Statistics report to claim that Black men rape 19,000 white women per year, while white men rape o Black women. It was a bad table, misleading and deliberately exploited by white supremacists. So, I wrote up an explanation of that on my blog, describing the data used and putting it in the historical context of anti-Black lynching.[33] This was more or less within my expertise, and many people have since used the blog post to counter the meme (which of course never dies), but I didn't go on to claim positionality as The Spokesperson Against Racist Rape Myths.

Entering—or starting—a current conversation can be as simple as adding your expertise to the news cycle around a public holiday. This common practice, hooking into holidays in the news, can promote your work and its lessons, and it has been well developed by organizations such as the Council on Contemporary Families and the Scholars Strategy Network, who specialize in getting social science research into the news. So, although not an abortion rights expert, I wrote an op-ed about the effect of overturning *Roe v. Wade* on modern families.[34]

And without knowing (or caring) much about Jeff Bezos's personal life, I used the Bezos's divorce to write about divorce trends.[35]

For a more substantial turn, consider generating questions for your discipline based on wider events. I'm not an expert on Ukraine, for example, but when the war escalated in 2022, I produced some rudimentary estimates about how the flow of refugee children fleeing that war might affect a country that already had one of the lowest fertility rates in the world.[36] Demographers looking for a way to make a contribution relevant to that particular crisis might jump into the subject of how refugee flows affect a population's age and sex composition. It's not my job to make a refugee expert listen to me pontificate on social media, but it might be helpful to raise the issue, in the process encouraging potential collaboration or consultation down the road. And using my fluency with simple descriptive statistical work and presentation (see chapter 2), I have a way to fruitfully apply a little expertise beyond my current research area.

4. *Collaborate*

Finding a way to get your message onto a public platform is one kind of entry into the swirling matters of the moment, but if we are to make deeper contributions by modifying our research efforts, we probably need to collaborate. I may have the skills to learn new things, but that doesn't make me an expert on everything I dabble in—and claiming false expertise would be bad both for me and for our delicate web of trust.

Some of us are trained to work in solitary conditions, especially in the book disciplines (humanities and some parts of social sciences). And some people work best (or think they do) when they are in charge of a project. But if you're accustomed to—or willing to try—working in teams, conditions of rapid change provide new opportunities for collaboration. When lots of people are trying to retool or change direction at the same time, they will be in a position to appreciate the value of new partnerships. If they're willing to play supporting roles, they may even be willing to jump into a project someone else is leading.

Jennifer, a tenured professor at a state university, channels her citizen scholarship into advocacy organizations in her field: "I am a pretty approachable person, and I've been able to build up relationships with nonprofits for the most part, where if they're starting a new campaign or if they're working on something, they tend to use me as a person who will sort of help them with whatever the numbers that they want to have. So that's the kind of engagement that I do and that feels best suited to my skills and talents, as well as sort of not taking up space that really should belong to people who've directly experienced the things that I've studied."

Besides its direct benefits, over time, such engagement helps shape your research agenda to be more relevant.

5. *Play a role*

Experts in the subject of scholarly communication have developed a great tool for thinking about the different kinds of contributions people make to research projects: the Contributor Roles Taxonomy (CRediT). They created this scheme to help systematize information about who does what with regard to publications, grants, and other research outputs.[37] This helps work around academia's long-standing reliance on *authorship* to determine responsibility and allocate rewards. Instead, they suggest, we can assess *contributorship*, recognizing the many different types of effort, skills, and knowledge that go into research projects.[38]

Repurposed slightly, the CRediT scheme provides a useful breakdown of contributions for potential collaborators. Consider the roles you might play in a research project that responds to fast-moving world events. How might you make your best contribution without having to conceive and execute a project on your own? Here are some of the categories of contribution, lightly adapted:

- Conceptualization: Formulating research goals and aims.
- Data curation: Managing, annotating, cleaning, and maintaining data and related tools (including code), for use and reuse.
- Data analysis: Formally applying analysis techniques to study data.
- Getting grants: Developing support for the project.
- Investigation: Performing experiments or collecting different kinds of data.
- Methodology: Designing the methods or models for the project.
- Administration: Managing and coordination for planning and execution.
- Resources: Providing subjects or materials, computing resources, or other analysis tools.
- Programming: Developing, designing, and testing computer code.
- Supervision: Taking responsibility for leadership and mentoring.
- Validation: Verifying the replication or reproducibility of the research and results.
- Visualization: Preparing, creating, or presenting visual presentation of the work.
- Writing: Creating original drafts or revisions, reviews, edits, and commentary at any stage of the project.

In short, if you're daunted by the speed of events or your lack of depth in the research methods or substantive background of an area of scholarship relevant to those events, that doesn't mean you have nothing to contribute. Imagine the aspects of your expertise that can lead to productive collaboration in one or more of these roles and consider making yourself available to teams or groups in formation. When I discuss open scholarship in chapter 3, I will return to the point that open research practices encourage the development of more branches of collaboration, including both active partnerships and the more passive encouragement and support that come from simply sharing your work and materials with other researchers.

Even if you determine that you have no research role to play, there may be other contributions you can make in riding the wave of fast-moving world events. Using your professional training and judgment, you can make good decisions about where to direct your energy. This might mean helping to organize conference sessions or special publications, working with students who are pushing into new areas of scholarship, or agreeing to extend the reach of your peer review effort. As a trained reader and communicator, you can help relevant organizations do their work, promote their efforts, or widen their networks. More actively and outside of academia, as I'll explore in chapter 6, you might volunteer, campaign, contribute money, and so on—all contributions that should benefit from and reflect your standpoint as a citizen scholar, with an ear to the ground and an open mind.

2

DOING DESCRIPTION

"Ordinarily, facts do not speak for themselves. When they do speak for themselves, the wrong conclusions are often drawn from them."

–Willard Brinton, 1914[1]

Sometimes a social scientist has an exciting new research result that still only represents an incremental advance over existing scholarship. If the research doesn't upend the prevailing wisdom, is it still news? The audience for a news story about the new paper might well be more interested in the first descriptive table or figure than they are in the original finding that follows, the importance of which they cannot grasp without additional context. One response is to exaggerate the importance or certainty of the new finding to make it more newsworthy.[2] My goal in this chapter is to convince you instead to lean into that descriptive material to make yourself a more general expert and give your research—even your incremental results—a better grounding in the real world. This isn't just a question of how to broadcast our findings to the public or the media after the research is done. If we want to increase the trust, and trustworthiness, in our work, we will need to improve how we produce and disseminate description.

One reason description gets short shrift is that academics often consider it an early stage in the research process, something you do before the real research,[3] like the literature review. That's a mistake—both about description and about literature reviews. The literature review is your reflection on the state of knowledge before your study, before the real work of advancing the state of knowledge. Obviously, for all but the select few readers who already know everything in the literature review, that piece of writing is vital not just for understanding your study, but for grasping its importance in the context of what is known already. In the normal course of science, a single piece of research adds an incremental drop in the ocean of knowledge. In the real world, being able to describe the state of the field as of the moment before you conduct your original analysis is itself a tremendous contribution.[4]

Descriptive empirical work sets research agendas, shapes media narratives, and informs students and the public. By *description*, I mean empirical reporting on a social field in a way that is not principally explanatory, theoretical, or prescriptive. It logically precedes these other types of work, which require a common understanding of an underlying fact pattern. And it is vital because the veracity of what follows depends on its correspondence to observable reality.

You can see this in biology, where description is part of the work of formal classification. Charles Darwin's descriptive work in the two decades before the publication of *On the Origin of Species* exemplifies the relationship between description and original scholarship. In sociology, W. E. B. Du Bois began his career with descriptive work, taking an inductive approach to the study of race inequality in the United States before moving on to more theoretical and political writing later in his

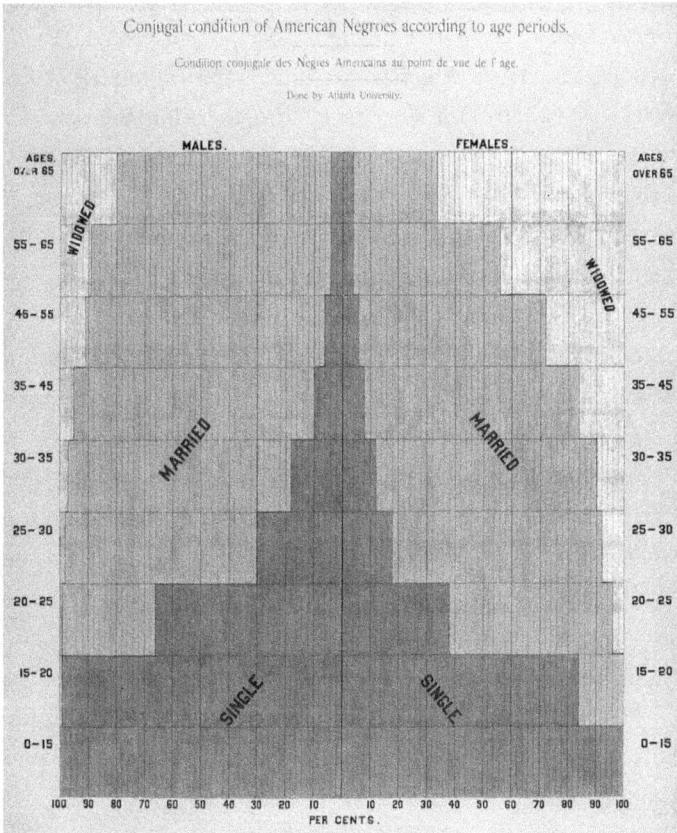

FIGURE 2.1 Du Bois data visualization prepared for the 1900
Paris Exposition.

I made an updated version of this figure, adding the category Cohabiting, with
2015 data (available at: https://familyinequality.wordpress.com/2017/04/13
/african-american-marital-status-by-age-du-bois-replication-edition/).

career (figure 2.1).[5] And in contemporary demography, mapping
the accumulated body of formal description to higher levels of
explanation or theory is a highly valued activity. Some of our
most useful demographic products—population projections—
are essentially descriptive representations of current trends.[6]

The relationship between description and explanation is complicated by the public nature of social science today. We do not have the luxury of quietly building empirical models of the social world, then examining and crafting them into theoretically demarcated packages, with layers of description and explanation, before releasing them into the view of the public eye. Insofar as we publish (in any form) our work along the way, it interacts with the heterogeneous publics in our environment. That is, whether or not we seek to do "public" work, we usually have no choice but to do our work "in public."[7] This means the intellectual model in which classification precedes theorizing is becoming obsolete as a workflow, even if it persists as a logical ideal.

But is it even a valuable ideal? A more dynamic vision of our research embraces the public engagement now inherent in the process of moving between description and explanation. The imagined purity of the research process of days gone by was of a piece with the story of unmarked privilege or the academic interest in disinterestedness—the researcher apart from the social world. Even if we hold in our minds the duality of description versus explanation, their intermingling is an invaluable conveyor of feedback between researchers and the public. To know what is important to describe empirically, we must know what is important socially.

If you are chipping away at the normal process of exploring the questions of the day, will your work speak to anyone outside of your field? Would the public, laboring under common misunderstandings of the trends in divorce, for example, be interested in the findings I discuss below? They might be, if the work includes a clear description of the underlying trends, engagingly situated in their social and historical context. Or, if I am interested in whether employer discrimination accounts for variation in gender segregation across different kinds of workplaces,[8] will

general-interest readers—who maybe aren't sure sex discrimination is even real—learn something from the paper or its accom-
panying popular essay? Maybe, if either describes the extent of
job segregation in clear terms and demonstrates the pervasive-
ness of the problem despite decades of legal protections.

Improving the use of description in our scholarship serves
our wider audiences, and it makes our work compelling to other
experts, editors, and reviewers, demonstrating mastery of the subject and establishing our expertise to address the pressing questions in the academic literature and the public discourse. Readers
of academic work should not have to turn away—to a newspaper,
government report, or think tank report—to get authoritative,
concisely described, current information on the topic. Producing
original, expert description is an opportunity to distinguish ourselves from the rabble of do-it-yourselfers who muddy the waters
in so much of the high-velocity online discourse.

Here's an easy example. If it was mid-2023 and you were
interested in the relationship between the age at which women
give birth and the likelihood their babies will die in infancy (an
issue pertinent to the Black–White disparities in infant mortality), what facts should you report in the introduction to your
article? You might start by citing the descriptive analysis I did,
which used 2013 data.[9] And your analysis might be an advance of
that done by Geronimus and colleagues, which used data from
2019, the latest now available.[10] But it's 2023, and your article
might not be published for months, so why not include the 2021
figures on infant mortality from the latest CDC report in your
introduction—or even run the new numbers from the CDC
databases.[11] Does that seem daunting or intimidating? It is a little extra work, but it's easier for you than it is for your readers, and
it will make your paper more valuable (including to a journalist
pitching it to an editor), so consider taking on the task—and

making it a habit of your research. Depending on your type of research, this may include getting data and performing descriptive analysis of your own or offering important context for your work by using the description produced by others. Either way, it's key to use your authority as a subject expert, your skills as a writer, and your access to publication platforms to broaden and deepen the impact of your work. Put your work in the flow of history. And, in the process, enhance your own credibility.

NO RESPECT

Including recent facts in your introduction is an easy step, albeit one too often neglected by working social scientists. Doing serious descriptive work requires substantially more commitment and effort (as you may notice when you find the available descriptive work by others falls short of your needs). Unfortunately, many social scientists' graduate school memories are haunted by professors deriding certain research as "descriptive"—or worse, "journalistic"—as opposed to serious, scholarly, and, maybe best of all, *theoretical*. This is changing, partly because of outside pressures, including pressure from the high-profile work of data journalists and think tank analysts who bypass traditional academic sources and use primary data to tell compelling and informative descriptive stories (often with powerful visualizations). And there is also increasing recognition that who controls the descriptive narrative often controls the political discourse—as Daniel Hirschman has shown with regard to the deployment of "stylized facts" about the gender wage gap.[12] But change is hard, and academia turns over slowly.

In a classically cranky essay, sociologist Stephen Cole argued that sociology differs from sciences such as physics because most of our work occurs on the "frontier" rather than addressing questions relevant to the "core" of the discipline. That is, our research doesn't change the common understandings and ways of thinking in the discipline, but merely addresses the issues of the day. For Cole, the emphasis on description rather than theory is the core of the problem: "Instead of sociologists selecting their research problems to address pressing theoretical issues, most sociologists do descriptive work that is motivated by their personal interests and sometimes experience. Most of this research has virtually no impact on the growth of sociological knowledge because its results are not relevant for any important sociological problems."[13]

By "sociological problem," Cole meant "theoretical problem," of the kind that could be tested and the results integrated into the canon of scientific knowledge. He believed that the pursuit of "personal or social goals" (such as feminism) rather than "cognitive goals" (such as theory) played well to the audiences for sociology, but did not advance knowledge. Thus, the pursuit of "social reform" rather than "theoretical questions" prevented development of "sociology as a science."

It is as if advancing knowledge requires distance from reality. Contrast this with the stance of W. E. B. Du Bois in his groundbreaking work of descriptive sociology, *The Philadelphia Negro*, published in 1899: "The final design of the work is to lay before the public such a body of information as may be a safe guide for all efforts toward the solution of the many Negro problems of a great American city. . . . I trust that this study with all its errors and shortcomings will at least serve to emphasize the fact that the Negro problems are problems of human beings."[14]

To go beyond simply talking to (or down to) the publics with which our work interacts, we have to expand the research process, not just distribute the publications further. The work you're sharing has to mean something to the people you're communicating with before there is a reason for them to read it. To make this turn, we need better description. *Effective descriptive analysis is foundational to the reflexive practice of social science.* One positive aspect of the bureaucratic imperative of "engagement" is that it presents opportunities for the citizen scholar to marshal resources and attention in support of real interchange with interested actors outside the research community—and that likely involves description.

The stigma of description mirrors the lower status (within academia) of scholars who work primarily to prove a point or teach a lesson rather than use science to "discover" knowledge. As we'll see, I don't completely buy the distinction (although I think we should be clear in our motivations). But even if one goal in your work really is to show the world something you already know rather than discover something new, that shouldn't be a marker of low status or intellectual weakness. We don't need to pretend that our research progresses from the beginning of an article, when we had a puzzle to solve, to the end, when we have solved it. The illusion—or performance—of discovery, and its exalted status in our disciplines, undermine the work of description and communication that is vital to fulfilling our role in society.

Our statistical training, generally built around null hypothesis significance testing, contributes to this problem as well.[15] To legitimately declare a fact as a fact (within some confidence interval, presumably) does not require a statistical test of its difference from something else. And the presence of such a test does not determine the importance of the number. Demographers may have embraced this reality better than other sociologists (although they suffer the "description" derision, too). When I publish a single number—such as the divorce rate—that is science, just as when the Census Bureau publishes an estimate of median family income.[16]

Null hypothesis testing science has its own problems, of course. This isn't the place to relitigate this entire issue, but some of it is relevant to the present case for description. In academic psychology, a generation of scholars has labored under the "replication crisis," in which major experimental research results could not be replicated; this disciplinary crisis contributed to a wider recognition that the scholarly record was systematically undermined by opaque methods, measurement error, publication bias, and worse.[17] One contributor to the problem of nonreplicability is the practice of HARKing, or hypothesizing after results known.[18] If everyone did experiments, concealed the experiments that didn't work, and only reported that they had tested the hypotheses that were confirmed, our scholarly record would be fatally biased and science would be mostly wrong. This is "drawing a bull's-eye around the empirical arrow."[19] Clearly, that's bad (although how bad, under what conditions, and the extent to which it is unethical versus merely poor quality are debatable[20]).

But a descriptive hypothesis test, of the kind I describe below, isn't the bad kind of HARKing.[21] As Moody and colleagues put it, the "idealized model" of "testing clear theory against newly collected data without any prior examination of the data . . . is impractical or even impossible [in much sociological research], because our data sources are collective goods used by many people in prior work."[22] We rarely produce data for a particular hypothesis test. Not only that, we get new data more often than society radically changes, so a lot of what we're studying is variations or updates on well-known phenomena—which takes a good deal of the suspense (or novelty) out of hypothesis testing.[23]

Sociologists trained to look down on description practice HARKing to pretend to distance themselves from description. The idea that description is not only less important but also easier to do than theory and hypothesis testing—and especially *causality*—leads a lot of researchers to dress up what are essentially descriptive findings in the language of theory and hypothesis testing, cluttering up the literature with pointlessly grandiose claims of causality and generalizability. The bias toward causality setting the standards for publication leads to researcher manipulations, especially *p*-hacking (torturing the data until it yields "significant" results) and publication bias.[24]

To make matters worse, our foundation for causal analysis is usually weak. Much of our normal research involves analyzing the relationship between (1) self-reported variables measured at (2) some level of aggregation (such as families, neighborhoods, cities, or countries), using (3) cross-sectional data. If the tests are significant and publication follows, disciplinary norms require us to caveat our findings by stating that they should not really be interpreted causally, but that is often treated as a formality. If an independent variable "shapes" an outcome, if the key variables are "associated," if the findings are "consistent" with the hypotheses, they may be said to "lend support" to a theoretical cause. The norms of the profession feed this kind of obfuscation and distortion. It's no wonder the literature is so opaque. People do descriptive research to make unsupportable causal claims, then immediately walk them back with jargon and technical doublespeak.

This is a deeply entrenched performance—a dance—passed down from generation to generation, at least since the mid-twentieth century, in the case of American sociology. And it is employed deliberately by social scientists who want to impress peer reviewers but also influence policy and politics. As Hirschman puts it, "social science research that explicitly disavows causality is still mobilized as causal for political purposes. We all know this."[25] If we took the caveats about causality more seriously (or more literally), we would reframe a lot of quantitative observational studies like this: We know a lot about how the systems we're investigating work. As a result, we have a theory about how something specific works. We can analyze the extent to which our new observations conform to expectations derived from the theory. And we can apply statistical tests for whether our observations are likely to have occurred by chance or random error. If we do this well, the result is an empirical analysis that helps assess the theory generally. It's good information that helps us understand the social world—that describes the social world. But it is a descriptive analysis, augmented with statistical tests, not in itself a *test* of a theory. If publications, grants, and academic glory more readily came from such a framing, we might appreciate descriptive analysis more in general.

The discipline of sociology, in which most research is not experimental, has mostly ignored the replication crisis in psychology. But there are lessons for us there, too. One lesson is to recognize what game we're in. We should explicitly conceive of more of our research as descriptive or exploratory than as theory or hypothesis testing. We should recognize, and valorize, work that is descriptive even if it uses the tools of null hypothesis significance testing to validate its results. Consider this common course of research:

1. Identify a problem, from history, the news, or the academic literature (e.g., gender inequality).
2. Compile relevant data that has already been collected for some other purpose (such as Census or CDC data).
3. Analyze the data in an exploratory way for insights into the problem and find an interesting statistical pattern (while arbitrarily setting other patterns aside).
4. Write up the results, with significance tests and p values comparing the observed pattern to a null hypothesis (e.g., no gender inequality).

In the terms defined by Mark Rubin, this research includes both CHARKing (constructing hypotheses after the results are known) and SHARKING (suppressing hypotheses after the results are known). These types of HARKing aren't *all* bad, so long as we are transparent about our reasoning and processes.

In the case of my 2019 divorce paper, which I discuss below, I already knew divorce rates had declined in recent years, from multiple data sources. What I contributed was a new set of measurements with newer data. For example, I reported that (net of some demographic controls), the annual rate of divorce for women fell about 10 percent from 2008 to 2017. I conducted a significance test using multiple logistic regression and reported that the likelihood of finding a result that big or larger, using my giant Census data sample, would be less than 1 percent if there were no such trend in the population from which the sample was drawn.[26] Was this discovery or exploration? Did the test support a hypothesis? If memory serves, I don't believe I SHARKed, but I did CHARK. That is, I already knew the trend from other sources and I had looked at the data in various ways before I conducted the statistical test of my pseudo-hypothesis.

In this project, it would have been wrong for me to write the paper like this: "I propose H1: Divorce rates are falling. . . . I analyzed the data, and hypothesis H1 is confirmed." However, I don't think it was wrong to say what I did: "The accumulated evidence [including statistical tests with p values] thus points toward continued decline in divorce rates." There is no getting around the fact that I used a null hypothesis test in my statistical analysis—a useful and recognizable statistical tool—but in this case, it served a purpose other than actual hypothesis testing. My p values were one indicator of my confidence that the pattern was not a statistical fluke. Their use was descriptive. And they were provided along with raw data, code, and other statistical indicators (especially sample sizes and standard errors) to facilitate alternative comparisons and assessments.

RULES AND NORMS

For the official view of description, consider a few applications from prestige publishing. The journal *Administrative Science Quarterly*, a top journal in the field of organizational studies, expresses in its author guidelines a grudging willingness to consider work that is principally empirical: "Theory is how we move to further research and improve practice," the journal intones, "but new empirical findings that disconfirm theory are also valuable. If manuscripts contain no theoretical foundation, their value is suspect." Under this regime, empirical work is judged based on its "theoretical contribution," and description is not mentioned. In practice, this is often a semantic exercise in which an author must first claim their empirical work is "generalizable," then use theoretical language to express the principle underlying that generalization. That explains the *ASQ* exception for disconfirmatory research—empirical findings that are theoretically relevant because they falsify existing theories. Of course, research that merely confirms existing knowledge may not be as exciting, nor as important, as that which challenges current understandings—but a publication standard that privileges the latter creates an arms race for inflated theoretical claims (while also institutionalizing publication bias). In addition, this kind of myopic rule drives academics to contort their research into three-dimensional, jargon-shaped puzzles, in the process erecting barriers to comprehension for nonacademic readers.[27]

More to my liking is the policy at the upstart journal *Sociological Science*, which includes this in its submission guidelines: "Empirical studies may be based on descriptive rather than causal claims as long as the described phenomenon is of sufficient sociological importance. For manuscripts that offer descriptive claims only, verbs such as 'affect,' 'determine,' 'influence,' 'shape,' and the like, should be avoided when describing and interpreting associations."

"Sufficient sociological importance" does not specify a relationship to theory, but rather to society. Constructing, confirming, and disconfirming theories is one part of our work, but it's not its *sine qua non*.

Scholars know that science proceeds by pushing the limits of received wisdom, especially through dramatic paradigm shifts, and this knowledge contributes to an antsiness that infects (or inspires) the process of normal science. This is a meta problem, or a problem of reflexivity, as researchers' inordinate focus on the place of their work in the big picture (with its implications for glory and success) can undermine their actual contributions. Researchers doing the normal science that Thomas Kuhn[28] described hadn't read his theory of scientific revolutions. Once the theory was known, however, it became possible for people to calibrate their career goals around christening a new paradigm (and naming it) rather than going through the painstaking process (which usually involves dying) of having mainstream science slowly evolve toward recognizing an organic transformation. Sociology is particularly prone to this tendency because of its nature as a "multiple-paradigm science," in which competing, announced paradigms vie for institutional influence and prestige within a single discipline.[29]

I don't want this critique to be read as opposition to new ideas or challenges to the status quo in social science, goals I cherish.

Rather, I want to argue that valuing empirical descriptive work is a vital part of those goals. Scientific development often does turn on theoretical innovations (which emerge from empirical work), but a given piece of research or researcher doesn't have to be practicing theory and hypothesis testing all the time. The idea that all social science—or all good social science—makes a "theoretical contribution" is the source of a lot of noise and puffery. We should step it down. As Max Besbris and Shamus Khan write: "Sociology should identify more specifically as a science and demand that the vast majority of research be purely descriptive; science, after all, is largely the generation of novel empirical findings. An ideal scientific discipline might be envisioned as a pyramid, built on a firm basis of description, with a smaller amount of reevaluation, and even less theorization."[30]

Ironically, the perceived need to produce new theory all the time contributes to a corpus of research burdened by petty, incremental theoretical claims, less ambitious and interesting than it might be if we focused on straightforward empirical contributions and demanded less theoretical innovation.[31] Certainly, if you engage with theoretical developments in your field, then your empirical work will reflect, and reflect on, the key questions of the day and contribute to new theory directly or indirectly—even without using the word "theory." An effective and important piece of descriptive work often waggles its head in the direction of the prevailing theoretical frame and asks, "What do you think about this, hmm?" But, again, "dressing up empirical findings as theoretical ones" makes our work needlessly self-referential, jargony, and exclusive in terms of audience.[32]

The question of generalizability is often where social science researchers have trouble speaking to the media or the public—and where the temptation to pontificate theoretically is highly salient. If you have conducted a study of a certain social group, place, or time, why does someone want to read about it in the news? To go back to the scenario that opened this chapter, the most important contribution you bring to an interview with a journalist might be contained in the literature review or Table 1 in your paper, even if your latest empirical findings are what led the reporter to call. Your coefficients (or equivalent) don't need to have predictive power for their lives for your information to be relevant, because you know a lot more than your latest results. You can give them context and explanation.

When the research is descriptive, it is easier to make this transition. It doesn't need to be proposed as a new theory. You can say, in effect, "We have been concerned about this situation for a while, because of what we know from previous research. This new research shows the problem is more (or less, or differently) serious when looked at in the most recent data." There is no advance of theory implied by such research, but it absolutely advances knowledge. Some work is principally theoretical, even if it uses empirical data. And some work is principally engaged with theory, even if it is not generalizable empirically (including, in sociology, much of ethnography). Just a single case study can be theoretically important, either through disconfirmation or elucidation, as we see not just in ethnography but in medical case reports. But all of it relies on descriptive work.

DESCRIPTION IN THE FLOW OF RESEARCH

"Facts are lazy and facts are late," sang David Byrne, expressing a common exasperation. "Facts are useless in an emergency."[33] Everyone needs facts, but how and where they land is crucial. We might think of explaining the value of our research to nonexperts as "translational" work. In medicine, translation refers to turning lab research into medical practice—"bench to bedside."[34] But in social science, translation should not imply a one-way communication flow. Indeed, a key theme of this book is that rather than just communicate our work outward, however persuasively, we should be looking for ways to draw ideas and information from diverse sources inward, integrating that information into our workflow. Doing good descriptive work—finding, analyzing, and presenting relevant empirical information in a compelling way—is an essential part of maximizing the benefits of public engagement, both for getting our work "out there" and for getting new ideas, strategies, and modes of thought *in here*. The common understanding of "translation" implies that the content of the research is completed and fixed, so that the work of discussing it with different people is not part of the process of discovery. This puts blinkers on our descriptive work.

Our descriptive work is truly foundational. "The construction of the object" is "the fundamental scientific act," as stated in *The Craft of Sociology*. For Pierre Bourdieu and colleagues, the idea that a researcher would "define in advance your objective and motives" was "the exact opposite of the real logic of the work of constructing an object, work which is not done once and for all at the beginning, but in every moment of research, through a multitude of small corrections."[35] Without getting carried away in every moment of research, we should nevertheless embrace this task of construction in Bourdieu's sense. As John Tukey wrote in a classic paper on the value of statistical exploration, "Finding the question is often more important than finding the answer."[36]

Figure 2.2 places the role of description in the knowledge creation cycle from the citizen scholar's perspective. The circular flow aligns with the research life cycle concept, which traces scholarship through its processes and products from concept

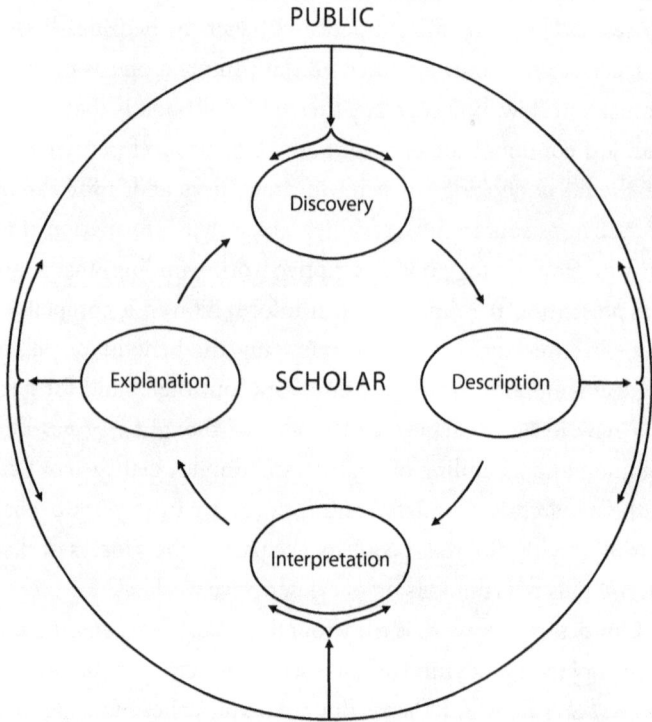

FIGURE 2.2 The scholar's perspective on information flows in knowledge creation.

development to public output.[37] Clockwise from the top, we move from lower to higher levels of abstraction: discovery, description, interpretation, explanation. I'll use my research on divorce trends as an example of the process.

A scholar *discovers* information about the field, through the research literature and existing data, but also through observation and public interaction. Information flows in. (Note this is the sense of discovery used by librarians—finding information already known by someone else—which is different from how scientists use discovery to mean knowledge never before known.)

In the case of divorce, we know it's a common topic about which many people have both experience and opinions, and these are reflected across the media. Most people have assumed the divorce rate is always rising (it isn't), like crime and laziness (they aren't). The presumed worsening trend is a bedrock of conservative criticism of modern family transformations, and it is a simplistic way of blaming feminism for civilizational decline. And yet, existing research shows that divorces in the United States peaked in the early 1980s and subsequently declined. Thus, although I stress the importance of listening, you need not believe all you hear. Often, our intervention is to oppose popular misconceptions as well as those who peddle them for political gain, but to do that well, we still need to take in information.

To generate a systematic understanding of a field, scholars first *describe* it, empirically manipulating and reassembling key information into an intelligible form that can be communicated to the public and among researchers. Hirschman calls this building "knowledge infrastructures."[38] Information flows out in this form. Since 2009, I have been engaged in an ongoing conversation around divorce statistics, on my blog, in essays and social media, and in subsequent research. This has included reacting to right-wing propaganda as well as interpreting social science research. I have reported on trends by statistically describing official data, as well as explaining the different ways divorce rates are calculated and lobbying for better data government collection.

My statistical work on the subject of divorce comprises this slicing and presenting of trends and fact patterns in different ways as new data become available and the conversation shifts, from stereotypes about Baby Boomers and feminists to tall tales about Millennials to recessions and the COVID-19 pandemic.

In each stage, the descriptive statistics go through a round of popular response and media coverage. At a certain point of maturity, we begin the phase of *interpretation*, which takes description to a higher level of abstraction, identifying the most important empirical elements and attributing meaning to them. This involves the scholar's examination of descriptive information as well as information drawn in direct or indirect engagement with members of the public who are responding to the description—over social media, through collective action and the news media, and so on.

Here is the key location for the exercise of reflexivity—when the proverbial person interviewed by a reporter in a local bar repeats back one part of the academic's interpretation of a finding. "I think it's better to get married when you're older," one woman told a New York TV reporter, confirming my research finding. "I think people don't know who they are when they're younger. And I think it takes a lot more time to be on your own, to learn who you are."[39]

With my work on divorce, the *interpretive* phase has involved publishing op-eds, teaching, and writing an undergraduate textbook, all of which entail interpreting the data in dialog with public audiences. The questions in this phase include: How much divorce is too much (or too little)? What does the evidence really show about children and divorce? Is divorce still a feminist issue? What are the other political and ideological interests of actors in the space?

The move to *explanation* requires a still higher level of abstraction, developing and deploying theory to provide systematic connections between facts and events and broadening those in the process of generalization. The explanation phase in turn yields distilled theories and fact patterns that inform (and constrain) future discovery. After some peace and quiet (or coffee shop writing) and some time for peer review or other academic interaction, the explanations are ready to flow out. The new knowledge thus produced—based on the interpretation of descriptive information as developed in part through public engagement—disseminates back to the public through the scholar's writing and, together with the scholarly record, builds the foundation for future discovery.

To wrap up the divorce work: My ultimate contribution on the question of divorce may have been the explanation that declining divorce represented the chickens of family inequality coming home to roost. The rise of divorce represented feminist progress but also reinforced inequalities between haves and have-nots, especially among children. As marriage became a more rarified status, divorce grew less common again. Married people today are more privileged and less prone to the causes of family disruption than they were in the heyday of the mid-twentieth century, when early marriage was virtually universal. Thus, we can read the decline in divorce as further evidence of growing inequality in family life, with a shrinking number of well-off people having stable, long-term marriages and a growing number of less-fortunate others struggling to piece together the family lives they see reflected in media depictions of privilege.

The phases shown here are not categorically distinct or linear but appear in continuous and overlapping flow. And they are not restricted to an individual scholar working alone. From the point of view of the citizen scholar, the important point is that we listen to the public primarily during the discovery and interpretation phases and disseminate our work in the description and explanation phases. An awareness of the overall cycle can help us look for moments of opportunity to advance our research and public understanding of the issues we study.

PRINCIPLES OF DESCRIPTION

On May 17, 1913, at the Municipal Parade, New York City's health department employees presented "many very large charts, curves, and other statistical displays . . . mounted on wagons in such a manner than interpretation was possible from either side of the street, showing in a most convincing manner how the death rate was being reduced by modern methods of sanitation and nursing." In fact, many city departments presented data and statements about their work on floating charts that day (figure 2.3). Despite the rain, hundreds of people crowded onto the streets to watch the data go by. "A great amount of work was necessary to prepare the exhibits," wrote Willard Brinton in *Graphic Methods for Presenting Facts*, "but the results gave ample reward."[40]

FIGURE 2.3 New York City Health Department parade float statistics, 1913.

Good descriptive work is clear and informative, but it also reflects less obvious traits. It involves selecting the right indicators for the question and describing them accurately, and it's based on an understanding of the wider context that frames the information. It's useful when it's relevant—which requires an understanding of the audience, which requires listening to them. And as the 1913 example shows, like any facet of language, description evolves with the culture of the audience and the available communication technology.

In graduate school, we learned that before presenting our regression results, we needed a descriptive table showing the characteristics of the sample and variables. This ritual "Table 1" was generally a boring affair. For experts to interpret your sophisticated statistical analysis, however, knowing the contours of the data going into the procedure is essential.

This kind of descriptive table performs another crucial function: to describe the state of knowledge before the cutting-edge analysis culminates your contribution. Because almost no one already knows what you knew before you conducted your analysis, it's worth pausing to do a little more explanation. Instead of (just) a boring Table 1, consider a dramatic Figure 1, graphically illustrating the situation you're investigating. Then, when you produce Figure X a few pages later—a visualization of what we have learned from your statistical analysis—the reader is better prepared to join you in a deeper understanding.

Over the course of my career, descriptive work has become more central than supplemental to my research, and I think that's both a matter of my development and a sign of the times. Maybe at the intersection of demography and inequality there is greater demand for timely description. But, along with social scientists generally, I've learned what aspects of the work are most interesting and influential to people both inside and outside of academia.

Not all descriptive work relies on data graphics, but much does, and most principles that underlie good graphs also apply to other kinds of description. With improving data visualization techniques and increased computer power, researchers are increasingly using, and presenting, results in graphical form. But descriptive results are generally much simpler than those used to present complex analyses. These more straightforward graphs may be appropriate for academic audiences, but they are essential for communicating with the public. Letting simplicity and clarity be your guide, here are some suggestions.

First, decide what you need to communicate, in words. Often, this can be reduced to three types of facts:

- Trend: Is the situation or problem changing over time? People often come to your work with an olden-days-versus-nowadays frame of reference. Anticipating that perspective can help you make your description clear. It can be misleading to reduce complicated trends to one stark comparison, and the choice of baseline is obviously crucial—as when people come to family research with a 1950s stereotype as their baseline. But if there is a clear direction of change, highlight it.

- Level: What is the scale? If we're talking about the United States, divorce is in the ballpark of 40 percent of couples, unemployment is probably between 3 percent and 15 percent, U.S. median household income is around $70,000. Before readers can understand the trend you're explaining, they need to have it anchored in a scale of magnitude. Jumping right to a depiction of ratios or differences can be confusing if the pattern isn't anchored in scale.

- Difference: Is there a gap, or a divergence, between situations or groups? This is often the story you're setting up. With the trend and level established, you should be ready to hit this point with clarity.

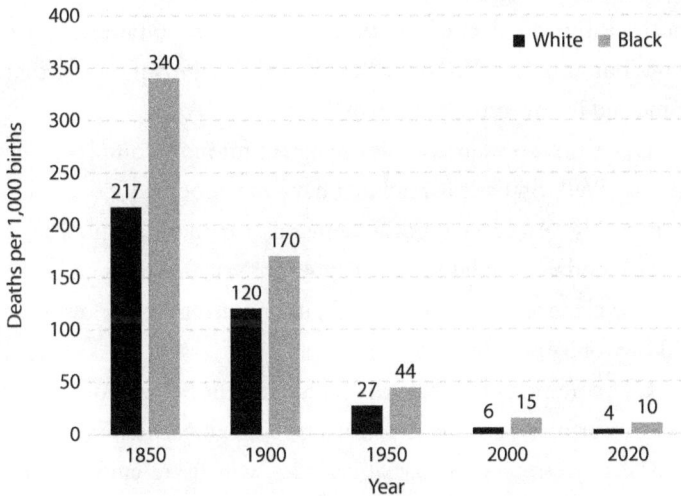

FIGURE 2.4 U.S. White and Black infant mortality rates, 1850–2020. Cohen, *The Family*.

To maintain clarity for your audience, it's important not to pack many trends, levels, and differences into one figure. Especially for people who aren't used to the visual presentation of data, a busy figure often presents an insurmountable obstacle to understanding. It may communicate your expertise and visualization skills, but it won't help inform your wider audience. And even for expert audiences, showing a simple graph can demonstrate confidence.

I have used this trend-level-difference guide for many figures in my undergraduate textbook and in training my students to study from data graphs. Consider figure 2.4, showing the long-term trend in mortality rates for Black and White infants in the United States. This figure clearly shows the trend (dramatic decline over the long run), level (now down to between 4 and 10 deaths per 1,000 live births), and difference (Black infants have always died at higher rates). This allows the reader to see that for both groups the decline has been greater than 90 percent since 1850, but also that the Black/White ratio has grown during that time and is now more than two-to-one.

Descriptive presentation is important for more complex analyses as well. Statistical methods have mushroomed along with computing resources (and as demands for more sophisticated causal models have taken hold). Now our visualizations can have a more elaborate foundation without cluttering up the result or taking forever to produce.

One common procedure that illustrates the benefits of simple, yet powerful descriptive work is age adjustment. Unlike many causal processes in the social sciences, which are controversial or unresolved, we all know that age increases the likelihood of death. When we make comparisons between populations, we often set aside the factor of age statistically so we can describe important social facts and patterns to nonexpert audiences.

Consider Burundi, Pakistan, the United States, and Japan. In table 2.1, I show the number of people in each country who died in 2020 (per 1,000 residents), the gross domestic product (GDP; national income) per capita, and the percentage of the population that is age sixty-five or older.

TABLE 2.1 MORTALITY, INCOME, AND AGE COMPARED IN THREE COUNTRIES

	Death rate	GDP per capita	% age 65+
Burundi	7.6	$ 234	2.4
Pakistan	6.8	$ 1,360	4.4
United States	10.3	$63,028	16.6
Japan	11.1	$ 39,918	28.4

Data source: World Bank estimates.

Among these four countries, people in Burundi and Pakistan are least likely to die—the poorest countries by a very large margin. They are also very young countries, with less than 5 percent of their people over age sixty-five. On the other hand, Japan, which has the highest death rate of the four, is the oldest country in the world, with 28 percent of its people over sixty-five.

Now, death rates are real information. This table is not wrong or misleading. It *would* be wrong to say, "See! The United States thinks it's *so great*, but it has a higher death rate than *Pakistan*." (And that's probably what half of social media would think you were saying if you posted the table without explanation.) But that information is still an important part of understanding health, wealth, and well-being in the world. And it's complicated. There are more old people in Japan and the United States because these countries have lower death rates at *younger* ages; their relative old age skews death rates. These relationships are the subject of voluminous ongoing research. However, because of the well-established and intuitive causal link between age and death, much of that investigation, whether by professional researchers or by lay people in adjacent fields, can proceed from a simpler descriptive comparison: death rates adjusted for age. This simple adjustment can be communicated clearly and descriptively to a general readership.

In the four panels of figure 2.5, I show that (a) rich countries have higher death rates, which seems counterintuitive; but, (b) they also have older populations; and of course (c) older populations have higher death rates; so when we isolate income from age, we see that, (d) at a given age, rich countries have lower death rates. Depending on the purpose, you could cut straight to the last panel and describe it simply: "Once we take into account their older average age, we see there is a strong relationship between national income and death rates." And the figure

A. Crude death rate by GDP per capita

B. Percent age 65+ by GDP per capita

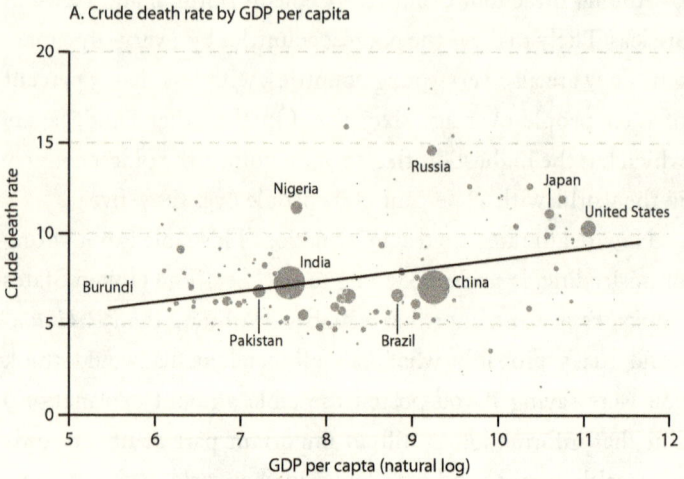

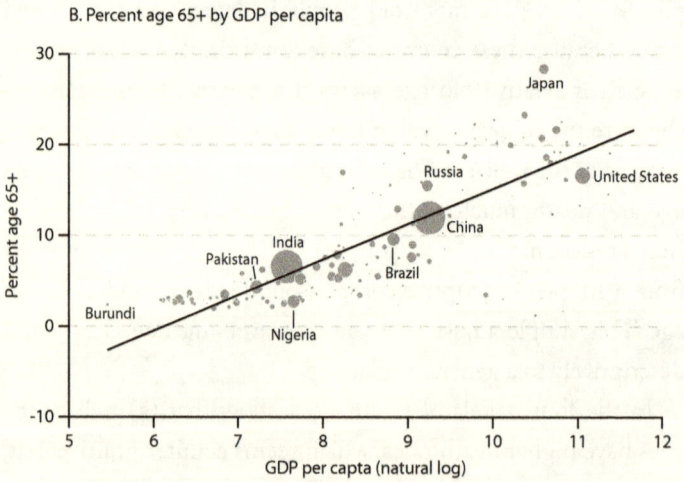

FIGURE 2.5 The relationship between gross domestic product (GDP) per capita, crude death rate, and percentage of population age sixty-five and older: 186 countries in 2020.

Note: Data source: World Bank estimates.

C. Crude death rate by percent age 65+

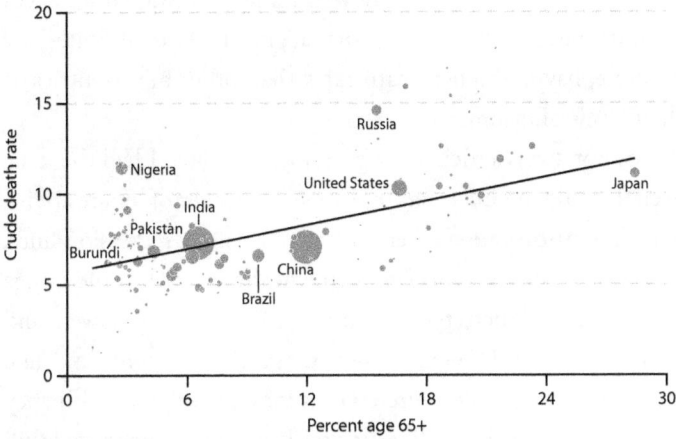

D. Crude death rate by GDP per capita, with age held constant at the mean

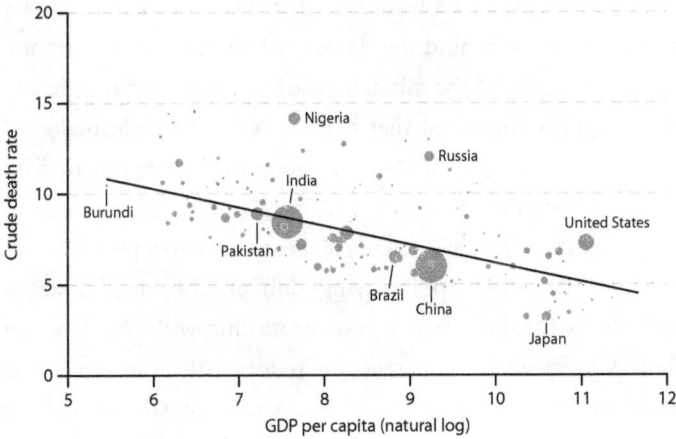

FIGURE 2.5 (*Continued*)

shows us what we may have wanted to explain from the start: "At a given level of income, however, there are wide differences in death rates, with Nigeria, Russia, and the United States, for example, having higher death rates than other big countries at their levels of income."

I'm not a very efficient programmer, but once I had the data, even I could produce figure 2.5—four panels of figures, with scaled, semi-opaque markers, selective labeling, regression lines, and titles—with just forty-nine lines of Stata code. Some things get better and better—like software, computing power, and transmission speeds—and other things change (fonts and line styles, shapes and colors, preferences for types of graph). Fluency in data communication, like writing, is not a once-mastered skill but an ongoing process of socially engaged development. As is the case with our professional attire, many academics have a knack for falling behind the times aesthetically—maybe from a self-isolating life of the mind, maybe because of social deficiencies or quirks correlated that balance out our intellectual acumen. That's all fine, but it's not a good excuse for out-of-date communication styles.

Our polarized public discourse means some people will react to your descriptive work by saying "duh" or "obviously," or argue with the point they assume you are making with the data you show. Clarity and transparency help anticipate, and direct, the likely reactions to your descriptive work. Social media have made us constant judges and objects of judgment, which is terrible for many reasons. However, if you're in the communicating professions (if you're reading this book), there is an advantage to that, too: practice.

I'll return to social media strategy in chapter 5, but with regard to descriptive communication skills, the ability to get rapid feedback on repeated attempts at disseminating facts and data is a great opportunity. To put this affordance into practice, I developed a social media post heading, "Now you know," and started the Demographic Fact A Day Twitter account (@demfactaday) for newsworthy statistics from secondary sources or my own calculations, presented without comment. Calling this informative data visualization series "Now you know" was aspirational. When people take issue with the presumed conclusions, my answer is in the title—at least we all have the same information now. This project served the dual function of intervening in the attention cycle of the moment without argument (I love to argue on social media, but not every minute) and practicing data presentation skills with a responsive audience. If looking back on these is cringe-inducing, that's instructive, too (I saved the ones that seemed effective at the time here: https://www.philipncohen.com /citizenscholar/now-you-know).

DESCRIPTIVE INTERVENTION

If we want to help move the public discourse along, or change its direction, then a well-placed, well-informed, descriptive debunking may be invaluable. Falsification as a scientific method may be a hassle for the modern working scientist (thank you, Karl Popper), but for debunking, it's the opposite—it's much easier to debunk things than to bunk them in the first place (a topic I return to in depth in chapter 4, with regard to peer review). To wit: theories or explanations in social science have to leap descriptive hurdles to gain traction. If you think women are disadvantaged relative to men because of sexist discrimination, for example, rather than because of their personality types or biological predispositions, how will you go about proving or testing this idea? First you have to show that women have less of some valuable resource (money, power, occupational status) and then show it again for men and women who are similarly situated (that is, entering into a set of interactions with similar skills or endowments). The first hurdle is descriptive. Of course, it *could* be the case that women have more of something than men do *and* that they suffer from sexist discrimination that prevents them from having even more, but it's hard to even get that theory off the ground if your first descriptive pass shows women dominating over men (and the problem wouldn't be as important in that case).

It's nice for the modern critical debunker to be on the other side of the burden of proof once in a while. An incisive descriptive analysis can construct a formidable obstacle in the path of any number of bad theories or explanations of social phenomena. Here again, our methodological skills, our contextual knowledge, and our ability to access relevant data combine to create opportunities for valuable interventions.[41]

Here are two bad theories I have encountered, then countered with descriptive analysis: mobile phones causing auto fatalities and single mothers causing violent crime. In the years between 9/11 and the pandemic, when existential threats were out of the headlines—when we should have been paying more attention to climate change—"distracted driving" emerged as the way "kids these days" were threatening to kill us all. Something *had* to be done! Food, makeup, and Palm Pilots were cited as threats to safe driving, but focus soon shifted most directly to mobile phones. A cadre of well-meaning journalists, lawmakers, and corporations eventually converged on the idea that people distracted by phones were causing untold deaths on the roads. It was a classic distraction, an outlet for venting about rapid social and technological change, a moral panic.[42]

The real danger on our roads, of course, is driving itself—our fatally underdeveloped public transportation, melting glaciers and boiling seas, and, yes, traffic fatalities are all caused by our structural addiction to driving cars and trucks. How we drive them is important, naturally (and we've made great strides in reducing drunk driving and improving vehicle safety), but secondary to the threat posed by the system itself. Like divorce and laziness, however, many people assume the roads are always getting more and more dangerous. Everyone knows mobile phones are everywhere, and everyone has encountered obnoxious drivers on the phone. Blaming them for the rising tide of dangers on the road was easy. In Washington, DC, the Diane Rehm show aired, "Distracted Driving: What It Will Take to Lower Fatalities," at a time when traffic deaths per mile were down 80 percent from historic highs. The *New York Times* columnist David Leonhardt called the upward blip in traffic deaths in 2015 and 2016 a public health crisis and ridiculously declared that "the only plausible cause is the texting, calling, watching and posting that people now do."[43]

At its most extreme, a chain reaction of telephone game–like errors committed by purpose-driven advocates (and their marketing arms) led to unchecked, preposterous claims. In 2013, *Mother Jones* falsely repeated an unsourced claim that "the leading cause of death for teenage drivers is now texting, not drinking, with nearly a dozen teens dying each day in a texting-related car crash." *New York Times* reporter Matt Richtel picked up on that for the subsequent marketing for his book, *A Deadly Wandering*,[44] with his website declaring: "texting and driving continues to claim 11 teen lives per day." For the truly curious, this was obviously false, as readily available federal statistics revealed that 7.7 teens were dying per day from *all* car accidents, regardless of their cause. But in a moral panic hype cycle, no one cares, and statistical naysayers can be marginalized as callous, pointy-headed hair-splitters.

Of course, distracted drivers cause accidents, and one thing they are distracted by is their mobile devices. I suspect that, in the same way that mobile phones have replaced so many other things, phones are displacing other distractions. More people are distracted by phones, and fewer are distracted by flashlights, compasses, slide rules, cameras, maps, car radios, and in-person friends. The much greater cause of America's (still high) road-way mortality is how much Americans drive (especially in large vehicles) and transport goods in trucks. Safety improvements are swimming against the tide: from 1981 to 2021, the average weight of new U.S. passenger vehicles increased by 6 percent, or more than 200 pounds.[45] How many people bought bigger cars—putting everyone else at greater risk—to protect themselves from the threat of drivers using their phones?[46]

Meanwhile, violent crime followed a somewhat similar path. In 1991, the official violent crime rate in the United States peaked at 758 reported crimes per 100,000 residents, an upward spike of more than one-third in just six years. That year, given the choice of whether the country was spending "too much," "too little," or "about the right amount" on "halting the rising crime rate," 68 percent of Americans told the General Social Survey we were spending too little. Three decades and tens of millions of prison stints later, 72 percent of people gave the same answer to that question—despite the fact that the crime rate had fallen by roughly half in the intervening years.

This is perhaps the best example of a near-perfect disconnect between public opinion and social reality. The moral panic about crime does not rest on crime rates. It attaches a constant fear of crime to the perceived moral decay of the moment and embeds itself in a narrative about the traditional past being degraded by the mores of the modern present. The public opinion equation was perhaps first described in England in the early 1970s by Stuart Hall: a perceived rise in violent crime, plus the soft ("modern") treatment of criminals by police and the judicial system, leads to the evergreen demand for a return to the tough ("traditional") treatment of the past.[47] In the United States, the moral panic about crime is heavily racialized, and it has attached specifically to the family structure and welfare status of Black families: single Black mothers on welfare (and irresponsible "absent" fathers) generate violent sons. Of course, it is quite possible that the children of single mothers are more likely to end up committing crimes than those raised by married parents (on average, they have harder lives, live in poorer areas, and are less well supervised). But there is no way the rise in single parenthood can account for the rapid rise and then fall of crime rates that peaked in 1991.

In both cases—mobile phones and traffic fatalities, single mothers and violent crime (figure 2.6)—there is both the possibility of real causal processes and the absolute reality of hype-driven, politically motivated panic narratives playing on the fears and assumptions of the underinformed public. And in both cases, there is a straightforward obstacle for the theory to overcome—the trends don't line up with the causal narrative. A plain descriptive debunking seriously undermines the simplistic story. Lots of false narratives do line up with time trends—like the proverbial correlation between rising organic food sales and autism diagnosis rates. So this method doesn't work for fixing all of our misinformation ills. But it's an important first-pass tool, and many social science readers of this book have the capacity to contribute such descriptive debunkings to the issues they confront.

A simple debunking obviously won't resolve either of these public debates because there are strong interests at work and they have their own momentum. But with descriptive analysis like this—playing the falsifying spoiler to the unproven hypothesis of

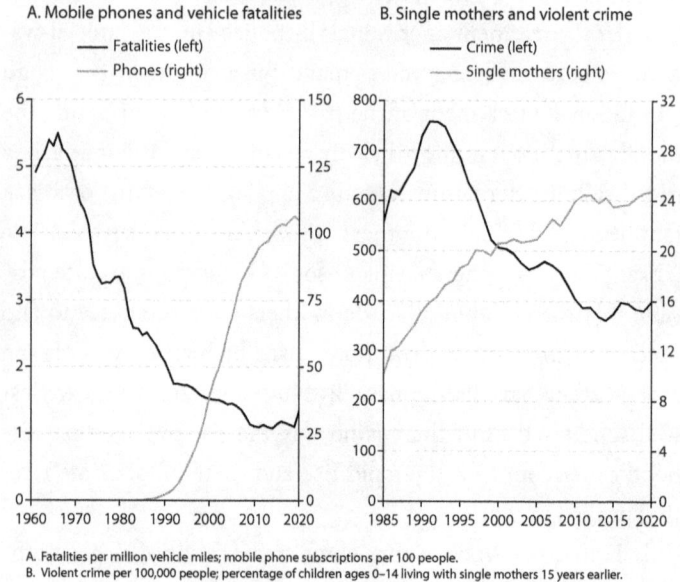

A. Mobile phones and vehicle fatalities

—— Fatalities (left)
------ Phones (right)

B. Single mothers and violent crime

—— Crime (left)
------ Single mothers (right)

A. Fatalities per million vehicle miles; mobile phone subscriptions per 100 people.
B. Violent crime per 100,000 people; percentage of children ages 0–14 living with single mothers 15 years earlier.

FIGURE 2.6 Mobile phones and traffic fatalities; single mothers and violent crime.

Note: Data sources: National Highway Traffic Safety Administration (traffic fatalities), World Bank (phones), Uniform Crime Reports (crimes), Current Population Survey (single mothers).

a pernicious media narrative—we can help anchor the debate and provide grounding for its potential deconstruction. Crucially, we don't have to be afraid or ashamed that the problem of explaining crime trends or traffic fatalities is difficult to solve, because that's not how we enter the dialog. We can show with straightforward statistics that single-mother families are not likely to be the root cause of the problem, that even if distracted phone users are crashing their cars, that can't explain much of what's happening on our roads. We can erect hurdles for the moral panic's hypotheses. Single motherhood became more and more common as the crime rate fell after 1991, and traffic fatalities were falling for decades, and continued to fall, after the invention of mobile phones. Simply showing the crossing trend lines at least makes the mythmakers run uphill. It's worth a try.

A citizen scholar needs knowledge and understanding both deep and wide. That is one of the great privileges of an intellectual career—a career in which claiming your newspaper subscriptions as a tax deduction is not a cheat, but an honest recognition of the true dimensions of the job. Being generally informed and widely engaged allows us to grapple with the contexts for our work and its implications outside our laptops. That's essential to our sense of place in the social world, and it creates an opportunity as well as an obligation to help others similarly situate the scholarship of the day in the stream of historical and current events. Being engaged with wider publics, reading the news a lot, and observing or participating in debates over trends and findings helps keep you current—and so does timely, relevant descriptive work.

To be more involved, and possibly even more influential, we can choose research topics that matter to people outside our workplaces. But to make that work, we have to produce research that they can read and respond to. One key element in that is high-quality description. Another is openness and transparency in our research, the topic of the next chapter.

3

OPEN SCHOLARSHIP

Professor Francesca Gino was one of the highest paid employees at Harvard Business School (with a university salary of almost $500,000) and listed a speaker's fee of $50,000–$100,000.[1] A behavioral economist, she had authored successful books and hundreds of studies, many of them about the psychology of cheating, dishonesty, and unethical behavior (you know where this is going). I don't know what exactly motivated Gino to fake data on her road to success. Maybe it was the money. ("Money can make us so focused on our selfish motives that it can lead us to behave unethically," she wrote in a 2014 op-ed.[2]) Or maybe she really did care about the truth and was just so sure she was right that she nudged the data to keep up with her insights.

In Gino's world, studies often consist of individuals—even just a couple hundred of them—filling out a survey or completing some online task disguised to suss out their underlying behavioral motivation, emotional state, or thought process. The research answers questions like whether people like cleaning products more after they write an essay they don't agree with,[3] whether people are more honest about reporting their expenses after they've had to make an ethics declaration,[4] and how people respond to a fellow participant who cheats for a higher reward.[5] As we have learned from unpacking the fraud Gino committed (along with at least one of her co-authors, Duke University professor Dan Ariely), success or failure at proving a hypothesis can turn on the responses of a few survey responses manipulated in a spreadsheet—maybe making the difference in a meteoric rise to academic stardom, with tens of thousands of citations, and book deals to match.[6]

Academic dishonesty undermines the entire scholarly enterprise by eroding public trust and confidence in researchers. "Trust is most relevant in situations when uncertainty is high," write Oliver Schilke and colleagues, "and it is in exactly those situations that trust is most difficult to produce."[7] Academic research is one of those situations because there is no way for readers to verify the information we get from the scholarly record, much of which (such as vaccine research) we desperately rely on. In response to this uncertainty, we have constructed elaborate institutional mechanisms to induce and signal trustworthiness (such as degrees, parades with medieval outfits, and peer review). As messy and inequitable as these mechanisms are, we know they are essential to the business of knowledge creation in part because of their trust function.

Crucially, Gino's fraud was only exposed because of the rules and norms in her professional field requiring transparency and data sharing. The "replication crisis" in psychology, and the subsequent generation of cultural and political intervention by open science advocates, created the context in which psychology and behavioral economics scholars performing empirical research became expected to provide open access to their data and other research materials. And infrastructure is now available to make that easily practical. In the 2021 fraud scandal involving her work with Dan Ariely, in which Gino was not directly implicated, she demonstrated her deference to this reality. "Though very pain-ful," she said in what we now know was a hollow apology, "this experience has reinforced my strong commitment to the Open Science movement."[8]

How would you know if scientific research was fraudulent? The 2011 case of massive fraud by Dutch psychologist Diederik Stapel, and the grueling investigation involving three universities that followed, was paradigmatic. After credible whistleblowers came forward with evidence of fraud in Stapel's work, investiga-tive committees assembled as complete a record as possible of the dozens of studies and experiments he had supposedly con-ducted. In many cases, original data and research materials were not available (if they ever existed); in others, only partial materi-als could be retrieved by his (perhaps innocent) co-authors. The limited documentation allowed only for probabilistic assess-ments of whether fraud had occurred, based on scrutinizing the data, attempting reanalysis, and performing other forensic work. Using a self-imposed standard of evidence, the investiga-tors declared fifty-five publications to be fraudulent. But they would have been much more definitive if his work had been done later, in the post-open era of psychological research. Maybe he wouldn't have committed the fraud at all.[9]

In another high-profile case, a UCLA political science grad-uate student, Michael LaCour, and a Columbia professor, Don-ald Green, published a 2014 paper in *Science* purporting to show that short, doorstep conversations with gay canvassers could have dramatic effects on individual attitudes toward gay rights. The finding, on a topical issue, was so striking (and the journal so respected) that the research was featured in multiple major media outlets. It also inspired several researchers to attempt a replication and extension—which is how the fraud was discov-ered. It soon emerged that LaCour (not Green) had not only fabricated data (which were never collected) but also lied about receiving multiple grants and created a fake paper trail to cover his tracks. Again, the fraud was only exposed because some data for the study were publicly available. Still, because he denied the fraud and the original data files were never recovered, the precise details of the hoax were never uncovered. *Science* retracted the paper, and LaCour's academic career ended.[10]

The varying trajectories of cases like these make clear that openness is an essential tool for the prevention and redress of academic fraud.

It is tempting to imagine that if all research materials were always already available to some authority in real time, fraud could always be prevented or detected. Maybe in the future our artificial intelligence overlords will impose such a system (though they won't need our research to know everything, so I'm not sure why they would bother). More reasonably, and realistically, we can continue to move the culture—the norms and rules—of scholarship in the direction of openness so as to reap the benefits of such scrutiny (including deterrent effects) without too many of the Big Brother downsides. More systematically, fraud is just one dramatic instance of our system's frailty, as a large literature now seeks to define and quantify a long list of (disturbingly prevalent) "questionable research practices" from failing to report contradictory results or disclose conflicts of interest to inaccurate citations and poor recordkeeping.[11]

In this chapter, I want to make the much broader case that our system of scholarly communication in the social sciences will work better in many ways if we subject it more rigorously to the principles of transparency and openness.[12] That term, *scholarly communication*, comes from library and information sciences, where it's used to mean the entire system "through which research and other scholarly writings are *created*, *evaluated* for quality, *disseminated* to the scholarly community, and *preserved* for future use" (emphasis added).[13] Openness throughout this process—carefully and appropriately, not carelessly and universally applied—is a vital component of our work as citizen scholars. In other words, we can't just disseminate our final products openly to achieve the benefits of open scholarship. We have to be more systematic than that.

SocArXiv, which I founded in 2016 with a group of sociologists and library leaders, was an intervention in that direction (it's pronounced *so-shARchive*). It is an archive for the storage and dissemination of social science (and adjacent discipline) papers, free to use and to read, posted at different stages of development. The service was the child of frustration and opportunity. To me and many other researchers, the idea that people couldn't read our painstakingly crafted work until after it was submitted, reviewed, revised, reviewed, revised (repeat), accepted, and finally "printed" had become untenable in an era when many news organizations were sharing sophisticated original data analyses with millions of readers mere moments after they got some half-baked idea from a Twitter thread.

Everyone has a story. Here's one. Lucia Lykke, then a graduate student in our program, and I wrote a paper called "The Widening Gender Gap in Opposition to Pornography, 1975–2012." It reported a straightforward, descriptive result: the proportion of respondents to the General Social Survey who say there should be laws against pornography had declined, but it had declined faster for men than for women, so the gender gap in this attitude had increased. We offered some theoretically informed speculation about why opposition to pornography was breaking down, even as women remained more likely than men to object to pornography, and used a sociological frame to explain why this was significant. We wrote it up and submitted it to *Gender*

& Society on August 6, 2013. Six weeks later, it was rejected based on reviews by four anonymous peers who critiqued how the paper was framed and how we interpreted the evidence. One wrote, "If the author wanted to investigate postfeminism and pornagraphication and the relationship to pornography, a much more nuanced empirical study would have needed to have been designed." All reasonable critiques of the paper, but not really reasons why *no one* should have read it in its current form.

Two weeks later, we submitted it to *Sex Roles*, and the editor returned it immediately, asking for, among other things, citations to articles in her journal. We ended up submitting it three more times to *Sex Roles*, which entailed a combined six months of waiting for reviews. After realizing we weren't making progress with one obstinate reviewer who did not understand the simple regression model we were using, we sent it to *Social Forces*, where it was rejected after seven weeks. Finally, in January 2015, we sent it to *Social Currents*. Three months later, the conclusion of the three reviewers was, according to the editor, "the paper needs better framing." We revised and resubmitted, it was accepted in July 2015, and finally it was posted to the journal website two months later—twenty-five months and thirteen reviews after our initial submission. The final framing was a little different, but the result we reported was unchanged from the first submission.[14] Since then, the paper has been moderately influential, with a few thousand downloads and about fifty academic citations.

The point of the story is not that our system of journal peer review is flawed, much less that peer review is bad (more on this in the next chapter). Rather, the lesson is that the system takes too long to produce unreliable results, opaquely and without adequate public accountability. What became of the many hours of review effort by these busy academics? If the result was to bounce the paper around for two years without it changing much, was their time well spent? Did anything or anyone hold them accountable (or reward them) for their actions, by holding the quality of their work up to scrutiny? Of course, we all know the answers to these questions. The peer-reviewed journal publishing system is rife with waste, fraud, and abuse.

If we are going to create a better system, we have to first develop an intolerance for the systemic problems of the current one. We have to stop seeing these as acceptable sacrifices for the greater good of a functioning academic peer review system. To change the culture, we have to embrace rejection of the culture as it is. We have to let our imagination of a new culture, led by openness, emerge.

OPENNESS AND TRUST

Even if we can imagine a better system of scholarly communication, it's difficult to build consensus on the first steps to take. We have had a breakthrough, however, in the recognition that we must make our work available to more readers, sooner. That's the story of "open access" publication, including and especially preprints. On one hand, the desire for researchers to have their work made available for free has coincided with the economic interests of journal publishers, who see a commercial opportunity in the political pressure to provide open access to their pages. In the case of prestigious publishers, this has been very lucrative, with high page charges to authors and their institutions, who pay to make the papers available for free. And a raft of less prestigious publishers have provided publication opportunities on an article-processing charge basis as well. By now, more than a quarter of major journal publications are free to read under article-processing charge arrangements.[15] Under pressure from the federal government and its agencies, and through arrangements between publishers and major universities to open access to their research, that number is certain to rise.

On the other hand, preprints represent a more radical intervention into the workflow of research publication, offering a path to both accelerated dissemination and free access. During the time scholarly work is in peer review, by convention, no one but the editor and reviewers are supposed to read it. The problems with that approach became more and more obvious as wait times increased and the global reviewer labor pool was stretched thin. By the time Lucia and I had our seemingly interminable experience, the system already was breaking down. More and more social scientists were stepping around publication delays to post working papers or drafts on websites and share them on social media. But too many of us were still doing our work in an inefficient, closed process that squelched the possibility of wider engagement with all but the "finished" product and, even then, mostly only involved those readers at institutions whose libraries could afford the spiraling cost of journal subscriptions. And all that was happening at a time when social science data, methods, and results were being disseminated faster and more widely than ever among the reading public by journalists and think tank researchers—increasingly leaving behind those social scientists who labored under academic conventions like journal peer review, making our research outdated before it is published and diminishing our impact in the public square.

The colleagues with whom I created SocArXiv in 2016 (in partnership with the Center for Open Science [COS]) wanted to make it easier, faster, and cheaper to share work in progress, as well as published work that was destined for a life behind paywalls. At the time, there were only a few such "preprint servers," as they are known: arXiv (pronounced *archive*) for mathematics and physics (that X is a Greek chi, which explains the pronunciation), bioRxiv for life sciences, and SSRN for social sciences (which was owned by the publishing monopolist Elsevier). Now there are dozens of such services, and the practice of publicly posting papers at (or before) the point of submission to a journal is widely accepted. That is how, during the pandemic, tens of thousands of preprints related to COVID-19 were posted, many of them generating important attention and influence long before they were published in peer-reviewed journals, as we saw in chapter 1. It is also extremely efficient. At SocArXiv, as of 2024, we provide free public access to our entire backfile plus thousands of new papers every year by paying COS the equivalent of one article-processing charge in a *Nature*-branded journal ($12,000) and contributing a few hours of volunteer labor per week to screen the papers.

BUILDING TRUST

There is an unfortunate association of science with arrogance. This no doubt arises from the arrogance of scientists. But it runs counter to the quiet essence of science, which is uncertainty. Once, when I spoke up for "scientific rigor" in sociology, a sociologist replied, "this pretence of natural science needs to be resisted not indulged." Another wrote: "I'm not here to perform 'science' so the public will accept my work, I'm here to seek truth."[16] But it's not just science—all types of research enhance their legitimacy by acknowledging uncertainty and practicing accountability, even if not all involve ideas like research replication and reproducibility. And the science practices around scholarly communication—openness, transparency, replicability—are more compatible with the underlying perspective of my critics than they sometimes admit. I am less interested in the epistemo-logical questions of what is meaning and truth, or a critique of positivism, and more concerned with basic questions like, "How do we know researchers are doing good research, or even tell-ing the truth?" And, "How can we improve our work so that it's more conducive to advancing research overall?"

It is in the nature of expertise that scholars know more than most of our readers about what we're studying. Sometimes the work produces its own legitimacy. If I explain something about your life to you, and you can verify it with your own senses, what I said is legitimated directly—and trust follows. The next easi-est thing is if I give you information to learn something new on your own or accurately predict a future event—your new capac-ity is verifiably attributable to my intervention. Think of weather forecasting. If I tell you it will rain, and it does, you might trust me again in the future. (And if someone teaches you to predict the weather and you do, even better.) Unlike weather forecasting, however, much of our transmitted knowledge cannot be directly verified or confirmed. For example, if I explain someone else's life to you—if I tell you the unemployment rate or describe the prevalence of viral infection or police racial bias—then verifica-tion does not come from your direct assessment of the knowl-edge I claim to have imparted. In fact, verifying my information often relies on information that I also provide. For example, I might tell you how the unemployment rate is measured, and link you to the data, and then tell you what the rate is, and then tell you its implications. Before you act on such knowledge that comes from an expert, you need a reason to trust it.

In general, people only enter into a trusting relationship with experts if their own ignorance requires it. Unfortunately, "igno-rance always provides grounds for skepticism or at least cau-tion."[17] This means people need to trust experts but are likely to doubt them. Scholars need the people who use our work to trust us. But our readers encounter that work in a social context of high uncertainty.

Trust is also delicate. Gil Eyal compares trust in science to Pierre Bourdieu's description of gift exchange.[18] Systems of gift exchange are generally reciprocal, as gift receivers are normally expected to return a comparable gift after a suitable time lag.[19] The right time lag is crucial because it creates trust. If you immediately return a gift of equal value, you are in effect negating the gift and converting it to an untrusting transaction, denying the original giver the opportunity to express their friendship; if you wait too long, you are untrustworthy. With expertise, similarly, you may appreciate the principle that a scholar's work is verifiable through an accessible mechanism (such as a trip to the library or a search engine). But if you always verify an expert's work, you are in effect denying their expertise and rejecting their institutional status as a trusted source of knowledge. This does not imply scholars should hold back our data; it means we have to understand its symbolic importance. Sharing the right information at the right time—in the right social context— matters more than sharing everything all the time in an impenetrable deluge.

To make matters more difficult—and to further raise the stakes—modern society imposes on people the judgment of the community for all life decisions and their outcomes, whether or not those outcomes are within individual control. In family sociology, for example, that means parents are judged for their children's success—along with their diet, their reading scores, their creativity, their health, and their gender identity—even as constraints on parental actions limit their choices.[20] (Worse still, the chasm between success and failure grows ever wider with advancing social inequality.)

People's success at life, however they conceive it, is wrapped up in the evaluation of others. As individual agents in an individualist era, they have to not only succeed but also justify their strategy for success (whether it works or not). If they acted on advice from experts, that choice, too, would be subject to scrutiny. Did they follow the advice of Dr. Fauci? Dr. Phil? In this high-stakes condition, there are lots of reasons to distrust scholars—either as individuals or as erstwhile representatives of the institutions to which they belong—before they act as public agents for our brand (social science).

The trust issue goes beyond the basic question of whether we are literally committing fraud or incompetently completing our research. It's related to the general phenomenon of "social trust," which is increasingly hard to come by.[21] If you think people in general can't be trusted, then choosing an impersonal expert to trust is even more fraught. And social scientists are impersonal. We collect and disseminate information readers can't see with their own eyes (which may involve ethical issues including harm to research subjects or threats to privacy). We are charged with policing our own biases and subjecting ourselves to scrutiny on conflicts of interest. And, generally, we are only held accountable for errors or misdeeds within institutional settings governed by people like us. If you don't know us as individuals, you have to trust the institutions charged with policing us—institutions we happen to run.

Trust in scholars as experts is a specific case of the general problem of trust and cooperation,[22] and it's not limited to medical science, social science, or even humans. Every creature that acts on information needs a reason to trust it. Without much working memory, as with schools of fish, individuals rely on instinctive cues about whom to follow. With a little more robust memory, one individual can remember who provided useful information in the past and decide to trust that individual again in the future. Using longer memories and the tool of gossip ("the exchange of information about absent others"[23]), we can build networks of trust, helping our friends, and their friends, make wise choices about whom to trust. In the process, we also encourage people in our social networks to behave prosocially, so that when we gossip about them they might be similarly rewarded. When memory becomes more durable still, especially in the form of writing that can be stored and transmitted widely, we can develop social systems of trust built on institutional reputations. Eventually, this evolution has given us a system in which phrases like "Harvard study" are widely understood to mean *trustworthy*.[24]

This institutional dynamic is essential. Despite the high importance of this question, if we as individual scholars devoted sufficient time and effort to building trust with everyone who reads or relies on our work, we wouldn't have time in the day left to do the research. Just like most of us can't build our own computers, we can't on our own construct the conditions for trusting us and our profession. We need a system. The system for building trust in scholarship includes technological tools, cultural norms, economic incentives, and organizational rules. Some of that is already in place, of course, in the features of our academic system, our institutional rewards, our publishing, and so on. But there are also contrary pressures, contaminating our efforts with a set of incentives that drive us toward bad practices, as in the Gino case.

We have seen the frailty of this trust recently in the success of right-wing ideologues in mobilizing large swaths of the public against academia by painting a fantastical picture of higher education as a vast system of indoctrination ruled by "critical race theory" and "diversity, equity, and inclusion."[25] Ideologues also turned people against "the science" of preventing pandemic virus transmission with vaccines, masks, and social distancing—a practical divergence that escalated to the point of physical threats against scientists and public health departments.[26] The problem has worsened more on the political right than the left,[27] with the gap growing during the pandemic,[28] but the pandemic wave of intense distrust and animosity occurred precisely when believing science was a matter of life and death. The paradox clearly illustrates how uncertainty raises the bar for trust.

As an aside, conservative critics like Stephen Cole (somehow, the people who complain about politics contaminating social science are usually hung up on the left-leaning form of this problem), discussed in chapter 2, have a point with regard to trust: one source of trust derives from the social or political positions we take—people trust us when we agree with them.[29] To Cole, this is a fatal weakness, but I understand that this kind of trust is important for some sociologists and truly valuable, although it's different from science. Maybe unreasonably, I want both (as I'll discuss in chapter 6). I am glad some people will give my work a hearing because I take antiracist or feminist public positions, for example. But I hope they will also do so because I practice science in my research, with the vulnerability and accountability that implies. Cole and others might say my public political pronouncements undermine not just my science but the reputation of sociology as a whole. I can't prove they're wrong. But I think the roles of citizen and scholar are ultimately compatible. Having a home in a discipline that embraced science and better communicated its value would help.[30]

SCHOLARLY COMMUNICATION

The problems of faster dissemination and open access without a subscription fee are only part of the motivation for open scholarship. Openness is a broader value orientation that seeks to address much of what ails our scholarly communication *ecosystem*—the network of communication around us and our research. Interventions like SocArXiv are intended to provide the tools needed to make sustained cultural and organizational changes to our institutional environment.

I said that we know things our readers don't; we're in the knowledge business. But if we know things the lay public doesn't, the reverse also holds—much of what we are trying to learn in our studies comes from the perceptions and perspectives of people with different experiences than us. Directly or indirectly, we learn together. This is one of the main reasons that doing better social science and establishing trust in that science through our openness are so tightly coupled. Building trusting relationships isn't just about preventing catastrophes or sussing out fraud; it's about opening up new worlds of knowledge and insight we would never see if the people we're talking so expertly about hold us in suspicion or assume we're unreachable.

The trust problem also includes the relationship between scholars themselves. This is crucial for those in the scholarly community whose work, and livelihoods, depend on our trustworthiness (and who are well aware of the incentives we face to skew, shade, manipulate, and cheat our way to success). If two researchers are exchanging views about the demography of Imperial China or about the DNA of a virus, neither of which can be verified by lived experience, they need a system for trusting each other's information.

Consider the preceding section. I knew the contours of my argument when I began work on this chapter, but to make these passages more valuable and more interesting, I decided to learn more and bring my existing knowledge up to date. I read some articles I hadn't read before, which I selected by doing some keyword searching in Google Scholar, for terms like *reputation management* and *institutions* and *trust*. I found a few articles that had been cited a lot by other scholars (thus relying on the wisdom of researcher crowds), and then looked for popular articles citing those that had "review" in the title or abstract. That led me to recent review articles that included a lot of relevant citations. At each step, I scrolled through many articles, looking at various other metadata cues: titles, abstracts, authors, and journal and book titles. In this process, I used a system for finding information (what librarians call *discovery*) that is inextricably tied to our systems of trust.[31] I relied on other scholars to have cited these works, journals to have published them, and, indirectly, universities to have credentialed and then hired the authors, and so on. (Of course, I also relied on Google and its algorithms, which gave me access to millions of documents, conveniently if opaquely ranked according to its self-fulfilling prediction of my clicking desires.)

I might criticize the workings of such a system, with its opaque biases and hierarchies, yet to make such a critique I would have to rely on this network of information. Fortunately, however, I am not entirely reliant on the formal, established scholarly communication system, with its corporate overlords and their hegemonic tools. I also communicate (often on social media) with a network of people with similar perspectives and concerns and can draw on *their* networks to gather information from different points of view. This set of resources—what you might call scholarly social capital—includes people in different academic disciplines, who work or study at different institutions, who interact with people in many different social positions. To my mind, this leaky, messy, inequitable system is essential for preventing the ossification of knowledge. But it still runs on trust, which requires openness.

NORMS AND PRACTICES

In our era of public scholarship, the communication between scholars—formal or informal—including the process and product of this book, is also often observable by the public. Other people have various entry points from which to engage the research community, from Google Scholar to social media, from drafts scholars post to course syllabi on the open web. And the principles that establish trust between scholars, based on formal processes of scholarly communication largely in academic settings, overlap with the elements of trust between scholars and the public. Chief among these principles are accountability, transparency, and openness.[32] In any social setting, norms are necessary to establish trust and promote social cooperation. We build trust by adopting the norms of open scholarship, and in so doing, we bring the practices of citizenship into our role as scholars.

Recognizing the value of norms doesn't displace the need for supportive institutional practices—a formalized system of rewards and punishments, infrastructure, and guidelines. In fact, rules and the training they require are a great way to teach norms as well as make them more effective. (Even Francesca Gino, who knew she risked the unearthing of a trove of fraudulent studies, was unable to resist the norm of open data sharing in her field.) In a brilliant essay comparing academic scholarship to used car sales, Simine Vazire explains that competition for academic success will drive researchers toward the lowest acceptable standards for quality and reliability.[33] If some people can succeed without devoting the effort to making their research transparent and reproducible, then those who do make such investments will be disadvantaged.

Without an enforceable requirement for higher standards, the average quality of research falls, and eventually public trust in the scholarly enterprise becomes impossible to sustain. In addition to the benefits of open scholarship for the quality of our own work (which I discuss below), Vazire's observation implies that *all* researchers—even those whose work is not the subject of widespread public scrutiny—need to meet high standards for *any* of us to be trusted. The wealth and status achieved by Gino is suggestive here, as she bested the competition by faking data. It's no surprise that her fraud, once discovered, was treated as an object of collective revulsion and led to her expulsion from the community. If Gino's violation of scholarly norms was allowed to stand, we would all be debased.[34]

Researchers sometimes think only a few people are interested in our work, so the effort to make it open has few benefits. But that microspecialization also means you don't know what other people might start thinking about or the connections they will suddenly draw. You can't know in advance how some small niche of people you don't know about might benefit from—and give benefit to—your work. It has to be open for that to happen, and not just open to read the final product, but open in the wider sense, so that people can find, reuse, and remix the data and materials as well. Yet we are right to limit our investment of time and resources so that we aren't devoting everything to future, hypothetical uses at the expense of getting our work done today—and putting ourselves at risk of losing out to career competitors.

In resolving this tension, institutional actors and policies are key. The only way to accomplish consistent high standards is through institutional action, by universities and other research organizations, by academic publishers, and by professional associations. As Jeremy Freese and Molly King put it, "transparency poses a collective action problem." Who goes first? They add: "Even when the benefits of increasing transparency to scientific communities are readily recognized, individual researchers have

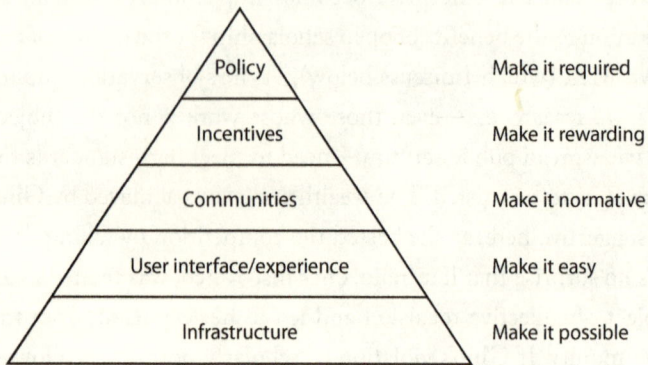

FIGURE 3.1 Brian Nosek's strategy for cultural change model.

pervasive incentives not to participate and may even perceive that providing more information about their projects poses risks. As such, exhorting researchers to be more transparent only goes so far. Instead, what are needed are institutional solutions."[35]

The psychologist Brian Nosek, who, with Jeff Spies, co-founded COS and its research-sharing platform, the Open Science Framework (OSF), has used the pyramid shown in figure 3.1 to show the relationship between technological innovation, normative change, and institutional policies in the effort to forge a culture of open science. Following the levels of the pyramid upward: When (1) *new infrastructure* makes improved practices possible, some people will jump in and take advantage of the new tools to improve their work. That's what Nosek and Spies did by creating the OSF in 2013. With enough users and support, they can generate the resources needed to make using the tools (2) *easier*, so that the number of users multiplies and their systemic advantages scale up.[36] As it grows, (3) collegial *communities* of practice can form, reinforcing effective and prosocial practices with emerging norms and expectations. That is the point at which my colleagues and I launched SocArXiv (which runs on the OSF platform). As successes compound, leaders in the space who seek to reward effective practices offer (4) new *incentives* to adopt them, which helps bring along those who have lagged behind the innovators. This is happening now, as academic leaders begin to recognize open scholarship practices as worthy of reward in the cycles of hiring and promotion.[37] And finally, (5) policies *requiring* the new practices can be implemented with broad support, serving to level the playing field and institutionalize the progress already made.[38] The wave of public policies requiring open dissemination of research—starting with publications and moving on to data and other outputs—will inevitably lead to adaptations by universities and researchers. That means the time to adjust our workflows is now.

ON QUALITATIVE RESEARCH

Many readers may have assumed the preceding discussion didn't involve qualitative research because social science research requires anonymous research subjects, which makes openness impossible. Like journalism, however, a lot of qualitative research does not rely on anonymity or masking the identities of subjects. It names the people involved and gets them on the record. This includes historical research (which may involve interviewing people involved in historical events as well as documents) or contemporary research on publicly recognized events in which the actors are already known. Still, that is not the case for many qualitative social scientists and ethnographers, who often feel on the outs in the practice and policy debates over open scholarship.

It may seem reasonable to construct policies that apply universally across different modes of data collection and analysis.

For example, any kind of research can be subject to an expectation that researchers will share data if it is possible to do so without compromising confidentiality. In that case, much qualitative work—where the data is riddled with direct and indirect personal identifiers—would simply be exempt. I do think we should do this, but also recognize that there are several problems with it as an approach. First, the burden on qualitative researchers may be greater, as preparing their data for public sharing is often more onerous. Second, researchers who routinely claim exemptions from sharing requirements might be perceived by their peers as untrustworthy or shirkers. Both of these may have the effect of discouraging scholars from entering into qualitative research projects. Such downstream consequences of a universal policy require attention.

More fundamentally, however, some qualitative data are simply not shareable or replicable—for example, interactions and interpretations that occurred in the moment between researchers and subjects just cannot be experienced secondhand. The idea of "replicating" a social observation undermines the practice of ethnography, which is built on conditional and contextual relationships that will never happen twice—as "ethnographers are themselves the instrument of data collection and analysis."[39] As Freese and Peterson write, "replication is simply the wrong language to apply to qualitative studies."[40]

The goals and practices of replication (or reproducibility, a term sometimes used interchangeably and sometimes differently) vary considerably. You can rerun an analysis of Census data using the same code to make sure it produces the same result (sometimes called "push-button replication," other times called reproducibility), but that's not the same as administering the Census again. And even administering a survey or other measurement again—such as doing an experiment in a different lab with new subjects or generating a new random sample to survey a month later—can never exactly replicate the conditions of the original data collection. So we should not fetishize replication as a perfect test or verification. In the case of qualitative work, by insisting on applying "quantitative logics to qualitative research," open science policies can threaten all that is good about ethnography.[41] All that said, however, there is a lively and useful discussion going on among qualitative scholars about transparency and accountability—a discussion that takes into account the essential nature of the work.[42] I return to this issue and offer a few suggestions for practice below.

EXPOSURE AND VULNERABILITY

While a member of the British *Terra Nova* expedition to the South Pole in 1911, George Murray Levick conducted an extensive study of Adélie penguins. In his published writings, he described the behavior of "'hooligan' cocks," unpaired males who "hang about the rookery in little bands" and "cause a great deal of annoyance to the peaceful inhabitants." And, he added ominously, "the crimes which they commit are such as to find no place in this book." He actually did write up the details of those crimes, it's just that the editor of the book at the Natural History Museum excised the section on "sexual habits." The section was instead printed as a pamphlet under the heading, "Not for Publication," and circulated only among a small group, "for our own use." As a result of that censorship, these observed behaviors— which included homosexual and other "non-procreative" sexual behavior (to use the clinical term)—were lost to science, and it would be decades before they were widely revealed and studied.[43] Levick was so disgusted and appalled by what he observed, apparently, that he wrote some of his observations in Greek characters, perhaps to protect himself or his readers who couldn't handle the truth. Needless to say, this is not how science works.[44]

We all understand the importance of openness to the extent that our work only becomes meaningful when it is "published." Knowledge is iterative and cumulative. If no one hears a research paper fall in the library stacks, it does not make a sound. But what is publishing? Publish means *to make public*.[45] Articles and books printed by academic publishers are published, but so are social media posts, blog posts, working papers, preprints, open educational resources, online syllabi, datasets, and code repositories. Some scholars want to opt out of all those and choose to publish only the "final" products of our work, that is, the versions that have been peer reviewed and edited—even if that means delays of months or years before people can read them, with final access restricted to subscribing institutions. But generally, we adopt some hybrid approach. That often means participating in conferences that are semi-public, giving lectures on campuses, and publishing essays, all while holding working drafts close. A very few are transparent at all stages of the work. But there is no working scholar who seeks to publish nothing. We all understand that the work of knowledge creation requires communication. "Not for publication" science is oxymoronic.

To build trust in our own scholarship, we need to find ways to adopt and communicate our adherence to the values of accountability, transparency, and openness in the short run, even as we contribute to the long-term work of reforming our institutions. For those of us who do work in and around the nonacademic public, the returns are clear. To win trust among people with whom we hope to work, people need to see our open practices, our shared data and code, and our willingness to admit mistakes, embrace uncertainty, and entertain alternative explanations.

So, why do some scholars hold back? There is a cost to open-ness in terms of investment, which I discuss below. But first consider the impact—positive and negative. Optimistically, wid-ening the circle by publishing more material, quicker and more accessibly, might just mean that fellow scholars interested in our work are more informed during the process of generation, lead-ing to more engagement and interaction, spinning off different ideas, provoking feedback, helping students get started with new projects, and so on. In the process, that may signal trust and con-fidence in our work, for example among those who are able to access our datasets and code for verification and extension. But openness might also bring an increase in public exposure and readership, dramatically changing the character of the audiences with which we interact. The nature of online virality means it's difficult to predict what material, in what context, will sud-denly, exponentially, attract attention. For some people that's the point—publishing op-eds, giving public lectures, engaging with journalists or activists online, and so on, is the result of a suc-cessful public scholarship strategy (which I will discuss regard-ing social media and activism in chapters 5 and 6). But there are potential downsides.

Many academics have experienced online harassment and abuse. Most of that stems from public engagement in the politi-cal realm, which attracts the attention of individual trolls as well as organized bad actors, mostly in right-wing media and its envi-rons.[46] However, simply being visible as a scholar—publishing research, sharing materials, presenting at conferences, and teach-ing courses—entails risks. These risks can seriously undermine individual researchers and—by differentially silencing people—perpetuate inequalities in academic and scholarly communities. Open scholarship makes us vulnerable because it brings more people into engagement with our work.[47] It is paradoxical that increasing the basis for trust also multiplies opportunities for malicious misinformation, but it's not contradictory. Being willing to face the public is one reasonable signal of trustworthiness. So, openness is a negotiation between different values and commitments.

In addition, maybe social scientists in particular—and especially those in the softer social sciences—are reluctant to open up their work because they risk more by engaging with people outside their fields. This might be because our authority is, frankly, more precarious.[48] Think about language. When physicists or engineers use language only they understand, it's not "jargon," it's "technical." When sociologists use fancy words, we just seem obnoxious to lay readers. Social scientists are usually talking about things that are closer to the consciousness of people outside of their disciplines. Our authority is more tenuous the more our work approaches intelligibility to nonexperts. This is compounded by race/ethnic and gender bias, which further undermines the legitimacy of social scientists in the eyes of many readers. And the incentive to attack us increases as our work becomes more critical (and more critical of those with more to lose from our work).

Perhaps this explains the tendency or inclination to lean more heavily on formal legitimacy, to only "publish" what has been formally vetted and approved by the institutions of authority in our industry, especially via peer review. Social scientists might thus be more reluctant to share work widely that has not been peer reviewed or published by a high-status journal or academic publishing house. These are reasonable responses, although they come at a cost.

On the other hand, open science is especially important for those who work in contentious areas, as Christensen and colleagues persuasively argue.[49] Open practices may help shift the burden from the individual to the research community, which can be a form of protection from social criticism. They quote Robert Merton's depiction of the scientific ethos, arguing that "the substantive findings of science are a product of social collaboration and are assigned to the community." By honoring scientific norms, in other words, we gain some community protection in exchange for giving up some of our individual claim to the ownership of our ideas. Merton further wrote: "Property rights in science are whittled down to a bare minimum by the rationale of the scientific ethic. The scientist's claim to "his" intellectual "property" is limited to that of recognition and esteem which, if the institution functions with a modicum of efficiency, is roughly commensurate with the significance of the increments brought to the common fund of knowledge."[50]

There's a big "if" in there. Consider some reflections from a woman I interviewed, Lauren, a graduate student in social psychology at an elite university. She had seen the upside of early research sharing on social media (Twitter specifically) in her career: "There have been some early career researchers who have shared their work most of the time. I would say most of the experiences I see represented are positive, people commenting on the work and congratulating the person saying, 'I can't wait to read it!' [and] occasionally bringing up points like, 'Oh, did you think about this?' And they're like, 'Oh.' Maybe it's a preprint and they'll incorporate it before they publish it or whatever."

But she had also been scarred just by observing bad experiences, as when criticism of work by an early career researcher, even when well-intended, had a negative cumulative effect at the scale of social media:

It wasn't someone I knew, but someone who was popping up in my feed a lot, who shared a publication, and then there were a few senior male academics who started mocking it and kind of like encouraging a pile on because they didn't see the research topic itself as serious. And then they were kind of attacking her statistical analyses and her, you know, approach to the analysis itself. And it, like, blew up into this huge, like, multiday thing where people were piling on from all across the psych community, and even people who consider themselves very, like, measured and respectful people, you know, like, someone did a podcast episode on it, and it was a podcast focused on methods and analyses. But this was like after days of people kind of running this woman through the wringer and so even what would normally be perceived as a respectful kind of engagement with the work and taking seriously the approach she took . . . after days of piling on, people saw that as additional piling on, even if the tone of it was respectful. And I know for the woman herself who was at the center of all of this, it was a very harrowing experience. And I think she left social media for a long time and didn't really talk about the experience publicly because of how poor of an experience it was.

I will return to the social media aspects of this kind of incident in chapter 5, but from the point of view of research openness, stories like this are important—and we should think about the contributions of our individual as well as institutional engagement in them. If we want to promote open scholarship practices for all the good reasons described here, we need to hear scholars who are concerned with these risks and acknowledge that they are hierarchically distributed.[51] If we persist in the effort, it is not because we discount the risks but because we think social science is too important to give up in the face of them. So it's good to be tenacious but not dogmatic.

The challenge is to move toward openness without incurring costs greater than the benefits. We cannot assume transparency is sufficient for trust or that it is an unqualified good. As Eyal argues, an undifferentiated document dump cannot replace a genuine re-embedding, in which experts routinely make themselves available to publics in response to specific concerns.[52] We also know that unfettered transparency—in the form of leaked internal scientific documents—can be disastrous, as in the case of the 2009 "climategate," which was used to drive skeptics away from action to address global climate change.[53] One innovation we need to develop further is the use of semi-private professional spaces, in which scholars can speak more freely and speculatively than they can in wide-open view.[54] These are tricky to establish and administer. Administration and moderation can't necessarily be done casually and are not free, but the effort may be well worth it.

Opening our work allows us to better build collaborative networks for intellectual, social, and political support. By sharing with each other, scholars can make the enterprise of social science stronger, partly because the work will be better and partly because we will have a greater pool of shared resources on which to draw in response to the opposition we may face from skeptical or hostile publics. This is easier said than done, but it's the basis for my optimism on openness.

SCOOPING AND HOARDING

Another reason to hold back from sharing research, especially before "publication," is the fear of having one's ideas stolen by unscrupulous competitors. Some people are especially afraid that senior scholars with the resources and wherewithal to capitalize on free ideas will convert them into status-bearing publications, thereby establishing precedence and depriving the early-career scholar of the credit they deserve.

However, at least with regard to posting papers early (preprints), the evidence suggests the opposite: preprints offer protection from scooping and idea theft. A survey of several thousand preprint authors at bioRxiv found that a majority were motivated to post by the ability to stake a priority claim to their research, and only 1 percent reported that their preprint had adversely affected their priority claims—in other words, led to scooping.[55] Those with experience using and promoting preprints universally argue that posting papers earlier—with formal identifiers, such as a DOI and timestamp—offers protection from having ideas stolen,[56] an observation that goes back to the first internet preprint server, arXiv.[57]

Sharing papers is less contentious than the idea of sharing research data and other materials. This is mostly because "publications" (supposedly representing "discoveries") rather than all the other valuable outputs we produce, are the coin of the academic realm. People don't cite ideas, they cite publications—so having an idea stolen and turned into a publication is a common fear. It doesn't have to be this way. The valuation of "publications" is not an accident, but the outcome of a successful campaign by the academic publishing industry. As journal peer review proliferated in the post–World War II scientific milieu (see chapter 4), publishers were positioned to capture the process—the reviews and editorial decisions—and create the explosion of academic journals. When their monopoly was established (there can be only one *Science*), they began ratcheting up the price of subscriptions, leading to what libraries called the "serials crisis"—the rising share of library budgets devoted to journal subscriptions. Libraries were trapped by this effectively involuntary expenditure tied to the structure of the organization.

A key element in the business model is the "version of record" concept—the idea that research culminates in the dissemination of a single, citable document. As Lisa Hinchliffe wrote on the publishing industry blog Scholarly Kitchen, "Subscriptions are payments for access to the version of record."[58] They are the business model. Academia, in its quest for a parsimonious (simplistic) system of credit and prestige, has acquiesced to this definition of production, but at the cost of a more dynamic system of scholarly communication. As others have argued, what we need instead of a "version of record" is a "record of versions"—a network of stable, citable documents, each with a clear provenance, and record of authorship, peer review (what has been reviewed and by whom), and other key metadata.[59] If we could escape the idea of One Version to Rule Them All, academics and their institutions would become more willing to engage with—fund, credit, cite, reward—different, equally valuable products of the research process.

As noted, with regard to data sharing, there is of course a legitimate concern with the security and confidentiality of research subjects. How to protect privacy while sharing (deidentified) data is complicated, both statistically and ethically.[60] Making data available can put vulnerable groups at risk. Theoretically, even reporting summary characteristics (without individual identification) can trigger state repression.[61] This was the case with Japanese Americans during World War II,[62] and possibly for Arabs and Muslims after the September 11 attacks.[63] Data sharing requires careful planning and training.[64]

Another source of temptation not to share data and research materials is simple hoarding. This stance was summarized by Glenn Firebaugh: "Why should I go to the effort to obtain grants and collect my own data if I am then required to share my data with others?"[65] Putting personal interest before the public good is common and unsurprising. But with good policies, training, and support, we can make the realization of this attitude rare.[66] Simple policies to require sharing are one approach—such as those imposed by journals before they will consider a paper. But a wide array of sticks and carrots will help. These may include, for example, technical support for data preparation and archiving, requirements to disclose the reasons for withholding access, and, if necessary, embargoes that allow researchers a limited time to publish more of their own work before making data available. The journals of the American Economic Association require data and code access before publication, for example (and they check to confirm the code works), while *Demography* gives authors six months after publication to share their data.

WHEN AND HOW TO SHARE

A book isn't the best place to run down technical systems and options, which change frequently, so I will focus on principles. The insight of the COS model described above is that infrastructure has to be ready before researchers need it. With some encouragement, and if the barriers to entry are low enough, people may choose to use already familiar services and platforms. However, most people are unlikely to search out, much less invent, new systems just to share their work, which many see primarily as a contribution to the success of others.[67] Ideally, scholars would integrate sharing options into their regular workflow, so that when it's time to share some part of our research output, we can just flip a switch to make it available. We can already do this with systems that run on your PC like Dropbox or Google Drive or other cloud platforms like Github or COS's Open Science Framework. These also allow a hybrid approach, such as creating a "to share" folder in your project space and dropping materials in it when they're ready. A key advantage of the academic systems, such as OSF, is the archiving and version record they provide, as well as the option to apply different use licenses, create DOIs, and affiliate projects with a university or institution—all features that increase both transparency and trust among users. We need to start thinking of these as essential elements of scholarly communication, which is why librarians are key actors in this reform movement.[68]

On one end of the transparency continuum, there is a lab notebook approach, where your workflow is documented step-by-step and recorded for posterity. Scientists do this in anticipation of patent or other intellectual property claims,[69] although they may not share such documentation publicly in real time. The social science version of the notebook may include the grant applications, survey protocols, registered hypotheses (tested and untested), different kinds of data (analyzed or unanalyzed), software and code, bibliographies (which may be annotated), paper drafts and revisions (including responses to editors and reviewers), and so on.

On the other end of the continuum is a workflow where researchers share nothing but "final" publications, which include whatever documentation their editors require to be disclosed at the point of publication. Sadly, this is how much of sociology still works. In this mode of scholarship, as Christensen and colleagues put it, the scholar is not really publishing the research, they are publishing a *description* of the research.[70] The machinery of scholarly communication at this end of the continuum is grotesquely slow and inefficient. For example, what happens to the work effort of peer reviewers if the work is rejected by a journal? It is not disseminated or credited, and authors frequently discard the reviews and move on to another journal. Other people working in the same field of research may go on to spend their time duplicating the creation of code and other tools and materials—unaware of and unable to benefit from others' unshared work. Our collective progress slows to the pace of the last reviewer.

In a more subtle way, such nontransparent work practices undermine our social cooperation and cohesion. Two scholars working on the same topic in isolation are in competition; the same two people sharing work as they go are more likely, or at least more able, to become collaborators. Such solidarity is hard to quantify or identify, but its traces are found in the scholarly record.

As you position yourself, or a given project, along the transparency continuum, here is a way to categorize the principles behind your sharing decisions:

- *Accountability.* What do you need to share for your research to have integrity and be trusted by your community and potential readers? This may include the editor of a journal or its reviewers, as well as your colleagues and the various public constituencies you hope to reach, such as journalists or activists.

- *Efficiency.* How can you maximize your sharing investment in ways that will promote the efforts of others? Posting deidentified datasets and statistical code gives others a leg up on replicating or extending your work. Would they also benefit from survey instruments, grant applications, or other materials that would be easy to share—in ways that would also come back to benefit your work?

- *Equity and diversity.* Your sharing enables other researchers to make more of their research investments. What can you do to empower scholars with fewer resources, such as less training or smaller budgets for research assistance? This can involve, for example, promoting the availability of your shared papers and materials on social media or within your professional societies.

In addition to first-order assistance, this can also widen and diversify your network of colleagues and collaborators.

- *Reward.* How can you make your work matter more, in ways that rebound to your benefit? When people use your materials, they should cite and credit you; when your ideas take hold, your reputation should improve. When your work appears in public, your dean should be impressed.[71]

The type of research, methods, and data strongly affect the nature of sharing you can and should do. If you're using publicly available data, then sharing your code is relatively easy and essential; there is no reason not to let others check your work and benefit from your efforts (although there are choices to be made about the right time to do this). If you have collected original quantitative data, such as a survey, sharing it is generally expected, although it takes effort and resources to do so—and you might wait until you have written up some results. If you have conducted in-depth interviews, you may make available redacted transcripts, as well as interview guides and summary data. If you are analyzing confidential data from another source, such as the employment records of a company, there is a more complex negotiation, and you might end up not being able to share the data while still providing access to your codebooks, code, survey instrument, summary statistics, and other useful materials.

And then there is ethnographic data. In Allison Pugh and Sarah Mosseri's words, ethnographers can't just dump a trove of "'facts' and 'fieldnotes' as if they were static and immutable," to establish trust in their work. Rather, in light of the "multiple, coexistent realities" inherent in social life and ethnographic research, they need to build trust in scholarship incrementally, in the text, by the reflexive practices that expose potential contradictions and differing interpretations. "If readers do not trust the ethnography by the time they finish reading," they write, "the ethnographer has already failed in their task."[72] I think this is great advice, which requires thorough training and time to do right—all of which I support. And ultimately, some of the "replicating" equivalent in ethnographic research is a longer-term, iterative, affair. Scholars working in similar social contexts compare their observations and results, not expecting identical outcomes but reflecting on similarities and differences that emerge across settings.

Nevertheless, there are important, concrete steps that qualitative researchers—including ethnographers—can take to improve the trustworthiness of their research. Regardless of the mode of research, there are at least some aspects of a scholar's work that are verifiable and should be subject to scrutiny. Murphy and colleagues[73] provide a set of suggestions to consider:

- *Using electronic recording devices for gathering and then preserving data.* This generally won't replace personal observation, interaction, or handwritten notes, but it can provide greater depth and reliability than the older practice of handwriting notes during a break or at the end of the day—and recordings can be used for verification if necessary.
- *Verifying facts.* This might mean checking that an interviewee correctly described a particular practice or event by talking to others involved or tracking down documentary evidence. It can involve hiring independent fact-checkers to run down specific accounts, as Matthew Desmond did.[74] At minimum, what (if any) methods of verification were used in a project and why should be disclosed to readers.
- *Preserving and sharing data.* Some ethnographers including, famously, Alice Goffman, have destroyed their field notes to prevent exposure that might jeopardize the safety or security of their research participants.[75] That should not be the default,

but how and what to store and share are complicated. There
is support and guidance available on this question, such as
resources shared at the Qualitative Data Repository at Syra-
cuse University.

• *Identifying rather than anonymizing research subjects.* This is
  perhaps the most contentious terrain in ethnographic methods debates. Deciding whether to name respondents depends
  of course on their permission, as well as authority from institutional review boards. But there are costs to the traditional
  practice of anonymization, too. In particular, the anonymization might give respondents a false sense of security that they
  will never be identified. And masking identities may encourage
  researchers to take on an exaggerated sense of generalizability,
  as if they are describing generic or universal types rather than
  specific individuals.[76]

I don't share Pugh and Mosseri's disdain for using "outside
experts" and "ex post facto stamps of verification."[77] In fact, these
can be a relatively unobtrusive part of the research process and
provide substantial benefits. Without having to hire an independent fact-checker to reinterview all your respondents—or
undermining the reflexive, interpretive practices that good ethnography provides—sound, open practices can provide a greater
sense of accountability and transparency to readers in the public
and scholarly communities.

PUBLISHING

Compared with sharing research data and materials, and the
complex questions of how and when to open the research process
to different audiences, the question of disseminating finished

(or draft) research products—chiefly papers—is relatively simple. But it still entails a series of choices and trade-offs. In light of the continued centrality of "papers" as units of scholarly output, we developed SocArXiv to promote a culture of sharing and openness in the social sciences without demanding a restructuring of the entire system. As decades of experience in mathematics and physics show, a norm of preprint sharing can happily coexist with a peer-reviewed journal system, without (for better or worse) threatening the business model of academic publishers (including the professional societies that live off their journal subscriptions). And SocArXiv includes infrastructure for sharing supporting materials, such as data and code, in an archivally responsible manner. So, by posting preprints, researchers can accelerate and widen their impact, signal their openness and accountability, and maintain academic career trajectories that require the status confirmation of peer-reviewed journals.

The transition to open access publishing has been led in large part by research funders, who began requiring outputs from research they support to be made freely available, first in the private sector and then in federal and other government agencies.[78] In parallel to these funder policies, a growing number of universities have implemented "rights retention" open access policies, which give the university a license to distribute the writing of its faculty (and sometimes other staff) that precedes the rights given to publishers. Beginning with Harvard, these policies have spread through many major universities, including the University of California system and about a hundred others at this writing (and to Europe, in different form). They usually mean that the university repository can hold and share the "author accepted manuscript" version (that is, after peer review) of any paper written by a member of their faculty even if the paper is published in a paywalled journal.[79]

If you are governed by an open access policy or mandate at your institution, it may set a floor of openness below which you may not sink. But you may want to consider going beyond the policy to share your work earlier in the process. Within a given project or workflow, I encourage authors to consider the right time to share papers publicly:

- *Early stage.* When you just want to receive feedback, to engage with or identify potential collaborators, or to plant a personal flag on a research topic or question for future reference, posting before (or in lieu of) any other process may be a good idea. I have posted a number of papers at this stage and then never submitted them to a journal because they served their purpose as stand-alone papers—getting them off my desk and into the public for some topical purpose without tying me up in months of peer review stress and labor. Some work doesn't need to be peer reviewed, especially descriptive work using well-worn data and methods, but it should still be shared and archived in a transparent and accountable way.

- *Conference stage.* If you are going to present at a conference, that means you're willing to have strangers know about your work. To increase engagement with the audience, draw people to your session, or help establish the precedence of your findings, posting a paper at the time of the conference can help. This also helps with the Q&A, as you can refer people to the full paper rather than appear to dodge technical questions. Ideally, more conferences would require posting papers (and would take responsibility for properly indexing and archiving them), which would remove the individual burden of this decision (with reasonable exceptions). A large QR code on your first or last slide can bring your audience right to the paper.

- *Journal submission stage.* At this point, you are ready for the complete paper to be evaluated by expert strangers, which means you are prepared to stand behind your work publicly. Preprint servers have promoted sharing at this stage by facilitating submission to journals directly from their submission platforms. Publishers that offer to post your submitted paper as a preprint hope to capture it so that, if it's rejected, they can convince you to submit it to one of their lower-status journals with just a few clicks. In disciplines with double-blind peer-review norms, such as sociology, some scholars balk at sharing submitted papers because Google-happy reviewers may discover your identity. But double-blind review is increasingly unraveling anyway. Have you presented the work at a conference or given a talk that's listed online? Have you applied for a grant or blogged about your project? You could refrain from all that, but it's a lot to give up for the sake of blind review, the benefits of which are probably overstated anyway.

- *Acceptance stage.* Any concerns you have about your work being good enough to share or about undermining peer review secrecy are alleviated by this stage. As long as you are publishing in a journal that does not require you to sign away your right to distribute a preprint (which I don't recommend), there is no reason not to share it now. Good preprint servers (including SocArXiv) allow you to link your preprint to the journal version when that is published, so that readers who cite the prepublication version will be contributing to the citations of the final paper as well. (Many journals have realized this and now post "prepublication" versions themselves.) Maybe there is some vanity or pride that motivates people to only want readers to see the beautiful journal version—especially for high-status journals—but you should not fall into that. You can say, "Forthcoming in the *journal of high status*," right on the title page of the preprint.

- *Postpublication stage.* This is for papers published in paywalled journals, when some readers will not be able to access the full paper. Some people post the journal version on their own websites, which usually violates their (rarely enforced) author agreements, but I encourage authors to follow their agreements and post legitimate versions—usually the final accepted version, before copy editing and typesetting—on authorized servers. If the journal doesn't allow this, again, I suggest a more public-minded journal.

My goal in this chapter has been to provide motivation, and some guidance, for opening up our scholarship, for the good of our readers, our colleagues, our collective accountability, and ourselves. The more we can cooperate and move forward in the process of opening together, the less risk we take as individuals and the more we can maximize the benefits of this social and institutional change.

4

PEER REVIEW, UNLEASHED

"Don't call bullshit carelessly—but if you can, call bullshit when necessary."[1]

What is true? *True* in general means "in accordance with fact or reality." Truth is the basis of knowledge. *Being* true is also important in relationships, especially families and romantic relationships, where we value loyalty and dedication. *True love* means love that is real and authentic, from the historical meaning of true as *faithful*, where being true to a marriage refers to sexual or romantic fidelity. The connection between knowledge and love also appears in the Torah, where a man "knowing" a woman meant he had sex with her. Was it meaningful when Adam knew Eve in Genesis—was it true? Yes, we are told, it was the opposite of what a spouse caught cheating protests: "But it didn't *mean* anything!"[2]

You can think of true ideas or facts as those that accurately reproduce reality—that are faithful to reality. Facts have fidelity. And the question for us is, how can we tell what's true? I have hashed this out for years with regard to studying families, where the issues involve contentious debates about how to describe and interpret the rapidly changing realities that so many of us experience in our daily lives. And of course, a lot of people are telling tall tales about families.

Before making the case for taking an expansive view of peer review and its uses in the public square, I will first discuss peer review in its formal, institutional setting: academia. Researchers and readers often interpret "peer reviewed" as a status to mean other scholars with expertise in the same field of study have evaluated the work and declared it to be true. More specifically, however, the peer reviewers are evaluating the methods used and the interpretation of evidence. If I say, "I analyzed the unemployment data and the unemployment rate is 5 percent," the peer reviewers are not evaluating whether the unemployment rate is 5 percent; they're asking whether I did the research right and interpreted it reasonably. As I mentioned in the previous chapter, the written article or book is better thought of as a description of the research. And that's what the peer review of publications is about.

Why is peer review necessary? As I discussed in chapter 3, in a world of highly specialized training, it's impossible for individuals intent on learning something to verify all the information they encounter. That applies whether we are doctors deciding what medicines to prescribe, airline manufacturers deciding what materials to use, or regular people deciding whether a viral outbreak means it's not safe to hug our grandchildren.[3] We need experts to get through every day. That's why "Do your own research," which pretends to be a call to independent thought, is actually the mantra of know-nothing conspiracy theorists. It signals disregard for systems of expertise, opening a back door to the dark world of ignorance.[4]

Our modern life requires systematically trusting people who know more about something than we do, people who have the legitimate role of exercising that expertise. We could seek out individual experts—asking them what food to eat, medicines to take, bridges to drive over, water to drink, and air to breathe. But instead, we rely on institutional systems of expertise in which groups of experts evaluate the information we need. This "trust in expert systems," which we learn to do without thinking, is not only necessary for survival but also has become a key component of the modern personality.[5] We are socialized to live under the protection of anonymous experts whose judgment is a daily matter of life and death, socialized at a level so deep we don't recognize it. Paradoxically, this can make it difficult for those very experts to convince the public to change routine behaviors.[6] People who don't realize that their "commonsense" practices were already based on expert guidance say, "You can't tell me what to do!" (Like the assistant in *The Devil Wears Prada* saying she doesn't pay attention to fashion as she shops in a discount store.) Although it might seem reassuring to have so much trust, there is also an inherent anxiety to this existence, because so much is out of our control. Trust is only necessary in a context of risk.

The experts who conduct peer review are supposed to have training related to that of the people whose work is under scrutiny—that's why we call them "peers." Engineers assess bridge design, doctors test medicines, chemists evaluate toxic hazards, family sociologists scrutinize divorce research. Among the millions of people laboring in the global scientific enterprise, peer review has been elevated to a defining principle, and for good reason. Only people with relevant skills and knowledge can effectively evaluate work in specialized topics. The stakes are high, for scientists and their careers, and for the people who live or die by the veracity of scientific research.

Evaluating scholarship is part of the machinery of knowledge creation, and it occupies a large part of the collective work of scientists and other scholars at universities around the world. In a recent year, there were almost 14 million peer reviews of research articles conducted, requiring sixty-nine million hours. That's the equivalent of thirty-three thousand reviewers—more than the entire faculty of the University of California system—working full time for the entire year.[7] Most of us who review do this work as part of our jobs, without additional pay, in service to our academic institutions and disciplines. We have a vested interest in contributing to the system, because scientists and readers of science benefit from the trust it generates. Or so we hope. People outside of academia know that peer review is at the core of science, where "true" has a special status and (unlike in the humanities) style and subjective impressions aren't supposed to count. Peer review has become part of the social contract between scientists and the public.

Albert Einstein, a professional scientist who wanted people to believe his theories, nevertheless wrote that, "a foolish faith in authority is the worst enemy of truth."[8] As a scientist committed to truth, he didn't want people to have *faith* in science as an authority—like the religious authorities whose leadership he rejected—but rather to have *trust* in science. You can think of "trust" as something that comes from evidence and conscious deliberation, while "faith" is something we don't need to think about to believe in. Religious faith may play a positive role in the lives of many people, but you can see why Einstein—a Jewish person who renounced his German citizenship and fled the country after Hitler rose to power—would be against "foolish faith in authority."

We can continue to trust what deserves to be trusted, while keeping a critical eye on the process and the people involved, because they have their own interests, too. But how? The imaginary attributed to John Stuart Mill, in which a cacophony of ideas in the public sphere competes for attention, propelling the most valuable to the top of the charts, might sometimes work in the realm of opinion, but it is decidedly ill-suited to the realm of facts.[9] Truth claims win out for the wrong reasons (actual truth is rarely the most salient value), and the playing field is decidedly unlevel. Free speech is a vital political principle, but it is not a neutral mechanism to establish veracity for which expertise is required. Experts have a crucial role to play, even when the state of knowledge is uncertain or in flux, but we cannot simply hand the reins to a cabal of experts.[10]

Thinking critically about expertise requires us to build trust in each other and our knowledge communities. And this commitment needs to run both ways, between experts and the communities they serve. Experts have to earn the trust they need to do their work effectively. In the previous chapter, I argued that the norms and practices of open scholarship were an essential element in securing this trust. Another way we do that is by engaging with the public in accountable and respectful ways.

ACTUALLY EXISTING PEER REVIEW

Despite its mystique as the one true way of publishing science, academic peer review in its current form is a recent innovation. For most of scientific history, the editors of academic journals decided what to publish and consulted with additional experts only at their discretion (sometimes anonymously, sometimes not). In some U.S. sociology journals, such as the *American Journal of Sociology*, editors began informally consulting their friends and colleagues about which papers to publish by the early 1920s— especially when specialized knowledge was required—and routinely relied on such consults (with escalating formality) after the 1940s.[11] The term "peer review" became common only in the 1970s, an adaptation of mid-century trends in science. There was an explosion of research after the end of World War II, and federal funding for that research threatened to put power in the hands of government bureaucrats instead of academic research-ers. So scientists sought to institutionalize their influence. Insist-ing on peer review meant scientists had to be involved at all levels in both funding and publication decisions.[12] The assump-tion that papers would be reviewed by outside reviewers (that is, beyond the editor and editorial board members) as a matter of fairness and integrity did not become universal until the 1980s. Put differently, the main purpose of the practice of peer review was not originally to address ethical or intellectual concerns, but to involve more professors in the work of reviewing the rising tide of papers submitted and marshal the growing technical spe-cialization required to assess them.[13]

In the humanities, formal peer review is even more recent; the practice spread from the sciences, becoming part of the concept of academic "rigor" more generally. And in these disci-plines, where book publishing dominates knowledge creation and subjective concerns are accepted as legitimate, outside review-ers evaluate scholarly quality on behalf of editors who are more concerned with readability, marketability, and sales. Interestingly, demand for blind peer review in the humanities also came from women who were confronting gender bias at journals.[14] So even though perceptions and debates about peer review generally focus on science, we should think of these issues with regard to scholarship and knowledge creation more broadly.[15]

Many people consider peer review to be the pinnacle of modern knowledge creation. While we debate that, we need to remember that putting peer review on a pedestal happens to be exactly what the companies that sell research publications want you to do. The five biggest publishers together publish more than 12,000 academic journals.[16] Elsevier published more than 600,000 articles in 2022; its parent company RELX turned a profit of $1.6 billion that year.[17] Their business model depends on the fetishization of, and control over, peer review—and the convention that it is provided as a free service to the research community. These companies, and the academic establishment more generally, are happy to control the definition of truth and sell its products to us. It's true that they play an important role, especially by organizing peer review and disseminating research. Similarly, the companies of Big Pharma develop and produce many of the valuable medicines that we rely on today. As critics of these systems, we have to wrestle with how to accomplish the good parts of what the profiteering companies do, while countering their harmful practices.

Regardless of its origins, review of research by other experts often serves both the research and the researcher well. Being a responsible researcher involves aiming to stop bad research (including your own) from misleading or confusing the public. Peer review is a way for us to work together toward this end. In our highly contentious social and political milieu, where researchers are sometimes depicted as just another interest group competing to establish their own self-serving version of truth, peer review sends an important signal that scholars aren't afraid of independent scrutiny and assessment of our work.[18]

The idealized form of peer review—in which anonymous professional academics conduct "blind" review to help editors decide what to publish in academic journals and books—doesn't apply to all the many ways information is created. *Publishing* used to mean having something printed in a paper journal or book, but now print is a minority share of what's published, and the volume of content has exploded. We need ways of differentiating quality among the endless supply of available published work. Practically speaking, this means research is often judged after it's published rather than before. Instead of telling us what people *can* read, we need peer review to help us decide what we *should* read and what we can believe. Ahead of her time, Kathleen Fitzpatrick put it this way in 2012: "Rather than focusing our efforts on importing traditional peer review to our new networked communication systems, artificially recreating conditions of scarcity, we need new ways of coping with abundance. In other words, we need filters, rather than gatekeepers."[19]

Treating peer review as a filter rather than a gatekeeper is important, because it democratizes the process of knowledge creation. A lot more people can be involved in both creating and assessing research—for better and for worse. The sooner we recognize that the importance of peer review, as a principle, extends beyond the decision of whether to publish research, the better we can improve our own contribution—as individuals and communities—to the massive, endless undertaking of global information quality control.

If the essence of peer review is experts using their expertise to assess work that other readers aren't qualified to review, there are a lot of ways this can happen—not all of them equally trustworthy. Consider this disparate set of apparently factual recent statements about poverty in the United States, which were produced by various combinations of academics, nonacademic organizations, and people with different kinds of formal and informal training (and axes to grind):

- The U.S. Census Bureau reported that the poverty rate in 2021 fell to a historic low level: 7.8 percent (using the Supplemental Poverty Measure). The report was based on a large sample survey, written by a team of analysts and subjected to strict quality review within the bureau before it was released.[20]

- I made a graph and posted it on Twitter, showing the trend in poverty rates for children, using the Census Bureau data.[21]
- The *New York Times* reported on the falling poverty rates, using the Census data to make their own graphs, interpreted by half a dozen professors and researchers they interviewed, who all agreed the big drop in poverty resulted from government assistance during the pandemic.[22]
- Brad Wilcox, a conservative scholar at the American Enterprise Institute and a University of Virginia sociology professor devoted to promoting marriage, testified before Congress that "child poverty would be markedly reduced if the nation enjoyed 1970s marriage levels."[23] What he didn't say, in his effort to turn back the clock, was that he based that claim on research conducted in 1995, using data collected in 1989—thirty-one years earlier. (Since those data were collected, child poverty has fallen drastically, despite continued decline in marriage rates.)
- Sociologists Deadric Williams and Regina Baker published an article in the peer-reviewed journal *Social Problems* reporting that racial hierarchy, more than family structure, is a systemic cause of poverty in the United States.[24]

No one formal system of peer review can regulate and control all this information. But in these examples, you can see different systems of review and evaluation at work—different kinds of peer review. At the Census Bureau, reports go through rigorous expert review before being released to the public. Experts check the technical aspects of the analysis, and administrators screen it to prevent political controversy. When I tweet a data graph, you know it's from me—a professor with a PhD and a publication record—and I link to my data sources (you also know I am a progressive who favors liberal social policies). The *New York*

Times reporters link to the data they present and often identify the experts they consult in their reporting. Even Brad Wilcox, the least reliable of these examples, cites his sources, allowing a critical reader to see how weakly they support his case. And if we are aware of the highly partisan political nature of the American Enterprise Institute, we can approach his work cautiously with an eye toward identifying bias. Finally, the sociologists Williams and Baker, publishing in a peer-reviewed journal, offer the purest form of what we normally call peer review—and by far the slowest. The journal does not have a transparent process—we don't know who the reviewers were or how thorough their review was—but we can decide to trust it based on its long institutional reputation and the credentials of its authors, editorial board, and editors. In each of these cases, we can make some judgments about the trustworthiness of the information. Yet many consider only one of these statements "peer reviewed."

I could list many other examples of scholarly experts involved in knowledge (or disinformation) production outside the idealized system of peer review, often with an academic imprint, a PhD after their name, or an impressive command of scientific terms and methods. The point is, there is a lot of important research working its way into the public eye outside the scrutiny of the academic peer-review system—such as the first three examples above—often having been reviewed by experts in ways not normally understood as peer review, which is all the more reason not to put academic journals on a pedestal of assumed superiority.

Indeed, academic journal peer review often fails comically. Bad actors sometimes get their work out under cover of peer review. Sometimes it wasn't seriously reviewed or was reviewed in corrupt ways, or it's fraudulent work that goes undetected, as we saw in chapter 3. This problem is exacerbated by the secret, and anonymous, nature of the process. Consider the case of a racist article by the political scientist Lawrence Mead, who wrote in the journal *Society* that "cultural difference . . . best explain[s] why minorities—especially blacks and Hispanics—typically respond only weakly to chances to get ahead through education and work. . . . The ultimate solution to poverty is for the poor themselves to adopt the more inner-driven individualist style."[25] He had no evidence to support these claims. Only after hundreds of people complained did the journal retract the article and admit it was "published without proper editorial oversight."

Family research has seen its share of deceptive or shoddy research published despite peer review. In particular, there was a long campaign by activists on the religious right to undermine the marriage and parenting rights of same-sex couples. They generated research, some of it published in peer-reviewed journals, claiming to show how children raised by same-sex couples suffered as a result. That included a number of papers by sociologists including Mark Regnerus and Paul Sullins—tenured professors—whose research was widely criticized (including by me) for its low quality and clear bias. In one case, emails later unearthed through public records requests revealed that Brad Wilcox raised the money for and guided the research design of a study, then served as one of the anonymous peer reviewers when it came time to publish the results. Once published, the papers ended up being used in the futile effort to stop same-sex marriage and parental rights in the courts.[26] In short, the formal, legitimate system of peer review is highly vulnerable to deliberate manipulation.

JOURNALISM AND CITIZEN SCHOLARS

Even when peer review works more like it should, the system has serious problems. During the COVID-19 pandemic, peer review buckled under the pressure of urgent demands for scientific output and the rush of scientists generating results. Papers backed up for months (even more than usual) waiting for reviewers to volunteer for the job and complete their work. As we saw in chapter 1, scientists posted tens of thousands of papers as preprints—made public before peer review—in the first months of the pandemic alone.[27] But this didn't mean we just jettisoned peer review. Rather, some of the best rapid peer review was coordinated by science journalists, who not only understood the pressing issues within the field but also had access to research that was not yet "published." Good journalists, aware of the importance of new research and the stakes involved, also understand the importance of getting it right (even if they were also motivated to get it done fast).

During the pandemic, these journalists worked with a gaggle of public health experts, epidemiologists, physicians, and related scientists who were speaking directly to the public on social media. Their tweets weren't peer reviewed, but their expertise was on public display, along with their credentials. Hundreds of preprints, posted without formal peer review on preprint platforms—especially medRxiv and bioRxiv—got run through a wringer of overworked, underslept peers who felt compelled to evaluate them publicly as rapidly as possible. Suddenly there were dozens of such experts with more than many thousands of followers each on Twitter, as the public demanded rapid information. In hindsight, we can see that the pressure of the pandemic pushed editors and reporters to radically shift their stance toward preprints—to start including them in news reports—dramatically accelerating a trend that had limited momentum to that point.[28]

Yes, they make mistakes, and, yes, they are vulnerable to the incentives of the click-driven information economy, but we have good colleagues in the news media who play a vital and powerful role in vetting and disseminating new science. I can't quantify the ratio, but it's safe to say that for every overhyped news story or breathless report on a study that isn't up to scientific snuff, there are many more irresponsible corporate or university news releases promoting unvetted research that is wrong, exaggerated, or unimportant that are turned away by good reporters and editors. As *New York Times* science reporter Apoorva Mandavilli tweeted, "People who accuse science journalists of chasing clicks must have NO IDEA about the dozens of bad preprints we pass on plus the hundreds of bad press releases we get pitched *every single day*. If what we wanted was clicks, you'd be seeing something else entirely."[29] Researchers should assist in this process as well. Despite the allure of being named in the news, it's vital for the circle of trust for us to also be willing to tell a reporter, "I would love to be quoted in a story, but I believe the study you are reporting on is not reliable."

When new research makes it through that gauntlet, and a responsible news outlet decides to do the story, the result may be a quickly assembled panel of expert reviewers commenting on the new research, either privately to the reporter or editor or publicly quoted in a story. The good journalists adjudicate the responses and make a judgment about what to report and how to describe the level of certainty. Yes, the experts they contact may have bad motives—to see their name in print, to debunk a rival piece of research for self-interested reasons, or to pursue partisan ambitions. And the constantly churning crew of experts (and people who say they're experts) unspooling capacious threads about the latest research on social media—where tempers are short and the incentives favor extreme positions—has many counterproductive aspects. But the alternative to this system is to squelch breaking-news research unnecessarily, leaving the field open for hucksters, think tanks, and other media outlets to take their cases directly to the public. Holding back also means not engaging with research in areas that may be genuinely unsettled, where public debate might actually move a field forward. Refusing to engage in this process has costs; just sitting back to wait for journals to conduct peer review is no longer a choice.

Formal peer review alone can't stop misinformation—which we saw time and again during the pandemic, as antivaccine conspiracies and other campaigns to undermine our public health response ripped through social media. We can't stop it, but we can respond.[30] We can be responsible consumers as well as producers of information—carefully deciding what information to spread and when to raise a ruckus. That includes exposing peer review itself, when necessary, rather than falling in line with deference to the information hierarchy. How was a study peer reviewed, and by whom? If it's not in an academic publication, was it produced by other people with trustworthy expertise or experience? Is there some system of accountability in place to correct or respond if it turns out to be wrong? We must use our knowledge and skills to help others evaluate and respond to what they're reading.

My expansionist view of peer review—which is not shared by all academics—should not be taken to diminish the more formal (and slow!) processes described above. In fact, being inefficient—slowing down the production of information and imposing quality hurdles—is important for impeding the spread of bad information.[31] But we should not kid ourselves about the formal peer review process, elevating it to an unrealistically precious status. The journal system fell down many times during the pandemic as well. Hundreds of pandemic-related research articles were subsequently retracted by their journals.[32] There are trade-offs to different kinds of review and commentary, and there are no easy solutions.

When we decide whether something is true, we often use the word *tell*, as in, "I can tell that's true." To tell something is also to know it, as well as to communicate about it. We have a social obligation to tell the truth about what we can tell is true. That requires listening and learning, but also talking and writing. In the end, the way we tell what's true is to speak up.

NEW APPROACHES

In the sausage factory of knowledge creation, we do peer review in all kinds of ways. Some is done anonymously by journals, but outside of the social sciences, most peer review is "single blind" (the reviewers know who the author is). Academic books and grants are often not reviewed anonymously at all, although the reviewers' names may be kept secret. Some journals stress veracity or reliability in their reviews—is this true?—but others focus on whether the work is novel, exciting, or clickable. Some peer review takes place in groups, such as NIH review panels. Sometimes people are paid to conduct reviews (usually they're not). Some journals publish the reviews they commission (at least when they end up accepting an article), while others keep them secret. The former journal *eLife*, in the life sciences, switched to "peer review after publication"—only considering papers that are already accessible to the public as preprints. Instead of "publishing" or "accepting" articles, it publishes peer-review assessments of preprints.

Although the essence of peer review remains experts using their expertise to review work that other readers aren't qualified to review, in practice we have many peer review processes. These include many variables—how anonymous it is, what aspects of the work are reviewed, at what stage of development the review

takes place, how secret or open it is, whether people are paid—
for different situations and to meet different objectives. But no
particular constellation of values on these parameters themselves
epitomizes peer review.[33] For all the different models of peer
review, it is remarkably hard to evaluate and compare their outputs systematically, even if we could agree on a common set of
goals (which we can't).[34] In light of this, we should not let one
group of self-interested, institutionally dominant actors—Big
Publishing—own the definition of this process, including when
in our workflow it should take place, but nor should we relinquish the principle behind it.

Consider PubPeer, a system that facilitates commentary and
discussion on already-published research, often amounting to
continuous postpublication peer review. In 2023, the president
of Stanford University, Marc Tessier-Lavigne, was forced out
of his job after image manipulation in many of his papers was
exposed on PubPeer.[35] People had started poking holes in one
of his papers on PubPeer back in 2006—a paper published in
Nature and cited more than 2,000 times. Commentators identified manipulation of images indicating likely fraud, leading to a
trail of apparently falsified papers by Sylvain Lesné and others,
which may have led to hundreds of millions of dollars of wasted
research funding.[36] Other initiatives, such as Plaudit.pub and
Hypothes.is, allow scholars to share their assessments of work
(in any stage of publication) in an accountable, transparent way.
Journal peer review stops when the articles are published, but
peer review goes on.

It's not just Big Publishing that wants to control this process. There is also a generation (or more) of established scholars who resent the loss of control they experience in this new,
disparate system of peer evaluation. I have already spilled thousands of characters on how antigay activists (including, as noted,

Mark Regnerus and Brad Wilcox) produced a terrible piece of research intended to persuade the Supreme Court against affirming the right to marriage for same-sex couples—and were roundly vilified by liberal academia.[37] But that case also produced a debate over peer review that is relevant for this chapter. Most critics of the research, who were incensed by the poor quality, obvious political machinations, and corruption in the relevant journal's peer review process, saw it as a case of anonymous peer review shielding the powerful from scrutiny. That's what occurred when Wilcox secretly agreed to serve as a peer reviewer for the study he himself had organized. But there also was a conservative establishment that was outraged at the outrage. In his subsequent book, *The Sacred Project of American Sociology*, which took the discipline to task for what he saw as lockstep leftism, Notre Dame sociology professor Christian Smith wrote, "no less important [than the attack on Regnerus himself] was the assault on the integrity of the double-blind peer-review process involved in those attacks."[38] Smith (who had been Regnerus's dissertation advisor) saw the public scandal as evidence of the tragic decline of authority for legitimate—that is to say, institutional, formal, hierarchical—peer review. He wrote:

> The Internet has created a whole new means by which the tra-
> ditional double-blind peer-review system may be and already is
> in some ways, I believe, being undermined. I am referring here
> to the spate of new sociology blogs that have sprung up in recent
> years in which handfuls of sociologists publicly comment upon
> and often criticize published works in the discipline. The com-
> mentary published on these blogs operates outside of the gate-
> keeping systems of traditional peer review. All it takes to make
> that happen is for one or more scholars who want to amplify their
> opinions into the blogosphere to set up their own blogs and start

writing. . . . No journal or book review editor has asked any of these sociologists to review a paper or book. What publications get critiqued and sometimes lambasted is entirely up to the blog owners and authors.

Smith was outraged that people who were not *invited* to critique work were nevertheless going public with their criticism. And that was before he found out about Twitter! His objections might have a quaint, get-off-my-lawn quality to them, but the expression of deep outrage directed at academic critiques delivered out-of-school is common. (The same complaint has been leveled at Data Colada, the blogging collective that exposed Dan Ariely and Francesca Gino.) Today's free-for-all is understandably stressful for a lot of people, who don't want their work peer reviewed from all directions at once—even those who aren't trying to protect their proteges from the accountability they deserve. But I use Smith's case because it illustrates the projection of the powerful losing control. They see the problem as debunkers run amok and complain that no one holds them accountable—but it's that accountability piercing their own impunity that is really getting under their skin. Even if you like "traditional" peer review, its advantages must be balanced against the absence of accountability for powerful actors in the secretive operations of the system. In the traditional process, the only real product open to public scrutiny is the published work. How it got there is kept under wraps, what's not accepted disappears, and the opacity of the whole process often works to the benefit of the powerful.

THE DAILY DEBUNKING

We don't have to live in Christian Smith's world of knowledge creation. When citizen scholars get involved in the public debates of the day—as scholars, not just as citizens—that's being true to the spirit and purpose of peer review. We should not shrink from the controversy or dismiss the discussion simply because the venue or format does not match the review process our guild masters say we should honor. Our smaller, sometimes indirect contributions through daily engagements matter. If you get on social media to say, "This paper is bad!" about a piece of scholarship that you are qualified to evaluate, that's part of the stream of discourse we can call peer review in the broader sense. Call it community-engaged peer review—or just debunking. Here are a few examples.

Ivermectin

As COVID-19 raced through Mexico in 2020, the population confronted the crisis with inadequate public health data and underdeveloped medical infrastructure, in a context of state corruption and political polarization. The personal response of the president, Andrés Manuel López Obrador, was Trumpian: scoffing at the pandemic and bragging about his good luck charms—although, unlike Trump, he kissed his supporters.[39] As the death toll mounted, desperately sick people stayed at home rather than face what they feared would be certain death inside a hospital.[40] But the government of Mexico City, run by an ambitious protégée of López Obrador, Claudia Sheinbaum, attempted to strike a different tone. A PhD scientist, Sheinbaum drew praise from experts—and international accolades—for funding widespread virus testing and contact tracing and requiring masks on public transportation (and in 2024 she was elected president of Mexico).[41]

But by the end of 2020, Mexico City's health officials had veered dramatically off course. They succumbed to a groundswell of popular sentiment in favor of ivermectin—a relatively safe, cheap, and popular deworming drug in a region with a long history of intestinal parasites, but one with no proven efficacy against COVID-19. They started a program to distribute the medication, and eventually more than half a million kits— including ivermectin as well as some combination of aspirin, Tylenol, azithromycin, and a pulse oximeter—were doled out to residents who tested positive at one of the city's pop-up health kiosks. Within a year, the bloom was off the rose for ivermectin, research showed it didn't work, and the program officially ended.[42] The authorities turned toward vaccination as their main strategy to suppress the pandemic.

Unfortunately, instead of admitting it was a mistake, in the fever months of 2021 before vaccines were available, the ambitious (arrogant) head of Mexico City's Digital Agency for Public Innovation, José Merino (a close ally of Sheinbaum's) promoted the ivermectin program as evidence of his effective response to the pandemic. To boost the party's political prospects, he led an ill-fated statistical analysis, with several co-authors within the bureaucracy, that they posted in un-peer-reviewed form on SocArXiv. (Papers on SocArXiv are "moderated" by volunteers, to weed out spam and fraud, but are not reviewed for quality.) The paper concluded: "The study supports ivermectin-based interventions to assuage the effects of the COVID-19 pandemic on the health system."[43] This reckless conclusion was announced at a press conference.

By the time the paper came to my attention at SocArXiv, it had been downloaded more than 10,000 times. And it was being widely used in the global Ivermectin Wars—a running series of battles against Big Pharma and "the science," waged by those opposing vaccinations, masks, school closures, or other public health restrictions. (In response to the controversy, one intrepid believer emailed me to demand, "Is there a double blind study that shows it does *not* work if used as soon as symptoms appear?") SocArXiv decided to remove the paper from our service on ethical grounds, and in the process, I wrote some essays and gave interviews explaining why the analysis and its conclusions were wrong, why the program was misguided and unethical, and how Merino et al.'s conflicts of interest disqualified their overconfident conclusions.[44] In response, Merino called me "colonialist" and "authoritarian," and López Obrador blamed the scandal on the opposition press.[45]

What can we take from this story? During the pandemic, online-active citizens engaged in many levels of unsupervised science exploration and dissemination, using a mélange of news reports, peer-reviewed studies, educated guesses, and anecdotes.[46] One response would be to identify the problem as the dissemination of scientific content without peer review, then bemoan the loss of "traditional" control over the production and dissemination of science—to look for ways to contain research within formal academic channels. But I see the incident as evidence that citizen scholars need to stay vigilant—and of the imperative to be prepared to call bullshit in the public square (in the spirit of peer review) when the need arises.[47] The instigators of this misleading research justifying a bad policy were governmental actors. They didn't need SocArXiv to get their research into the public square; they owned the public square. They held a press conference. They could just as well have created the *Official Journal of Mexico City Public Health Studies* and published the paper as the lead article. Merino did not need peer review, or SocArXiv, to tweet, "It is GREAT news to be able to validate a public policy that allowed reducing health impacts from covid19."[48] More broadly, when have authoritarian (or genocidal) governments needed peer review to justify their abuses of science, or scholarly journals to disseminate those justifications to the public? And when have online mobs, cults, or social networks heeded calls for caution and restraint?

Those who would mislead us—in government or otherwise—have better tools for dissemination than they used to. But we have those same tools to use in our debunking efforts. It is true that, in the era of modern science, public health authorities in democratic societies have an admirable record of subjecting research to public scrutiny. And some members of the public now expect compliance with scientific norms, including peer review—which is a positive development. But the digital horses of irresponsible or malicious information long ago left the musty barn of academic journals. We can't stop them, but we can respond. We can compel our governments to subject themselves to scrutiny and transparency. We can also bring our knowledge and expertise, our communication networks, and our reputations as responsible citizen scholars to the scrum of public debate. If we recognize that imperative and are willing to embrace it, we can develop the habits, tools, and training to increase our chances of success in the information wars of the future.

Generations

Many social scientists know that the generation labels (like "Millennial" and "Gen Z") with which marketers have so successfully infected the public discourse are essentially bunk. In the process of social change, generational change matters; generational labels are trash. To use the terms of demography, cohort change is a key mechanism for social development, which we often conceptualize with the idea of age, period, and cohort.[49] The *cohort* in which people are born determines the *age* at which they will experience the events that occur in different *periods* in history. The bunk part is slotting cohorts of people into broad groups arbitrarily labeled "generations" and given names (such as "Pandemial") without any empirical or theoretical basis. This results in blinkered thinking about the mechanisms of change, and it promotes stereotypes in the popular imagination.[50]

I chipped away at this problem on my blog for a few years, as the terms and their pseudoscientific applications spread through popular media and into academic research. Eventually, having failed to make the public see reason, I finally put together a petition for social scientists to sign. Many of us have felt hampered and annoyed by the endless listicles, stereotyping, labeling, hairsplitting, and debating that follows these pointless concepts like a cloud of toxic gas, so the first few hundred signatures were an easy sell. The petition asked the Pew Research Center to stop using generational labels, and I briefly spelled out why in a *Washington Post* op-ed.[51]

Where was formal peer review? There is no real research to argue over. No one has published academic articles systematically interrogating the appropriate length of "generations" or empirically establishing their dividing lines to see whether the common definitions fit the data—and the names are just farcical. Researchers normally debate categories such as race, ethnicity, gender, and family structure—to name a few prominent examples—but with generations, this discourse is completely absent. And yet you can always make the generations look real because they are correlated with time, which is the conveyor of social change. So if you only show generation differences according to your fixed categories, they look impressive. (Obviously, more "Millennials" than "Baby Boomers" identify as transgender.) We know that creating categories is a serious business in social science, or any science, but these categories are anything but serious. So, how do we debunk something that has never been properly bunked? How do we use our expertise to stop the spread of something that was never subjected to peer review?

After years of media use of these labels, a lot of people can identify the generation name that has been applied to their birth cohort.[52] But simple descriptive work establishes the vast gulf of experience that separates people under the same tag. For example, early and later Baby Boomers experienced a 30 percentage-point difference in rates of military service. "Millennials" include people who graduated before and after the Great Recession, people who were in elementary school or done with high school when the September 11 attacks took place—huge gaps in life experience. The birth rate for women at the age of twenty fell 42 percent between 1980 and 1996, representing a world of difference in the lives of women considered part of the same arbitrary "generation." It doesn't take peer review to get this kind of debunking out to the clicking public. In fact, the hucksters and consultants using these terms have simply avoided formal peer review for the most part. But the statistics I just reported are not controversial or difficult to ascertain. They don't need a journal editor, they just need to be compiled and communicated—often quickly, in response to media attention. A blog, an op-ed, a social media campaign—all these are legitimate tools to use against misinformation. And by publicly rallying around a well-justified counternarrative, responsible scholars can help.

GET INVOLVED

The old norm in which you wait politely to be asked to do a review, and then and only then do you respond with your opinion about a piece of scholarship, is—thankfully—crumbling. The stodgy complaints about critics who don't go through "proper" channels are becoming rarer. These archaic notions no longer fit in our contemporary information ecosystem. In their place, we are even beginning to formally value the critical reading of other people's social science, in many different formats and venues, as a vital contribution to knowledge. Tenure and promotion guidelines increasingly make mention of public visibility as a valued outcome. This fast-paced, decentralized system is chaotic at times, but the alternative is not a smoothly functioning, carefully supervised system; it's one dominated by more aggressive actors filling the vacuum left by our misguided sense of decorum.

Joseph Bak-Coleman and colleagues have argued that information systems require collective stewardship to protect against the pernicious effects of disinformation, stewardship that goes beyond traditional peer review to involve formal and informal mechanisms of dissemination and error checking.[53] This can include systems of verification before publication and rapid review after the publication of new information. (They also point out that universities and other knowledge-creating institutions will need to formally reward this work if we want it to become institutionalized and normative; I return to this in the conclusion.)

By speaking up in response to research that pops up in the news, social media, or political or policy channels, we are in fact acting in the spirit of peer review and exercising the values that it embodies, even if not under the supervision of an academic journal or publisher. It remains, however, our responsibility to behave ethically, to consider the implications of our public words and deeds, and to face the consequences. That means carefully considering our actions. Here are some principles for speaking up, publicly, about someone else's work.

- *Consider whether to get involved.* If something is out of your area of expertise or you're not sure what the correct take is, hold off. This doesn't mean you have to have done the exact study before, or even worked in the precise area, but you need to be able to assess what you're talking about—someone's research methods, someone's models, someone's description of the implications of their work. When pressed, it's fine to say that you aren't ready to judge a piece of research. (This doesn't mean you have to censor your own perspective or political views, of course.)

- *Don't exaggerate, needlessly impugn motives, heckle, or harass.* If research needs to be debunked for the public good, so be it. But don't debase yourself or your work by stooping to low levels of discourse.[54] Look for role models who offer criticism constructively in the appropriate venue or medium and emulate their style and approach.

- *Don't pass up opportunities to be constructive and helpful.* We all love to get positive peer feedback, so pay it forward. If you only have something negative to say, carefully consider whether problems in the research are consequential enough to justify damage to someone's life or career—especially someone with a tenuous or subordinate career status. If they are working in your area of research, you might do better in the short run— and make a friend or collaborator in the long run—by tempering your public criticism and instead reaching out to help them (and let them help you) in future work.

- *Practice open scholarship in your critiques.* If you do a reanalysis or offer a differing take on the data or methods of a study you're critiquing, be transparent and trustworthy. Make yourself vulnerable to the same kind of critique you're offering. Lead by example.

- *Carefully scrutinize the role of journalists.* Some journalists want to work with scholars to get the story right, and they need our help. Others may be looking to stoke conflict or jump in over their heads for the sake of a quick story. If a journalist gives you a chance to bash a new study, it's okay to bow out, ask not to be included, or simply decline to comment. You can always offer your response to the research in another venue.

- *Listen as well as speak, and admit when you're wrong.* We need to lower the stakes and normalize the experience of openly correcting errors. Your status, advanced training, and/or university affiliation are assets, but they're not evidence that you're right in a particular instance. Don't pull rank or demand deference in lieu of offering reason and compassion. When you turn out to be wrong, admit it in a form as prominent as your initial claims.

The decorum assumed in the staid, formal peer review process often serves as a fig leaf for nasty behavior, underhanded machinations, and rigid hierarchies. If we're going to extend the (positive) spirit of peer review, to widen our reach of influence and deepen our contribution in the public sphere, we need to be better. The informal give and take of public debate offers plenty of opportunities for politics and conflict—many of which are worth taking. But in the critique of research, we should adopt a gentler baseline, at least sparing the cutting vitriol for the truly bad actors who really deserve it.

A lot of the daily debunking we do, as well as our work with journalists and other interested parties, takes place on and around social media. Some of these principles apply generally to social media discourse, but the medium of exchange in that sphere imposes its own logic. In the next chapter, we'll talk about the form and substance of social media interaction.

5

SOCIAL MEDIA

My goal for a chapter on social media and citizen scholarship is to offer a model for how scholars can use these tools and platforms to disseminate their work, but also to listen and learn—to find the balance between these multiple types of information flow, to make meaningful a complex set of interactions across the collapsed context of overlapping audiences. Since I first pitched this idea, of course, social media blew up (again), especially the app formerly known as Twitter (now X), which was the network tool for which my model was designed and upon which it was tested. Twitter was the one place, especially, where academics, journalists, and political people talked to each other in public; this situation might or might not reemerge on another platform. But the key concept underlying my approach is the multiplicity of audiences, so I think—and, tentatively, hope—that such a situation will persist in some form, wherever the current platform wars land.

In the Facebook (and similar) context, "friends" are the people with whom we agree to enter into an ongoing relationship. On Twitter, Instagram, and TikTok (or comparable), "followers" are people who already know about us and elect to be exposed to the next thing we write. When friends and followers share our work in their networks, and network algorithms repackage and redistribute it according to their own priorities, our actual readers—the broadest group—is our *audience*. (In influencer-speak, this is sometimes called your "platform.") As scholars, this should work for us. The audience is our readers. We write because we want readers, and usually we always want more of them. So far, so good. The problem with social media is that the speed and simultaneity of dissemination across these audiences—and their multidirectionality—makes them unpredictable and unknowable. So we have to perform as if the whole world is watching.

It's one thing to want as many readers as possible to read your book and something else to want that for every half-baked thought you can't resist sharing—and also for the hostile screeds from every critic and troll who accosts you in public.

As Alice Marwick and danah boyd put it so perceptively in 2011, introducing the concept of context collapse, "Twitter affords dynamic, interactive identity presentation to unknown audiences."[1] In this environment, you can be flexible and experiment. The good news is you'll meet and have the opportunity to learn from new people, who will interpret and react to your work in unexpected ways. That's also the bad news. This is writing *in public*.[2] In principle, this dilemma applies to any genuinely public presentation (which excludes most academic writing). However, on social media, where the audience is simultaneously interacting across audiences among themselves—that is, in the hyperconnected digital universe—the interactions and impressions expand geometrically and chaotically.[3]

On the plus side, I guess, this is what enrages old(er) people like Chris Smith, whom we met in chapter 4, who are *shocked* that academics are reviewing books on their blogs, uninvited by any editor, without the authors' consent or participation. Where is the decorum, the deference, the predictability, the hierarchies, the elbow patches? That kind of reaction is what made social media adherents out of a lot of people—myself included—who were focused on the democratizing element of the hyperconnected world. Not coincidentally, that spirit had a pronounced peak at a moment when the democratic system, in America as well as many other societies, faltered or collapsed—the moment of Trump. (I return to Trump and Twitter in the next chapter, in which my epic legal battle against him makes it to the Supreme Court of the United States.)

Time for a timestamp: As I was drafting this chapter, Twitter was renamed "X" by billionaire owner Elon Musk. He eliminated "verified" accounts and much moderation from the platform, and he made other technical and political changes that drove many reasonable scholars—including me—off the app. Many academics, researchers, and journalists still use Twitter, or X (as do many news organizations, politicians, government agencies, and other companies), while also experimenting with other platforms, principally older platforms such as LinkedIn and Reddit, Threads (by Facebook), TikTok, Bluesky, and Mastodon. Most scholars seem to be looking for the good parts of heyday Twitter without the (increasingly) bad parts: they want community (the networks they already have), openness, serendipity, buzz, reliable technology, and decent moderation to cut down spam, trolling, and abuse—a combination they have not, as of early 2024, been able to find.[4]

The distinctions among these alternative platforms include their technical features, but mostly their governance and control, culture, and community. I prefer the Mastodon model because it is a decentralized online social network—part of the Fediverse, on the ActivityPub protocol—with noncentralized platform governance.[5] This allows a social network app to have no ads, no content algorithm, no centralized corporate ownership, and a choice of community norms. I favor the view that decentralized, nonprofit ownership offers our best chance to make social media a force for good in the scholarly community and the world. My hope is that, with such guardrails and supports, we can break the cycle of what Cory Doctorow has the called "enshittification" of social media platforms: "First, they are good to their users; then they abuse their users to make things better for their business customers; finally, they abuse those business customers to claw back all the value for themselves. Then, they die."[6]

SURVEY AND INTERVIEWS

In this chapter, I include information from a survey of researchers I conducted in 2022. By sharing a link on my social media accounts, I generated a convenience sample of about 400 academics and researchers who used social media for professional purposes. About half were sociologists, and most of the rest were social scientists in other disciplines (Black [4 percent], Hispanic [6 percent], and Asian [8 percent] scholars were underrepresented). Using this (nonrandom) sample, I set out to identify patterns unfamiliar to me; then I followed up by interviewing a subsample of respondents. In the survey, I offered fifteen possible reasons to use social media in our professional work, each of which addressed types of information gathering, interpersonal networking, and research dissemination. I clustered the respondents into five groups by their level and type of engagement and then interviewed people from each cluster.

In the end, I interviewed thirteen people for about an hour each. Their use patterns ranged from a low of, "I never post, I only look at things on Twitter when my colleagues send me links to things" (public health scholar, white woman, age forty-eight), to a high of, "Twitter is the primary means by which I learn about new research, hear about academic debates in my field, and participate in those debates" (economist, white man, age forty-something). The purpose of the survey and interviews was to help make sure I wasn't missing large swaths of experience among the likely audience for this book—and I am confident that the exercise accomplished at least that. A handful of interview excerpts—those insights and examples that stood out or illustrated a point particularly well—appear in this chapter (and a few elsewhere), though a lot of what we discussed became obsolete in light of events at Musk's Twitter.[7]

SCHOLARS IN SOCIAL MEDIA CITIZENLAND

Fruit was designed by natural selection to entice animals to carry seeds away and deposit them in piles of fertilizer.[8] Humans are the descendants of frugivores, and today, eating fruit is good for us not just because it provides sugar, but because it's high in fiber. So if you want to moralize your way to a better diet, you can think of juice as evolution's way of getting humans to eat fiber—and drinking juice without pulp is everything wrong with modernity. It gets worse, because our ancient hominoid ancestors probably used the smell of fermentation to find ripe fruit, planting the seeds, so to speak, for alcoholism and possibly other addictions in our gene pool. (In evolutionary addiction research, this is known as "maladaptive cooption of ancestrally advantageous behaviors."[9]) Next thing you know, you wake up in the

Anthropocene, and the number one cocktail "perfect for day drinking" is the Mango Guava Ombre.[10]

The positive view of social media is similar. We crave attention (sugar), and in seeking it, we sometimes get the human interaction we need (fiber). I can't say how much of this is evolution as metaphor versus the actual biological kind of evolution, but it works either way. We chose this history, but not under circumstances of our own creation. Social media gives us the opportunity to strive for attention, complete with perfectly intermittent reinforcement, and when we fall for that, we get the social interaction we need. In turn, all this provides a reasonable personal and professional justification for our shameless behavior.

Unfortunately, evolution also set us up to be suckers in the presence of abundance. Just as we famously undermined the productive collaboration with fruiting plants by separating juice and alcohol from pulp and calling it progress, so, too, did we bobble the evolutionary handoff on calorie storage generally, so that our clever metabolic tools for famine preparedness made us patsies for the obesogenic foods industry. When it comes to Twitter and its ilk, we can see that we love attention, and we'll do stupid things to get it—even reshape our brains in the process, making newly tailored behavioral and linguistic patterns automatic, built-in elements of our personalities.

A common perception among Twitter users was that they learned to "think in tweets," something that seems obvious to people who used that platform a lot and perhaps (I wouldn't know) impossible to imagine for people who didn't.

- "I was tweeting so much that I was even starting to think in tweets."
- "Everyone who knows me knows I'm obsessed with Twitter. . . . I'm told I think in tweets."

- "Ever think in tweets when ur really frustrated? Happened this morning as dentist was ½ hr late. Thinking angry tweets somehow consoled me."
- "I feel like it has overtaken my brain, so that I think in tweets. I'll see a thing in the world and begin thinking about a tweet-able way to say it."
- "I think in tweets now. My hands start twitching if I'm away from my phone for more than 30 seconds."[11]

We don't need to delve too far into our brains and their decomposition in the maelstrom of social media. But before we can productively discuss useful advice about citizen scholarship in this context, we have to grapple with the systemic elements of the digital platform age. In his book, *Hyperconnectivity and Its Discontents*, Rogers Brubaker distills five themes for our time, which can serve as helpful guideposts for work on social media: abundance, miniaturization, convenience, quantification, and discipline. Brubaker doesn't devote much time to the implications for scholars working in online environments, so I will refocus his themes for our purposes.[12]

ABUNDANCE

That satiating, calorie-rich, "cacophonous glut of information," in Brubaker's term, ends up flattening communication and reducing its value. This is emptiness in abundance. As we both consume and produce social media, we want the knowledge we produce to appear in the doomscroll but stand out from it as meaningful to the right audience at the right time. How to figure this out without simply collapsing into our own doomscrolling is profoundly perplexing.

The abundance problem is apparent on all the platforms to different degrees. It also involves the choice and mix of platforms. Do we want separate platforms for different feeds and functions (friends, family, professional, news, music, etc.), though this risks losing serendipity and cross-pollination? Or do we want everything jumbled together, which means Nazis and cat pictures mix in with news and tenure congratulations? By the time I interviewed Eugene, a tenured white male English professor who often used Twitter to share and discuss methods and materials in the digital humanities, his survey responses had landed him in my low-engagement cluster. He explained that the hodgepodge of his feed was one of the main reasons he had stepped back from Twitter: "Just that feeling—the big news would come in and how could you not say something? Because the timeline is filled with it. . . . There I would be tinkering away with some totally inconsequential, completely technical, silly thing. And there's the latest blaze up of the world [I had just mentioned mass shootings]. But Twitter was the way I was circulating the technical thing—the only possible way to reach anybody else who is interested in it. So I certainly felt it as a kind of dissonance."

It is not enough that we consume information in a jumbled, undifferentiated stream that removes it from its essential context. We also have lost the ability to maintain separate identities, or subidentities, in the various aspects of our lives—the bits of content we create are also undifferentiated. This is by design. "You have one identity," Facebook's Mark Zuckerberg said in 2009: "The days of you having a different image for your work friends or co-workers and for the other people you know are probably coming to an end pretty quickly. . . . The level of transparency the world has now won't support having two identities for a person."[13]

So the Eugene who is sharing a bit of code for text analysis is the same Eugene—in the same feed, at the same time, in the same voice—offering obligatory outrage over the latest mass shooting.

The wide openness of social media differs from a classroom or conference presentation especially in the way it creates an unsettling free-for-all. With so many people there for different reasons, there is no one set of norms. "Twitter's public nature enables users with vastly different views to interact without the constraint of shared purposes or identities," write Moran Yarchi and colleagues, "resulting in heated controversy and growing polarization."[14] Without common norms, you have to watch your back for unexpected problems; the result is a heightened state of watchfulness and anxiety.

What Twitter and other open platforms definitely don't have—and probably never will—is organized peer review to limit the flow of information. As we saw in the last chapter, this is a core function of the academic journal system—mostly helping us decide what studies to read rather than blocking bad studies from ever coming out. But on social media, we don't have that, so we need to rely on signals of reliability and trust that can be embedded in the bits of content we pass around. Those signals include information attached to the links themselves, such as the names of journals, publishers, and research institutions. But lots of important information will not have that quality branding.[15] This opens a key role for scholars in this public space. As participants in this public discourse, our training and degrees, our titles and affiliations, and our proven records of responsible conduct all contribute to the quality of our feeds. This helps our readers as it helps us build trust with them.

MINIATURIZATION

Abundance is partly achieved through miniaturization, one of the key innovations of social media apps that Brubaker describes. Tiny bits of information and communication worm their way into every crevice of our attention, bringing with them little nuggets of advertising as well as data collection devices that bind like integrins to the information receptors of our brains. In the decomposition of information, courses are broken into lectures, books into chapters, journals into articles, albums into songs, careers into jobs. Then they are broken down again into slides, tables, factoids, claims and counterclaims, riffs, tasks— memes. Attention is similarly carved up, until it is reduced to a series of glances, as exemplified by the Instagram scroll.[16] Like microplastics working their way up the oceanic food chain, the value of this miniaturized content is less than the sum of its parts, and its toxicity is enhanced by its fragmentation. If we're not vigilant, our ability to devote sustained attention to complex information atrophies from underuse even as our brains are overused to the point of exhaustion against the onslaught of information.

There is little social upside to miniaturization. There is no getting around the fact that longer stretches of concentration are better for us and our work, and for addressing the issues that concern us—including fixing the information ecosystem itself. Context is, of course, the first victim. Tragically, my own discipline, sociology, has claimed that context is the one thing we can reliably add to The Discourse. (That's why the American Sociological Association created the magazine *Contexts*, of which I was once co-editor, which was designed to swim against this insurmountable, context-crushing tide.) Nevertheless, we need to keep focused on this problem so that we can raise it on the agenda of any future interventions in the regulation or governance of social media platforms.

CONVENIENCE

"Convenience resets expectations, forms habits, and insinuates its way into our routines," writes Brubaker.[17] We're all on a treadmill: digital platforms provide convenience and then become the target of our demands for greater convenience still. Why do people actually want "threads" instead of essays? The imperative of convenience justifies the miniaturization of abundance with respect to information. What we are conveniently serving—the substantive content and its vital contexts—becomes lost in the undying, round-the-clock quest for the faster, easier, and ultimately frictionless form that it takes on social media.

When I first joined Twitter, many years ago, I called my account @familyunequal because I was planning to only use the platform to broadcast posts from my blog, Family Inequality (the name was just too long for a Twitter handle), which was itself a stream of miniaturized information nuggets produced in the service of my real project, a textbook on sociology of the family.[18] I didn't have time or energy for daily back and forth with strangers, I thought. Needless to say, that didn't last. You can't successfully run a social media account as a broadcast device alone. I eventually did develop a successful presence—at least in terms of followers and engagement—but only with a much greater time investment. Many of the strangers with whom I interacted became differentiated into friends, professional contacts, enemies, and so on. The audience became connected, to me and to each other.

There is no avoiding the fact that we as citizen scholars enter social media platforms as readers as well as content providers—everyone does. We all suffer consequences of the same type, but for those of us whose primary mission is generating and disseminating new knowledge, this is costly. We want to put our research in front of the right people at the right time, and the slightest misfire in time or pitch apparently makes the difference between success and failure. However, because our successes and their rewards are intermittent, and the threat of invisibility appears greater than the risks of oversharing, we respond by producing more and more content. As a result, we both work and live in a firehose of conveniently available information of diminishing average quality.

Many of us have experienced the simple email interaction with a student who innocently asks something like, "Quick question: What is the difference between Foucault and Marx on the issue of false consciousness?" It's a fourteen-word question that requires a fourteen-week answer. In public, and especially on social media platforms that encourage this kind of interaction, the same economy applies with personal attacks as with innocent questions, and the difference between the two may be moot. This defines the form of trolling known as "sealioning."[19]

So, the firehose is also a shitstorm boomerang.[20] Because when we try to make ourselves and our content conveniently available, we also make it much easier for people to waste our time, as well as harass and attack us. And, as we have all learned, the social media economy serves the interests of these bad actors all too well. The people criticizing, attacking, or threatening the person at the center of the interaction have much less to lose in the exchange. And they can cause harm far out of proportion to their investment, especially when they swarm together.

QUANTIFICATION

You don't have to care about the metrics that quantify all aspects of your work. The machines and people who count everything about you don't care if you care—they'll take care of it. And they speak to each other about you without needing to bother you in person. In addition to all the regular consumer and law enforcement surveillance you get for free by using social media, your academic work is also counted. The research impact score-keeper Altmetric, for example, analyzes posts on the app formerly known as Twitter to see how often a paper is mentioned in the news and elsewhere and generates a summative impact score. Maybe these social media mentions will turn into "citations," if the right person sees the right tweet at the right time and mentions your work in a publication that counts. Then those mentions might be counted by Google Scholar,[21] Web of Science (the Clarivate company that produces the journal impact factor), or Elsevier's CiteScore (powered by Scopus). Ultimately, datasets of millions of articles (including yours) are scraped and merged with government records, patents, and social media mentions, with machine reading to determine the quality and quantity of research impact across all academic disciplines.[22]

Are we using social media to increase our metrics? Years before impact shows up as "citations," it germinates on social media. Follower counts become data points in publication contracts and even some tenure decisions. If no one "reacts" to a post, the emotional feeling of invisibility may be crushing; if just a few people do, it might be enough to drag you further onto the platform.[23] And, of course, the platforms use the numbers for everything they do, whether we like it or not. This is to say, even if *you* don't look at the numbers, they reflect (and create) the reality we all work in. Everyone sees the numbers, and everyone is always already trained to react to them, to compare themselves to them, and to shape their own behavior around them (see "Discipline," later in this chapter).

Social media interactions are made—by us, the content providers—to be engaging, as determined by the behavior of readers and the algorithms they serve. One obvious outcome of the quest for quantified confirmation is conflict and polarization. In short interactions with strangers, it's hard to be noticed or make a difference when so many people have similar opinions. When 1,000 people don't like someone's comment, the only way to stand out is to make your reaction more extreme. So "I disagree" quickly devolves to "DIE MOTHERFUCKER." By shouting at someone and moving on, anyone can help build "the ratio"—a quantifiable metric aggregating shame and disgrace—with only a tiny individual investment (see "Convenience," earlier). For those involved in one-to-many interactions, this can become overwhelming, exhausting, or terrifying.

Again, even if you think you don't care about the metrics, you probably actually do, because you don't want to waste your time on social media. When a lot of academics moved from Twitter to Mastodon, one problem stood out: Mastodon users could not "quote tweet" someone else's tweet (or "toot," on Mastodon). That means when you share someone else's post, you don't get quantifiable credit for doing so. The likes and boosts and comments all redound to the original creator. This was a deliberate feature of the platform, designed to cut down trolling and pile-ons. But it had the effect of silencing a key feedback metric: Did anyone appreciate that I just shared something? *Hello?!* It is not an accident that the same platform affordances that promote healthy engagement also enable an app's weaponization.

DISCIPLINE

Digital platforms, Brubaker writes, get under our skin. "They draw us into their orbits, condition us to desire the gratifications they provide, and channel our interactions into the surveyable, calculable, and manipulable forms and formats" they construct.[24] In short, they are agents of the pervasive sort of modern discipline that Michel Foucault warned us about. We have learned to coerce ourselves into the shape demanded by our structural overlords. We think in tweets.

But do we have to do this? Can't we just keep our professional work separate from our social media? We are being pressed to participate by the gravitational force of network effects—the weight of those in our actually existing social networks who are already there, which increasingly relegates refuseniks to an outsider status. And many of us, directly or indirectly, are being cajoled into "outreach" or "engagement" activities by our universities or professional obligations—largely on and through social media. In Tressie McMillan Cottom's categorization, that encouragement includes two strains. There are the institutions' academic capitalists, who want to promote their universities, building engagement metrics to evaluate faculty based on their contribution to the prestige economy of academia. And there are the populists, who want to democratize knowledge and "tear down institutional barriers of access."[25] If I had to choose, I'd rather be a populist, the sorts who Cottom writes have better motives, though they have failed to grapple with the stratification of academic "microcelebrity" along the lines of social inequality, such as race and gender. (This means the populists are inadvertently pushing academics into an inequality-reproducing buzzsaw.)

Clearly, one answer is: no, we don't have to do this. Those with the self-discipline to stay off hyperconnected digital platforms can have functioning research careers, albeit with some (often large) loss in their social influence. And some people are successful dabblers, keeping up appearances without getting pulled whole hog into the social media cesspool.

But the deeper answer is that we don't have a choice. We are on the platforms whether we choose to be or not. Regardless of where or how you publish your work, the products of your efforts will be "on" social media and related platforms—shared by others, discussed (or not), counted, aggregated, and served up to audiences without your input. And regardless of how you interact with people in the academy or other publics, you will be the subject of their social media communications. If you field a survey, the respondents will talk to each other about it on social media. If you write a paper that engages a research literature, its practitioners will happily hop on the nearest platform to discuss its implications. If you have students, well, you may already know how that goes. All this interaction may or may not get back to you directly, but it is in your information ecosystem and it involves people important to you.

The platforms condition our behavior and identities through the actions of (human and nonhuman) others, whether or not we commit our bodily presence in their service. In our era, hyperconnected media is to communication what capitalism is to economic activity. It's the social infrastructure that undergirds a core component of human society. There is no way for individuals or organizations to function without relying on social media platforms' affordances. This system is something we can learn to work with, but not something we can learn to work without.

Thought of in this way, the question is not "Do we have to do this?" but "*How* should we do this?"

Note: I do not mean to say the current social media configuration, in terms of hardware and software (social or technological),

is permanent or inflexible or that it should be accepted unques-
tioningly. It's here right now, like the oceans and democracy and
cancer. We should devote some of our energy—and the energy of
our institutions and organizations—to the democratic effort to
regulate and reform Big Tech and its platforms and to supporting and building alternatives. As citizens, we need to help generate the responsible stewardship social media platforms need
to function as public utilities,[26] defined as such because they are
ever present and essential and therefore necessarily amenable to
democratic control.[27] Just because they generate wealth doesn't
mean they should be in the unchecked hands of a few billionaires, or anyone else.

Citizen scholars' attitude toward social media should be that
we will use what we may, change what we can, and set both individual and institutional goals accordingly.

LIVED EXPERIENCE

Consider two responses from my interviews with researchers.
Here is how Twitter provided a basic level of mundane social
and professional connection to Daniel, a thirty-something Hispanic sociologist in the nonprofit research sector. I noted that on
the survey he had said Twitter increased his work satisfaction,
and he replied:

> Oh, yeah, the work satisfaction is, like, a couple of things. One
> is general awareness of the field and understanding or situating
> myself and my organization in terms of this bigger field, and hav-
> ing that better clarity on what's happening and who's talking about
> it—which is nice, just as a professional. And then there's, I would
> say, like, little ego boosting stuff, like a colleague's congratulations

or thank you for helping with something. Or people are Tweeting an academic paper, or like a blog post that you wrote, and you see that others are reacting to it and taking it seriously. That kind of stuff. Yeah, that kind of stuff is also nice to see: connecting the dots and seeing your work, like, being engaged with.

Reading and listening on social media can be part of becoming a more open-minded person. George, a forty-something, white male sociology professor who studies issues related to gay culture, told me:

So, I follow a lot of academics of color, and I don't participate in those conversations at all because they're not for me. But I feel like it's a water cooler where I get to hear things that I am not privy to. I'm probably not friends with enough Latinx academics here at my institution, or the relationship that we have, or the infrequency with which we see each other. I don't get to hear the complaints about the microaggressions or, sometimes, the joys. And so I feel like, at a personal level, Twitter has been very helpful for me to be a more empathetic person, to have information that I might not have been privy to otherwise.

These are the interactions and relationships that help sustain us in our work. I don't want us to give them up just because the platforms we use are designed to convert the last drop of love wrung from our souls into a microcent of ad revenue. We have to find a better way.

In this chapter, I'm focusing on big-picture questions of hyperconnectivity and technology, rather than specific apps and features, because these things are changing rapidly and we need a solid grounding to confront the entire landscape. The details of our platforms and their features matter for whether they are pushing in the good or bad directions on these issues. But we need to be systematic and maintain a perspective on their structural role. If we are automatically coming to think and speak in 280 characters, that is awesome for conciseness and clarity but probably bad for deep thinking. If we are accustomed to a high metabolism and level of visibility, we come to anticipate different responses to every sentence before we finish it. That might be good for reflexivity and openness, but bad for new ideas and risk-taking—and it's just an exhausting way to live and work.

Beyond the technological features of the social media apps, with their idiosyncratic advantages and problems, there is our real life in and around their platforms. There is a unique culture and milieu to the social spaces they erect and facilitate. Even before Elon Musk bought Twitter, Carl Bergstrom, a prolific Twitter presence who rose to social media prominence on the strength of his pandemic-related expert science communication, believed the bloom was off the rose. "By early 2022," he writes, "the value I found on Twitter had fallen off. It was harder to find productive scientific discussions. Posturing, virtue-signaling and name-calling increased. Some of my colleagues left or locked their accounts. Coordinated harassment quashed nuanced debate."[28] Changing usage and interaction patterns shifted Bergstrom's experience of Twitter as a social space.

For example, we know there usually is a low cost to launching harassment and threats and a structural imbalance between the effort expended and the harms caused. The individually weak troll is drawn to this environment and feeds off its affordances. And yet the volume and intensity of their collective behavior vary dramatically according to a chaotic list of inputs that are difficult to pin down, much less predict. Whether to put up with trolling depends on the benefits we're receiving, in general and at a specific time. Sometimes we have no choice but to simply step away and protect ourselves.

Trolls can be scary as well as exhausting, annoying as well as life altering. I have had people maliciously subscribe me to hundreds of free mailing lists, vandalize the Wikipedia page about me, falsely accuse me of sexual assault, threaten to blow up my campus, make antisemitic memes about me, and so on. In most cases, simply logging off social media (principally Twitter, at the time) instantly quieted the deluge. In extreme cases, I reported threats to the police. But the advice to step away from social media devalues our work. If the work is important, then letting the trolls win is an important concession—one not to be taken lightly.

Harassment on social media usually doesn't fit legal definitions of harassment or, often, the definition specific to platforms' terms of service. For example, if 1,000 people each insult a person once, that is a wonderful community-building exercise for the mob, allowing them to reinforce their collective goals and norms while at most representing a mild violation of the system rules.[29] It is nonetheless a very bad day for the victim.

Social media platforms provide individual harassers with a nearly frictionless opportunity to pursue their ends, which often involve tormenting women it would be much riskier to accost in person. Indeed, women academic experts are a common target. Jennifer, a forty-something white woman social scientist, told me: "I don't receive the level of vitriol that I think other people do, but it's a weekly thing. It's just a weird thing. Yeah. But it is something I navigate in that space, which I don't navigate in my daily life to any great degree. . . . I guess, men regularly send me direct messages with pictures of their body parts and/or trying to ask me out, sort of things like that. . . . I would say once a week or so they come in."

Once-a-week unsolicited body parts photos may not be the worst harassment people get on social media, but it's awful—and enough to have an impact on Jennifer's public work:

> The way it presents for me is it constrains what I'm willing to talk about on social media. So, as one example, well, intellectually, I think it's really important that people share their abortion stories. Right. Because I think it's really important that everyone understands how many women have had one and how many men and women are affected and all this sort of stuff. But I would never [tweet about] that because of the level of sort of blowback that would involve. Yeah. So, there are just things I do not comment on because I don't want to deal with what the DMs are going to look like.

When the research topic is adjacent to the harassers' interests, the platforms offer convenient access to abundant targets. Jamie, a white woman who works in medical sociology, told me about people insulting her body on social media: "I don't care. Even if they think they've called me like a 'fat hag' or whatever they wanted to say, I would have been like, 'Yeah, okay.' I've had almost 40 years of people insulting my body size, whatever. . . . I think I just have so much practice with that. I'm like, 'Yeah, whatever. You can say literally whatever you want to me about that, and it will not hurt me.' . . . [And] unlike basically all of my colleagues of color, I've never gotten death threats from anything I've Tweeted or anything."

Jamie may be used to managing it, but she still finds herself in a workspace that creates a welcoming environment to those who would cause her harm. This is similar to what Candice, a multiracial Black woman who left academia but still follows research, told me about the casual racism she encounters on social media:

"People would say to me, who do you think you are just because you have letters behind your name? Well, you're going to call me doctor, that's number one—I don't care who you are. And so I would get in circular battles like that because people did not respect—Twitter highlights that Black women are not respected. And that is what it is."

Of course, such experiences disproportionately fall on women, sexual minorities, and people of color, and those who offer the public their expertise are clearly very appealing targets. But anyone can be vulnerable. Several people I interviewed said what they see and hear about the harassment of others makes them more cautious about putting out their work. Sophie, a thirty-something Hispanic woman in a junior faculty position, wants her work to be influential and reach people outside academia. But she is tentative about getting more involved in social media because she isn't sure how to manage her presence, given the risk of harassment as well as unclear social norms. Compare that with Richard, a forty-something white male economist in the nonprofit sector with a large Twitter following: "I constantly read about what a hostile environment Twitter can be for certain people, and I put full stock and trust in that experience. And it's just not that way for me. And I think there are obvious reasons why that would be the case. But it is just striking how I don't get harassed."

The same affordances that facilitate harassment also offer opportunities for interaction and growth, especially the convenience of quick responses to strangers. A quick correction can leave a mark, for the better. Jamie recalls: "An interaction that was, like, emotionally challenging was when I got called out for some language I was using by a Black woman in a thread. And she was obviously, like, 100 percent right. So that was, like, challenging, but honestly was a reason for me to stay more engaged in the platform, to do better in the future. So, while that was hard and I can remember that visceral feeling of like, 'Oh, God, I've messed up!' it made me want to engage more and listen more, learn more from the people I was following."

It isn't possible to design and maintain a platform that encourages such interactions while preventing harassment and bullying. It's just human interaction—but with high speed and simultaneity, and the potential for exponential reach. A supportive, inclusive social dynamic one moment can swing suddenly toward performative monoculture when people start piling on. Lauren, a white psychology graduate student at an elite university, says the social dynamic is usually positive, but she relayed:

> I don't usually entertain a lot of criticisms of cancel culture. You know, I just think generally people are trying to be more mindful of, you know, the words that they use and the way they engage with people around them. And I think that's fine. I think that's generally good, prosocial, and that's great. . . . But sometimes it does really feel like a one-sided kind of engagement with whatever the issue of the day is. . . . It is a little strange to see people who I consider rational or measured also get a little rabid with you know, like, "there's only one right way to feel about this [and] there's only one right way to talk about it."

TURN THE TABLES

Unfortunately, the excellent content of our scholarly communication alone isn't enough to build a better ecosystem. On one hand, we have access to the awesome power of free, nearly universal dissemination of information. On the other hand, we—the scholarly community—have relinquished control over the means of dissemination. On social media in particular, the algorithms are most likely to share our content with the people most prepared to trust us already. We used to publish journals and books and distribute them to a tiny information elite of our choosing. Now we produce knowledge in more formats than we can count, but we have to beg Elon Musk to distribute them for us.

As I wrote in the introduction, the appearance of the citizen scholar—in human form—can be a profound moment of re-embedding, bringing the expert system to life in the minds of those who are considering whom to trust. And social media provide the means for that, for injecting our voices into the feeds of the doomscrolling publics. If only we could make the platforms see it our way. We can try to change our training, practices, and habits, but ultimately, we're also going to need to change the way the platforms work (or build new ones).

Writing in *Science*, Dominique Brossard and Dietram Scheufele[30] identify several key problems for us to overcome:

- *Information siloing.* Social media algorithms love preaching to the converted, because it drives engagement. And we are tempted to love it because it drives our sense of community, which is truly valuable. But that doesn't allow us to expand our reach.
- *Context.* Researchers want to "tell stories," use compelling anecdotes, and cite multiple studies, but our miniaturized bits of knowledge get lost or, worse, get repurposed for misleading narratives. A key intervention here is for those of us who want to reach more people to create (write, review, publish, and reward) review pieces and descriptive work (see chapter 3) that go beyond single empirical findings.
- *Targeting.* We can't fight the algorithms on the current big platforms. We can train up and learn how to do social media better, but that's a Band-Aid. "When world chess champion

Garry Kasparov lost to Big Blue," Brossard and Scheufele write, "no one called for better training for the next generation of chess players, for developing strategies to outsmart super-computers at chess, or for blaming Kasparov for not understanding what the machine was up to." We need to use the institutions of democratic governance to shape the information ecosystem.

Social media training isn't going to solve our structural problems, but there is a lot our institutions and employers can do to help. This includes training, but also emergency services to help manage harassment and abuse, staff support to handle high-volume situations, technological tools, and public support when faculty or staff are under fire. If our employers want us to see and be seen in public, they need to take responsibility for the consequences of that engagement—and that includes recognizing and rewarding the time it takes. Some schools or departments erratically reward social media effort under "public engagement" or similar categories of accomplishment, but the assessment of this work is not systematic or rigorous. And many universities' social media policies amount to little more than warnings about protecting the reputation of the institution.[31]

That brings us to the specter of professional rebuke: hanging over all of us is the list of academic employees "fired for a tweet" (or at least punished a little). These include Melissa Vanden Bout, an assistant professor at Trinity Christian College, fired for tweeting things like "fuck the police" and using the phrase "transphobic bastards."[32] The faculty handbook at her school exemplifies the contradictions in many policies, which elevate both freedom of expression and institutional reputation and leave their employees guessing which way the wind will blow in any given situation: "When faculty members speak as citizens they are free from administrative or institutional censorship, [but] as members holding a special position within the community they incur special obligations. As scholars and educators, both their professionalism and that of the institution will be judged by their actions. They should be accurate in their statements, exercise restraint in their opinions, and give due regard to the opinions of others."[33]

Of course, politics matters, as we'll discuss in the next chapter. No one gets fired for militantly representing completely mainstream political views in public. A few notable examples cover some of the spectrum of what universities do punish faculty for—and the punishments they can dole out. These include faculty accused of racism, such as Columbia University Psychiatry Chair Jeffrey Lieberman, who lost several administrative posts (but not his faculty position) for suggesting on Twitter that a dark-skinned model was a "freak of nature."[34] (Someone on Twitter told Columbia, "you need to fire racist Dr. Jeffrey Lieberman IMMEDIATELY.") Or Charles Negy, fired from (but then reinstated at) the University of Central Florida for anti-Black tweets during the George Floyd murder protests.[35] And for anti-Israel statements, most famously, Steven Salaita, who lost a job *offer* at the University of Illinois for tweeting against Israel's attacks on Gaza and Zionism generally.[36] And for fat-shaming, Jeffrey Miller was sentenced to sensitivity training at the University of New Mexico and required to apologize for a tweet directed at applicants to his graduate program.[37] There are many others.

We may arrive at a point of public regulation of social media, which in my view is clearly needed, but we have to recognize that subjecting the platforms to the process of democratic control could be terrible, too. So, we can't wait for that solution. The actual policy approaches and debates are beyond my scope (and expertise) here, but the point is that we can develop a fundamental understanding of the system we're operating under, then develop the tools and practices we need to make the most of it in a responsible and effective way, all without losing sight of the need for change.

ADVICE

Some of what's awful about social media is also what's good about it. If you are tempted to shout online, "Hey sushi chef, if you're going to charge $100 for a piece of sashimi, how about some real wasabi?!" it's a good thing that the voice inside your head asks, "Am I sure social media will like this?" Discipline is how norms evolve and persist, and that's essential. Nevertheless, it takes a thick skin and the ability to face your own mistakes to reap the benefits of hyperconnectivity without imploding under the weight of its totalizing pressure.

Sometimes it seems the social media advice for early career scholars is just a contradictory mishmash of common sense and impossible-to-balance sensibilities. Be involved but not too involved. Don't screw up by saying the wrong thing but definitely have a presence—because either saying the wrong thing or not having a presence at all can hurt your career prospects and undermine your important work. If all that seems impossible to juggle, it's still good advice. I would add to it: if you find yourself feeling you have to engage with every little thing, then you need a sustainability adjustment. Even at a lower level of commitment, you can help keep yourself in touch with what's happening and expose yourself to different people and ideas in a positive way.

That's the case with Richard, a forty-something white male economist in the nonprofit sector. He has a heavy presence online, and he manages to keep enough distance while still benefiting from the wider discourse: "I'm unidirectionally putting out commentary on Twitter a lot, but I'm not often really engaging my audiences in a kind of discussion or consultation which takes up more energy and I think generates—we all know that social media can lead to kind of fights and emotional volume can kind of take unexpected turns. And I actually have quite a bit of aversion to that. And so I think in very subtle ways, you can just sort of be there and be talking, but never really engaging in the back and forth."

Developing a presence provides an opening to the kind of connections that can make your work much more effective and rewarding. For example, social scientists who wade into the platforms may find there are activist organizations that can make good use of their skills and knowledge and bring immediate relevance to their work. This is what Jennifer, mentioned earlier, recounted: "I've been able to build up relationships with nonprofits for the most part, where if they're starting a new campaign or if they're working on something, they tend to use me as a person who will sort of help them with whatever the numbers that they want to have. So that's the kind of engagement that I do and that feels best suited to my skills and talents, as well as sort of not taking up space that really should belong to people [who are directly affected]."

Despite a set of productive working relationships, Lauren found Twitter personally upsetting and disruptive, so she cut back on her political follows: "It was just like my timeline was just, like, filled with despair. And so at times like that, I think I'm still going to feel really negative, but that's more a reflection of what's going on in the world around me, not necessarily the social media itself."

Managing information flows around your personal tolerances is difficult but crucial. The algorithms will always try to provide you with solutions to the problems they cause, and sometimes they can be tuned to your needs. But often the solution is distance, time off, and a deliberate effort to modify your habits of interaction.

Here are some stripped-down suggestions, dos and don'ts for the productive, respectful, and sustainable use of social media:

- Be generous. Lift others up, especially those from marginalized groups and those who have smaller established audiences than yours. Share things that are helpful to readers.
- Be shameless. Promote your work—that's why you do it. Share positive things people say about your work. Don't be afraid to delete posts that didn't work out, like unfunny jokes, times you jumped the gun, embarrassing statements, or things that hurt other people's feelings. We should all delete more.
- Follow exemplars. Find some people who are more successful at doing what you're trying to do, acknowledge them, and then do what they do. Accelerate social learning by making it explicit.
- Be a friend. Develop reciprocal relationships with people in adjacent roles, like other academics, journalists, activists, and individuals who are vocal on your issues. Offer them support.
- Don't overreact to negative things, but develop a thick skin and try to let things blow over.
- Reach beyond your network. Don't just talk to people outside your network; listen to them and observe their norms. Find ways to help others by promoting their work, doing descriptive analysis for them, and sharing readings and resources. Don't expect immediate rewards, and don't grouse about not getting credit.
- Don't punch down. Don't make jokes at the expense of weaker people or direct harsh criticism at junior scholars or non-scholars—unless they are truly bad actors. Err on the side of

kindness, and consider the possibility that someone means well even if what they said lands badly.

- Help people do the reading. When you're promoting scholarly work, write short versions, in whatever medium, to tell the story simply, ideally with pictures. Make it easy to understand and convenient to share. Let people know the type of publication you're linking to and its peer-reviewed status.

- Don't post paywalled links. Sharing things people can't read for free is rude and contributes to an exclusive milieu, unless you make it clear you're giving them information about something to buy. If you are promoting something to sell, be brief and direct—"Here's a link to my new book." If you're sharing a journal article, find an open version to link to. If there isn't one, ask the author to provide one instead of putting that awkward task on your readers.

- Set limits. The platform was there before you got there, and it will be there after you leave. Spend time away and don't try to catch up when you come back. Don't let others suck you into their level of engagement. Pick your pace. Even taking one day off can be an important way to reinforce the value of limits.

We're in the knowledge business, and working on and around social media is increasingly part of our jobs. But how does that overlap with our citizenship? Does our activism, our political voice, coexist with, contradict, or contribute to our scholarly voice? That's the subject of the next chapter.

6

ACTIVISM AND
ACTIVE CITIZENSHIP

This chapter is mostly aimed at scholars who are worried that being too political in their public life will undermine their status or legitimacy as scholars or harm their careers. For you who are cautious, I want to urge a more open attitude toward an activist orientation, regardless of your political perspective, and help guide that choice. If we only have one identity across our various platforms and modes of communication, then you can't separate them, can't leave your scholar identity behind. So the alternative to speaking out "as a scholar" is silence, which is not acceptable for a citizen. Meanwhile, a smaller contingent of academic scholars, including "scholar activists," sees its scholarship *as* activism. In the second section, then, I will argue for maintaining a distinction between different forms of speech and communication, so that your active citizenship does not in fact compromise your scholarship.

IDENTITY

Why do we put our names on our work? There is nothing morally wrong with anonymity. It does reduce your accountability, but sometimes anonymity is necessary, for example in the case of state repression or illicit political work—think of the Russian band Pussy Riot or the Anonymous hacker collective. Or it may be merely useful, as in the case of a well-known writer who wants to escape public expectations for their work. Of course, writing under false pretenses, with a fake identity, is wrong, but that's because it's deceptive, not because of the anonymity itself.

Named authorship—and the risks that come with it—is a built-in feature of modernity. As Michel Foucault put it, historically, books were attributed to authors "to the extent that authors became subject to punishment, that is, to the extent that discourses could be transgressive."[1] Naming authors was also a significant step toward the commodification of ideas, according to Karl Marx, who wrote with regard to newspapers, "Through the signature of every article, a newspaper became a mere collection of literary contributions from more or less known individuals. Every article sank to the level of an advertisement."[2] The risk of punishment institutionally morphed into the right to profit from written work, which is probably not an accident. (And that was before Substack.)

A citizen scholar is one person, with one identity, doing two different things, the interdependence of which is vital. The tension between them is highly productive. Citizenship and scholarship are governed by different dominant norms. We are expected to exhibit tendencies toward positionality in our citizenship—meaning we take a particular stand in the social milieu. But in scholarship, it is the norm to at least lean toward universalism rather than privileging groups or group identities—a posture that's often labeled objectivity. How do these arenas work together, then? When we test the limits of the norms in both. Scholarship is best when it engages with civil society, which risks positionality. And citizenship is impoverished without a grounding in knowledge creation, which privileges universalist views. We gain strength as intellectuals from mining these intersecting veins.

Speaking out in public entails risks that many people desperately fear. If you say something stupid or wrong, especially on social media, or change your opinion about something you said in public, will it come back to haunt the evaluation of your scholarship and jeopardize your career? This risk causes anxiety, one reaction to which is to seek safety in speaking only through a narrow medium, such as (paywalled) scholarly work, and doing nothing else. You may argue this is sometimes necessary or reasonable, but don't elevate it to a principle, especially if it entails a stance of indifference. That's a huge, likely untenable sacrifice in terms of citizenship and social life. Will you not attend meetings and make unplanned remarks, comment on politics among friends (in ways that are archivable and discoverable), or volunteer for nonprofit organizations? What about the value statements you make through your visible actions, such as the clothes you wear, car you drive, neighborhood you live in, places you vacation, spouse you marry, schools your kids attend? What of the ways your whole consumer existence is archived, aggregated, and discoverable, beyond your foresight and control?

The defensive crouch is not a happy existence. You can't work as if social media does not exist, and you can't live as a scholar outside of citizenship if you want an engaged life. But the life of an active citizen does not require an activist identity, in terms of deliberate participation or membership in social movements.[3] The responsibilities of citizenship don't necessarily include individual leadership. We can support institutions, be part of teams, and do our work in active consideration of its social impact, without stepping out in ways that many social scientists find uncomfortable.

For some intellectuals, the separation between politics and scholarship doesn't exist, which doesn't mean it's easy to manage. Consider W. E. B. Du Bois, whose career was a difficult series of transitions between academia, various organizations, and independent scholarship. Sometimes such intellectuals are journalists, like Christopher Hitchens or Ta-Nehisi Coates, who are good enough, with ideas that fly in the market, to make their own jobs. They may be think-tank scholars whose scholarship is funded conditional on its propagation of certain political values, like Charles Murray (American Enterprise Institute) or Isabel Sawhill (Brookings Institution). Academic philosophers (Martha Nussbaum), historians (Rashid Khalidi), or law professors (Catharine MacKinnon) can play this role as well, although only within the bounds acceptable to elite universities. And some are activist writers like Richard Hanania, the right-wing pontificator who was outed for having previously written under a different name as a fascist,[4] or the left-wing pontificator Freddie deBoer, who writes as a Marxist. Mostly, these are not social scientists; those who are were likely hired into a specific institutional setting rather than a university (well-compensated jobs in this category are hard to get!).

But those are *exceptional* cases. My approach is more strongly pragmatic, intended for the rank-and-file intellectual. In it, you use the skills and knowledge you have to make the best contributions you can. If I'm a social scientist who studies demography, say, I have some master of social theory and methods. I also have personal morals and beliefs. I can put all that together and offer a relevant critique of Jordan Peterson or welfare policy. If you have a reputation in one realm, it's fine to use it for influence in another—like a pro athlete who speaks out on police brutality. As we will see, I stood up to say, "As a sociologist, my opinion is that Donald Trump is terrible." Those statements are the product of a whole person, even if only one aspect of your identity made people listen to you. There are costs to this, of course. You can't expect people to love you as an athlete, or love your scholarship, if they hate your politics. Politics is not, to coin a phrase, a dinner party—it's real life, with stakes.

SCHOLAR ACTIVISTS

Is a citizen scholar an agent of human liberation? In my conception here, adopting the position of citizen scholar does not imply an activist political orientation. But it does imply active citizenship, which may include attending (or organizing) a protest, but more likely means writing or engaging in political discourse and opinion-making in public or pseudo-public settings (like online professional or friend networks). In this vision of the citizen scholar, I differ from those who adopt the identity of scholar activists, those who are not only "interested in the emancipatory project of knowledge creation and dissemination" but also see political activism as intrinsic to their scholarly careers.[5]

On the left, the scholar activist identity is anchored in the work of Du Bois[6] and Paolo Freire, among others. Freire's *Pedagogy of the Oppressed* depicted the revolutionary educator as the handmaiden of emancipatory consciousness.[7] In that vein, historian Robin D. G. Kelley challenged Black student activists "to not cleave their activism from their intellectual lives."[8] But in so doing, the students' task is not to reform the university so that it truly cares for them as human beings—a fool's errand—but rather to use it as a tool for liberation. Kelley also quotes Stefano Harney and Fred Moten: "It cannot be denied that the university is a place of refuge, and it cannot be accepted that the university is a place of enlightenment," they wrote. "In the face of these conditions one can only sneak into the university and steal what one can."[9] This activist orientation is outward looking, from the university to the community.

One thing I share with this perspective is the idea of the citizen scholar as working at the intersection of individuals and their social worlds—not necessarily by being "of the oppressed," but by helping to produce and disseminate the knowledge they need for liberation. In my view, the citizen scholar may be the person of "true solidarity," in Freire's words, who enables or facilitates that reflection—albeit from a discrete status position, embedded *in* but not necessarily *of* the social world of the oppressed. Freire believed educational projects for liberation were possible within an oppressive system of education, and I similarly imagine emancipatory scholarly projects within the freer spaces of our variously precarious and unfree institutions.

Doing your scholarship *as* activism is a tenable practice, compatible with even mainstream success under some conditions—and it does not require a naive position with regard to institutional belonging. The main condition for that success, however, should give activists pause: your politics have to be acceptable to your professional overlords. That is, the scholar activist who supports causes within the Overton window of the day may be granted free rein to speak out, but that freedom is always conditional. If you are pounding the pavement for diversity every day, your provost may applaud. If you dedicate the same energy to a communist party or against Zionism, maybe not. For scholar activists with tenuous or unstable positions on and around the margins of establishment academia, consider Du Bois himself—or many others with sixties-era radical political backgrounds who adopted more mainstream stances later in their lives and had academic careers, including Angela Davis, Kathleen Cleaver, Bill Ayers, and Bernadine Dohrn.

The contemporary career course I am describing takes a middle ground on the melding of citizenship and scholarship that is not without risk, but perhaps allows more range of political motion, which is more sustainable and, I think, more intellectually and politically valuable. The key point is to treat your work in a more modular way, separating aspects of your writing into different—but transparently interconnected—streams. I especially want to dispel the idea that being true to a radical political agenda requires melding (and subordinating) scholarship to activism. Noam Chomsky, to choose a prominent example, was a social movement activist whose academic work in linguistics remained clearly distinct from his political writings.

With regard to scholarly writing, here are some suggestions for the line I'm trying to walk.

1. Challenge your assumptions. If you are doing empirical research and you know the results before you start—or the conclusions you will draw from them—then you probably aren't challenging yourself intellectually and your scholarship will read as advocacy rather than discovery. (It may also be boring.) There is nothing wrong with that (see chapter 2 on descriptive research), but it should be clearly identified so you don't appear underhanded or mislead your audience. Sometimes, there are obvious conclusions: the United States has too much poverty relative to the levels achieved in other rich countries, for example, and the government could take immediate steps to fix it. This can be in the "policy implications" of a lot of papers. But a research agenda, while contributing to that understanding, should push further intellectually.

2. Be open to being wrong. It's a sign of weakness if you never change your mind or admit you were wrong. Being wrong isn't good, but if you're always right that means you weren't

trying hard enough to learn (and teach) new things. There is a general principle that if you are too cautious you miss out on life's opportunities. But in the intersection of scholarship and politics, this principle is a bit nuanced. If you're never wrong in your political conclusions, you may be compromising your intellectual development for political expediency, which in the end undermines both. If scholars are to be involved in politics to optimal effect, they should be the ones to take intellectual risks in the development of new ideas—and to shoulder the blame for being wrong.

3. Attend to your biases. Another way scholarly work differs from activism is in the consideration of alternative explanations and implications. In scholarship, this is explicit and central to the process. When testing your results against your own expectations, you should be more careful and more critical if the results easily fit—you must account for your own biases. In activism, you don't have the obligation to lead with your weaknesses and give equal space to your opponents (although failure to consider opposing views won't help you in politics, either). In the ideal, these two aspects of your work fit together. Having been circumspect and thorough in considering alternatives in your scholarship, when you turn to political speech, you can refer to that work without dwelling on it: "We have considered the alternatives (cite), and let me tell you why this cause I'm fighting for is right today."

4. Stake your positions. Out of fairness and for legitimacy, you must be open about your value positions. This doesn't mean every piece of scholarship or every interview you conduct needs to lead with your political opinions. But they should be clearly discernible somewhere, such as in your professional profile or in a prominent essay. If your scholarship is all about poverty and you are active in antipoverty politics, give the readers of

your scholarship that information so they can hold your work up to critical scrutiny—or celebration—in that light. (The rare case in which all of a scholar's work has absolutely nothing to do with their political views may be a reasonable exception here, but those people probably aren't reading this.)

5. Don't privilege your own research—unless it's warranted. If you're engaging in public dialog on the issues of the day, you may be most qualified to discuss your own research and questions central to your research agenda. However, once you're outside of your academic research writing, you should only privilege your own work if it's the most relevant work for the debate you're having. Remember: A lot of what you bring to the table is in your literature review and descriptive figures, not the final results of your own research. One of the advantages that an active citizen scholar brings to the public sphere is a wide background knowledge and the ability to critically evaluate and disseminate research by others. Just because you are most invested in your own research is not enough reason to privilege it in your political speech.

6. Play a role. I said this in chapter 1 when discussing how to use a division of labor to move into unfamiliar areas of scholarship. Here, as a scholar, you may have a unique contribution to make within activism, but it's likely as a team member rather than as an independent actor. When I gave a talk about mass incarceration to a campus NAACP chapter, my job wasn't to intervene in the organization (which I support), but to provide them with empirical data and analysis for deeper understanding, to help them succeed.[10] Being willing to contribute that effort to one organization but not another is a political decision that also matters, and it should be acknowledged.

7. Don't assume consensus on goals. Social movement actors may make the choice to privilege a set of social objectives as

axiomatic, but as scholars, we need to acknowledge their social construction and contestation. As Monica Prasad writes regarding academic sociology, "Emancipatory perspectives . . . have never sufficiently answered how to determine what would constitute emancipation if norms are socially constructed and people disagree on what emancipation means."[11] The citizen scholar keeps wrestling with this even after the activists have set their course. Crucially, Prasad adds, "provisional" determinations of normative ends result from community engagement— to which I think citizen scholars can meaningfully contribute.

Scholar activists are a subset of citizen scholars, with their own set of strengths and weaknesses. As citizens, actors in civil society, we all have commitments that are subject to negotiation and change, and this is no different for citizen scholars. However, a commitment to the role of scholar implies a specific commitment to transparency and accountability. It's a principle of scholarly work that one source of its veracity lies in its openness. And the openness provides the means for social interconnection and genuine engagement, rather than the broadcast-style dissemination of "settled" knowledge.

TEACHING AND PREACHING

For those of us who are also teaching professionals, there are a related set of questions about the appropriate and effective deployment of our political views. Even though teaching has not been the focus of the book, teachers also have to manage the interaction of discovery versus persuasion in our work, and so I include a short discussion here. I mostly treat teaching—especially undergraduate teaching—as hewing closer to the category of scholarship rather than citizenship (much less activism). That may be because most students are not choosing my courses to debate my political perspective (which they usually don't know before the semester begins); they're just trying to fill out a schedule with tolerable courses that meet their major requirements. In short, they're a captive audience, and I should not abuse the privilege of their attention. Teaching in a classroom comes with different ethical responsibilities than speaking at a rally, obviously. However, just as in my scholarship, this does not mean I must keep my political views secret.

Let's return to Max Weber's classic essay, mentioned in the introduction, "Science as a Vocation" (or, alternatively, "Scholarship as a Profession."): "Politics has no place in the lecture room as far as the lecturer is concerned," he writes. "Least of all if his subject is the academic study of politics." Does that mean we must refrain from engaging in politics in our public lives? Absolutely not, Weber insists. In fact, it's our obligation to be forceful and persuasive: "If you speak about democracy at a public meeting there is no need to make a secret of your personal point of view. On the contrary, you have to take one side or the other explicitly; that is your damned duty. The words you use are not the tools of academic analysis, but a way of winning others over to your political point of view. They are not plowshares to loosen the solid soil of contemplative thought, but swords to be used against your opponents: weapons, in short."

So, why is it crucial to leave our politics out of our lectures? It's about the relationship between the lecturer and the student, and Weber's point is pedagogical as well as ethical. He adds: "Our aim must be to enable the listener to discover the vantage point from which *he* can judge the matter in light of *his* own ultimate ideals." The ethical problem arises from the privileged status of the lecturer. "I think it irresponsible for a lecturer to exploit a situation in which the students have to attend the class of a teacher for the sake of their future careers but where there is no one present who can respond to him critically."

Under the presumed requirement that students remain silent in the classroom, it seems clear that imposing our personal beliefs is an abuse of power. If a professor "feels himself called upon to advise young people" and "has a vocation to intervene in the conflict of worldviews and party opinions, [then] let him do so outside in the marketplace of life, in the press, at public meetings, in associations, or wherever he wishes," Weber argues. But that professor should not "display the courage of his convictions in the presence of people who are condemned to silence even though they may well think differently from him." Fortunately for higher education, times have changed. Most people now agree we should allow students to respond critically to their instructors.[12] That doesn't mean there is no power to abuse, but it's a big step up from mandatory silence. It also does not settle the issue of whether we are abusing or undermining our status as reliable truth-tellers by advocating political views, though it helps prevent some egregious abuses. To go further, we might say that, as instructors, as in our research, we are compelled to fall back on openness. Just as we nowadays recognize the benefit of allowing students to offer critiques of our viewpoints when we teach, we should also embrace as an ethical matter the right of any public with which we communicate—in the classroom or in the streets—to access the information underlying our conclusions and the sources of our beliefs. To prevent the reality, or perception, of imperious authority, the practice of transparency is just as important in our public advocacy as it is in our scholarly research.

That is one principle in Weber's distinction between our political public selves and our circumspect teaching personas. The other is the distinction between facts and values, which has been litigated at least back to David Hume.[13] Wherever one falls on the ontological status of these concepts and the nature of human reason, we can, in practical terms, maintain at least a sketchy boundary between teaching people useful things about how the world *does* work and proselytizing to them about how the world *should* work. Even if you do not agree that facts and values are strictly separable as a matter of philosophy, this is still useful advice as a matter of tone and demeanor—pedagogy, broadly defined. If our research cannot determine the ultimate morality of our ends, it can explain what the means to those ends must be and help the reader decide whether those means are morally acceptable. As Weber writes: "Does the end 'justify' these means or not? The teacher can demonstrate to you the necessity of this choice. As long as he wishes to remain a teacher, and not turn into a demagogue, he can do no more. . . . we can compel a person, or at least help him, *to render an account of the ultimate meaning of his own actions.*"

As noted earlier, however, in much of our work as citizen scholars, we embrace value propositions that can be elevated to levels of abstraction at which there is nearly a universal consensus. Human suffering should be minimized, human freedom should be encouraged, equality is better than hierarchy, arbitrary discrimination is immoral, and so on. You can safely say to a classroom full of American undergraduates: "We all probably agree that raising life expectancy is a good outcome for social policy. Here are some policies that would probably help achieve that goal and what their likely consequences would be." That leaves plenty of room for debate about the costs and benefits of different approaches—evaluations of means—which are susceptible to research. On such questions, we often have reasonable authority to express our personal views without abusing our authority or undermining trust in our work.

POLICY IMPLICATIONS

What are we doing when we write—or speak, communicate—*as* a scholar? Here I argue that the staid format of "policy implications" is just an academic's normatively straightjacketed form of political expression, often poorly executed and reasonably left behind. More pointedly, having a "policy implications" section in our work is unlikely to satisfy our desire and obligation to make our work impactful.

If work can accumulate into a larger agenda, it can also be broken down into tiny bits. In the digital, hyperconnected information landscape, our work is miniaturized into smaller and smaller, modular pieces—on social media and elsewhere (see chapter 5). And it is condensed, for example into a short video, university press release, or AI-generated summary.[14] With appropriate metadata (and convenient links), prepared and presented responsibly, *maybe* these pieces can stand alone in the public eye. Of course, we don't think this is ideal for all of our needs. As scholars, we want some people to read the whole work—and the background material and appendices—but outside of a very small professional circle, that will not happen (nor should it). The expert division of labor requires us to divide the intellectual tasks of the day between people with different skills, knowledge, and needs. It's even more horrifying that the individual chunks of our work will be judged by ad hoc juries (more like posses) in whatever fora they appear, according to norms and standards and types of expertise we can't control, and without our consultation (as in chapter 4). Political activists will scoff at the framing or draw harsh conclusions from the terminology used. Competitors will nitpick the methods. Graphic designers will take apart the figures. Large language models will ingest the entire contents and froth them into the corpus of knowledge. And so on.

Assume a case in which everyone is acting reasonably and responsibly. The research is well described, the methods are appropriate, the results are clear, and the conclusions are justified. In that case, what authority does the author have to draw "policy implications"? The granting of space in a journal or book to pontificate about "implications" is a courtesy, a historical holdover from a time when publishing was slow and expensive, readers didn't have access to professional opinion on every subject at all hours of the day or night, and deference was given to scholars (and teachers). In today's information system, I can't see how that privilege is justified, at least not exclusively. Anyone can speak to the implications of a piece of research and use the tools at their disposal to get people to listen to them: credentials, strength of evidence and argument, and a ready audience to spread the word.

To make this more concrete, I looked a little deeper at "policy implications" in academic journals. In empirical studies, this section seems to have been introduced by economics journals in the 1950s. From there, it became a fixture throughout social science research.[15] The first use of "policy implications" in a sociology journal was a 1971 article in the *Journal of Health and Social Behavior.*[16] It projected a tone that persists to this day. In a paragraph tacked onto the end of the paper, the authors speculated that inflated claims about the dangers of marijuana "may actually contribute to dangerous forms of drug abuse among less well-educated youth. If this is the case," they continued, "then the best corrective may be to revise law, social policy, and official information in line with the best current scientific knowledge about drugs and their effect." The analysis in the paper had nothing to do with antidrug policy. It was an interesting examination of the relationship between ideology expressed in a survey (rebellious versus authoritarian) and self-reported drug use. The "implications" are vague and unconnected to any actually existing policy debate (and none is cited). Being in this case both banal and hopelessly idealistic—two terms that find themselves miserably at home together in the space many in the public deride as "academic"—it's hard to imagine the paper having any policy effect (not that there's anything wrong with that.)

More than fifty years later, "policy implications" is a recurring feature of the landscape, demanded by some editors, reviewers, advisors, and funders. The prevalence of this trope now overlaps with the imperative for "engagement," driven both by our internal sense of mission and our capitulation to external pressure to justify the existence of our work in something like market terms. These may be admirable impulses, but they're poorly served by many of our current practices.

There is a very wide range of applications of "policy implications," from evaluations of specific local policies to critiques of state power itself. Here is a very prominent example, from a classic article, "Social Conditions as Fundamental Causes of Health Inequalities: Theory, Evidence, and Policy Implications,"[17] which has been cited thousands of times. The promise of policy implications is right in its title. But here is the list of policies intended to reduce inequality in social conditions as written: "Policies relevant to fundamental causes of disease form a major part of the national agenda, whether this involves the minimum wage, housing for homeless and low-income people, capital-gains and estate taxes, parenting leave, social security, head-start programs and college-admission policies, regulation of lending practices, or other initiatives of this type."

In the conclusion, the authors explain that, in addition to leveling inequalities in social conditions, we need policies that "minimiz[e] the extent to which socioeconomic resources buy a health advantage" (in the U.S. context, this is interpretable as a recommendation for universal healthcare).

The ends are not really contested—better healthcare for everyone. But these implications are almost broad enough—considered together—to constitute a worldview (or perhaps a party platform) rather than a specific policy prescription. If this were actual policy analysis, we would have to be concerned with, for example, the extent to which policies to raise the minimum wage, raise taxes, house the unhoused, and expand educational opportunity actually produce reductions in inequality, and which of these is most effective, or important, or feasible, and so on. But this is not policy analysis, and none is cited. This is almost equivalent to documenting wage disparities and offering socialism as a "policy implication." The paper has been very influential, reaching thousands of students and researchers, and eventually people in policy settings as well, by helping to establish the connection between health inequality and inequality in other areas of social life. It is important work, but the "policy implications" in the paper don't do the title any justice.

I looked further at the "policy implications" of 127 sociology papers in peer-reviewed journals that used that term in the abstract, published in the years 2010–2020. Only 40 percent of the papers had a substantive policy discussion or specific recommendations that followed from the research. Some of these papers were program evaluations, such as one that found prison-based dog training programs were well received.[18] It's possible, as in this case, that there are very specific "implications" that follow directly and logically from a piece of research, in which case the author may be able to provide them without stretching beyond the results. But that's not really how policy works, and the majority of papers I reviewed reflected that. Most offered either no policy implications (sometimes merely asserting that the results *have* policy implications) or general value statements that didn't rely on the results in the paper. Some scholars perform an empirical analysis, find an effect of an independent variable on an important outcome, and essentially offer as a policy implication the idea that we need more or less of that independent variable. Poverty causes poor health; this implies we need policies that reduce poverty.[19] The end.

One lesson is that a given piece of work doesn't have to do so much. This is an important point for scholarly publishing in the social sciences, especially sociology. Empirical papers usually should be shorter, without all the different parts that are often bogged down in peer review. Having different kinds of work reviewed and approved together in a single paper—a lengthy literature review, a theoretical claim, various empirical analyses, and a set of policy implications—creates inefficiencies in the peer review process. Different reviewers, with different strengths, could work on these components separately. In other words, miniaturization can be our friend here. Why should a whole sixty-page paper be rejected because a statistician with no policy experience hates the policy implications? Or because a policy analyst follows different statistical norms?

The other, more liberating realization is that we don't have to limit ourselves to offering implications of our own research. Just as we can write separately about methods or theory—which has been recognized as legitimate academic work—we can jump into someone else's work to offer our own policy implications. Anyone can read parts of one of these articles, such as the theory and results, draw the same (or different) policy implications, and write a paper to that effect—or paint them on a protest sign or post them on social media. Being the person who did the analysis only gives you more license to state that conclusion because of archaic publishing norms. If I as a scholar read a hundred articles and then make a t-shirt that says, "Child Tax Credit to Reduce Poverty!", the question is not whether I did those analyses, or whether my demand belongs in the same paper as the analysis, but whether others put stock in my credibility and trustworthiness as a scholar and citizen.

Here are my policy implications from an analysis of "policy implications":

1. Don't try to pin big conclusions on a single piece of peer-reviewed empirical research. In the old days, you devoted years of your life to a small number of "publications," and those were the sum total of your intellectual production. We have a lot of other ways to express our social and political views now, and we should use them. If you have a PhD, a job, and published peer-reviewed research, you may have earned the legitimacy for people to pay attention to your writing in different contexts.

2. Write for the right audience. If you are serious about influencing policy, write for staffers doing research for advocacy organizations, activists, or campaigns. If you want to influence the public, write in lay terms in venues that draw regular people as readers. If you want to set the agenda for funding agencies, write review pieces that synthesize research and make the case for moving in the right direction. These are all different kinds of writing, published in different venues. Importantly, none of them relies only on the empirical results of a single analysis (much less only yours). Discussing policy implications in the last three paragraphs of your narrow empirical research paper—excellent, important, and cutting-edge as it is—will not reach these different audiences.

3. Stop asking researchers to tack superficial policy implications sections onto the end of their books or papers (or dissertations). If you are a reviewer or an editor, stop demanding longer literature reviews and conclusions. Start rewarding the most important part of the work: the part you are qualified to evaluate.

4. If you are in an academic department, on a hiring committee, or on a promotion and tenure committee, look at the whole
body of work, including the writing outside peer-reviewed journals. No one expects to get tenure from writing op-eds alone, but
people who work to reach different audiences may be building
a successful career in which peer-reviewed research is a foundational building block. Look for the connections and reward the
people who make them.

POSITIONLESSNESS

What are we doing here? The dances academics do around the
concept of objectivity are repetitive, symbolic, and ultimately
vacuous if they don't confront the position of power in the construction of legitimate position-taking. There are many layers of
interest underlying our work. If I write a fear-mongering book
about how aging white male academics don't get any respect
anymore, you might pin me as a disgruntled activist researcher.
But if I write a staid tome about how meritocracy is the highest
ideal of modern society and universities have a special obligation
to put its tenets into practice, it's a little harder to label that a
self-interested effort, though the effect is substantially similar.
But the bias in these two assessments is not just about tone, it's
about power. Affirming the status quo, passively or actively, is
objective; challenging it is *advocacy*.

Pierre Bourdieu put the position of disinterestedness in its
institutional context like this: "If disinterestedness is sociologi-
cally possible, it can be so only through the encounter between
habitus predisposed to disinterestedness and the universes in
which disinterestedness is rewarded."[20] This is why the objectivity dances are endless, as people attempt to position themselves

as truly positionless, to achieve that specific kind of legitimacy that comes from a position of institutional centrality. You end up saying, "I'm not saying poverty is bad, morally, I'm just saying it increases mortality." Or, "people think this is a problem, so it's important—my feelings are irrelevant."

This is not a new critique. People from marginalized or subordinate groups have long been stigmatized for "mesearch" when they pursue social problems related to those groups. This was the theme of Mary Romero's presidential address to the American Sociological Association (ASA) in 2019. She outlined the historical abuse of "objectivity" as a weapon against applied sociology, the sociology that seeks to directly intervene to improve society, especially for the dispossessed, from Du Bois and Jane Addams in the Hull House through C. Wright Mills and the Vietnam War to the present.[21] The ASA's "vaunted empiricist tradition of objectivity," she wrote, "in which sociologists are detached from their research, was accomplished by a false history and sociology of sociology that ignored, isolated, and marginalized some of the founders. In the past half-century, scholar-activists, working-class sociologists, sociologists of color, women sociologists, indigenous sociologists, and LGBTQ sociologists have similarly been marginalized and discouraged from pursuing social justice issues and applied research within our discipline."

Going against the social justice warrior stereotype, however, Romero added, "We stand for data; we stand for evidence; we stand for critical thought; and we stand for an open and transparent presentation of research findings so they can be replicated or disconfirmed."

Romero attempted to walk a fine line, taking a stand for social science but against objectivity. She did so with a historical analysis that showed how the objectivist critique of applied sociology, against sociologists who worked for social change, was weaponized by the political right. This does not imply that progressive social science is above criticism for biases that compromise its veracity. But objectivity, or positionlessness, is neither necessary nor functionally achievable. Just because you're a social justice warrior doesn't mean you're not doing good social science, and Romero's inclusion of openness and transparency here must not be an afterthought.

The debate over objectivity and the imposition of a positionless stance is mostly distraction, a way of undermining the political positions actually at stake. If someone says, "Decolonize sociology!" the response, "You're not objective!" is a way to avoid arguing over the substance of the demand. Let's argue about decolonizing sociology instead.

I need to add here, again, that there are many scholars for whom active activism is not central to their scholarly work. Many of my students and colleagues have ended up working in the bureaucracies of the modern state, producing data and analysis that undergird the work of many others, myself included. I don't subscribe to the position that taking a value-neutral tone in our work necessarily makes us activists for the status quo. But equally important, these scholars must not relinquish their right—and, in my opinion, obligation—to speak out as citizens on the issues of the day, using the knowledge and expertise that they have to bring weight to the argument. They can write different things. You don't need to be a scholar activist to be a scholar who is an actively engaged citizen.

DISSEMINATION IS NOT ENOUGH

The clash between staid technical analysis and radical ideology has arisen in demography in recent years with the rise of "great replacement" theorizing among the white supremacist right.[22] A single, boring demographic report from the United Nations in 2000 used the phrase "replacement migration" to refer to "the international migration that a country would need to prevent population decline and population aging resulting from low fertility and mortality rates." One of the findings in that report was: "The levels of migration needed to offset population aging . . . are extremely large, and in all cases entail vastly more immigration than occurred in the past . . . [and the challenges of falling birth rates and population aging] require objective, thorough and comprehensive reassessments of many established economic, social and political policies and programmes, [including those] relating to international migration, in particular replacement migration, and the integration of large numbers of recent migrants and their descendants."[23]

As this report percolated out among academic demographers, surprising no one but putting some numbers to a well-known problem, the concept of "replacement" metastasized into a totalizing view of race war, in which European whites were the global victims of a plot to undermine their societies by flooding them with migrants from everywhere else.

The idea that elites—and, inevitably, specifically Jews—are scheming to replace whites has been cited repeatedly by mass murderers, including in El Paso and Pittsburgh in the United States and Christchurch in New Zealand.[24] The idea was first used to justify mass murder by Anders Breivik in Norway: "This crisis of mass immigration and sub-replacement fertility is an assault on the European people that, if not combated, will ultimately result in the complete racial and cultural replacement of the European people."[25]

Breivik was quoted by the Christchurch murderer, and then by the man who killed ten Black residents in a Buffalo, New York, grocery store in 2022.

Any demographer who works on questions related to birth rates and immigration has likely encountered racist responses that take advantage of every dramatic projection or turn of phrase suggesting falling fertility and increasing representation of non-European populations. Boring demographic reports, as important as they are, will not stop this tide. (Neither will passive interventions—I blocked many white supremacist Twitter followers of my Demographic Fact a Day account, but I doubt that did much good.)

The sociologist and demographer Douglas Massey was a generation ahead of me in academia. He set an example as a mainstream academic who directed his work, and his public voice, to public issues, especially immigration. In a 1999 article, he offered four ways of "addressing the public": testifying when asked, giving media interviews, sharing data online, and writing for general audiences. "Unlike some of my peers," he wrote, "I do not see a conflict between the roles of social scientist and social critic. On the contrary, I have always felt obligated not just to undertake the most rigorous scientific research, but also to disseminate the results of that research to the widest possible audience. After all, some aspect of demography underlies nearly every political issue of import, and as a concerned citizen I have a duty to speak out whenever demographic facts or analysis are relevant to an ongoing public debate."[26]

Valuable as I find this sentiment, it reflects a pre-hyperconnectivity perspective, focused on dissemination rather than engagement. Looking out at the world, and the role of social scientists within it, I have to conclude that we have tried dissemination, and it's not enough.

As a scholar of family inequality, I've been agitating for many years against the idea that social policy should focus on getting people to change their family structure as a means to improving

family and child well-being. In 2016, I offered the simple cal-
culation that the total annual income shortfall of poor families
with children in the United States was $57 billion, or roughly one
year's tax on the amount of money Apple had stashed overseas
at the time.[27] Federal efforts to reduce child poverty often took
the approach of fixing rather than assisting poor people, including by wasting hundreds of millions of dollars training, nudging,
and coercing poor people toward marriage. That approach attri-
butes poverty to the personal choices of poor people, stigmatiz-
ing populations with lower marriage rates (principally African
Americans)—and doesn't reduce poverty.

At the time, and in the years since, a consensus of academic
and policy experts was building that we could do much better,
more efficiently and humanely, by giving families with children
money. At the height of the COVID-19 pandemic, this consensus had a policy breakthrough moment, and the American
Rescue Plan passed, with provisions to radically expand the
Child Tax Credit (CTC)—raising the amounts, making it fully
refundable so more low-income families would benefit, and
making the payments monthly instead of annually. In 2021, that
policy lifted several million children above the poverty line, low-
ered the child poverty rate from 8.1 percent to 5.2 percent,[28] and
drastically reduced food insecurity.[29] Despite conservative concerns that the policy would discourage poor people from working, employment rates were not reduced.[30]

In short, the expanded CTC was a phenomenal success. It
offered a great return on investment and immediately made the
lives of millions of people better—just as experts (academic and
otherwise) had predicted. And Congress promptly killed it. The
expansion, passed only temporarily to make it palatable to conservatives in Congress, was allowed to expire after one year.[31]
Scholars did the work. They analyzed the world and proposed

the policy. Real-world evidence confirmed the policy was suc-cessful, scholars disseminated that evidence, and then . . . politics happened. A similar story could be told regarding gun control policy—great science, sound policy proposals, political defeat. Science and its dissemination are not enough.

The intellectual development Du Bois followed on the issue of politics and science is interesting here. In 1898, at the start of his career, he had insisted on something like "value-free" science: "Science as such—be it physics, chemistry, psychol-ogy, or sociology—has but one simple aim: the discovery of truth. Its results lie open for the use of all men—merchants, physicians, men of letters, and philanthropists, but the aim of science itself is simple truth. Any attempt to give it a double aim, to make social reform the immediate instead of the medi-ate object of a search for truth, will inevitably tend to defeat both objects."[32]

But by 1944, in the face of continued racial subjugation in the United States, he reflected that life could not always wait for science:

I suddenly saw life, full and face to face; I began to know the problem of Negroes in the United States as a present startling reality; and moreover (and this was most upsetting) I faced situa-tions that called—shrieked—for action, even before any detailed, scientific study could possibly be prepared. It was as though, as a bridge-builder, I was compelled to throw a bridge across a stream without waiting for the careful mathematical testing of materials. Such testing was indispensable, but it had to be done so often in the midst of building or even after construction, and not in the calm and leisure long before. I saw before me a problem that could not and would not await the last word of science, but demanded immediate action to prevent social death.[33]

This is beautifully stated, and it captures the reality that judgments about the role of science and scholarship in democratic and social contestation cannot be made in isolation from real human events and the emotions they inspire. You can't apply a scientific formula to life as it is lived. Du Bois's was a brilliant expression of what—in my own, tiny way—I felt around 2016. My response, naturally, was to get on the app formerly known as Twitter and start hollering.

TRUMP

The year 2016 was eye-opening for the secular Jewish progressive intellectual crowd. For those my age, more than at any time in living memory, antisemitism exploded into the sunlight—arriving directly, personally, and intimately at our (mostly online) doorsteps. Growing up in the 1970s and later, in liberal parts of the country, I had no experience with anything other than casual antisemitism, such as bullies spitting out my last name when threatening to meet me after school. But now that I was speaking out against the rising Trump phenomenon (not in an organized way, but in several op-eds, blog posts, and Tweets), I became identified as one Jewish face of the nascent anti-Trump movement.[34] That was enough to make me a target of virulent antisemitism, which in turn goaded me—(((Cohen)))—toward greater political efforts.[35]

In early 2017, with Trump in the White House, I articulated a new political alignment for myself, taking Adam Gopnik's advice in the *New Yorker*: "The best way to be sure that 2017 is not 1934 is to act as though it were."[36] In other words, united front politics. If you are against Trump, I wrote on my blog, you are on my side. Not on my side in every way or every issue, but where it counts most right now. If you're against abortion rights, against welfare, against environmental protection, I disagree with you on all those things, and I'll say that when we get a chance to talk. But to the extent that you march against Trump, vote against Trump's agenda, speak out against Trumpism, or give money to organizations that do those things, you're on my side. And if you're poor and your community is being left behind by global capitalism, with rising mortality and drug addiction, disappearing jobs, and crumbling infrastructure, but you support Trump and his movement—you are not on my side. If you're marching or voting for Trump, or supporting candidates or organizations that do, or fighting against immigrants or democratic institutions, I'm against you. We can work on your problems later. This position was truly a bitter pill to swallow, because it meant setting back progress for many things I valued, on an emergency basis, to try desperately to salvage democracy so we could live to fight another day. But I felt I had no choice.

I don't want to exaggerate—it's not like I quit my job and committed myself full time to The Resistance (which might have been the right thing to do). I just shifted a lot of my attention and energy in that direction. As it happens, my previously (perhaps misdirected) energies spent developing a Twitter following were fortuitous. I was "verified" in the old system and had a relatively large following (about 8,000 when Trump took office). That seemed to work for the platform's algorithm, and I discovered that if I replied to a Trump tweet within a few seconds of his posting (his timing was extremely predictable, so this wasn't hard), my tweet might sit at the top of the thread for a while, and thousands, or hundreds of thousands, of people would see it.

The work was not very sophisticated (figure 6.1), certainly not impressive to most of my academic colleagues (if they even noticed it), and it was completely ephemeral. But I took it

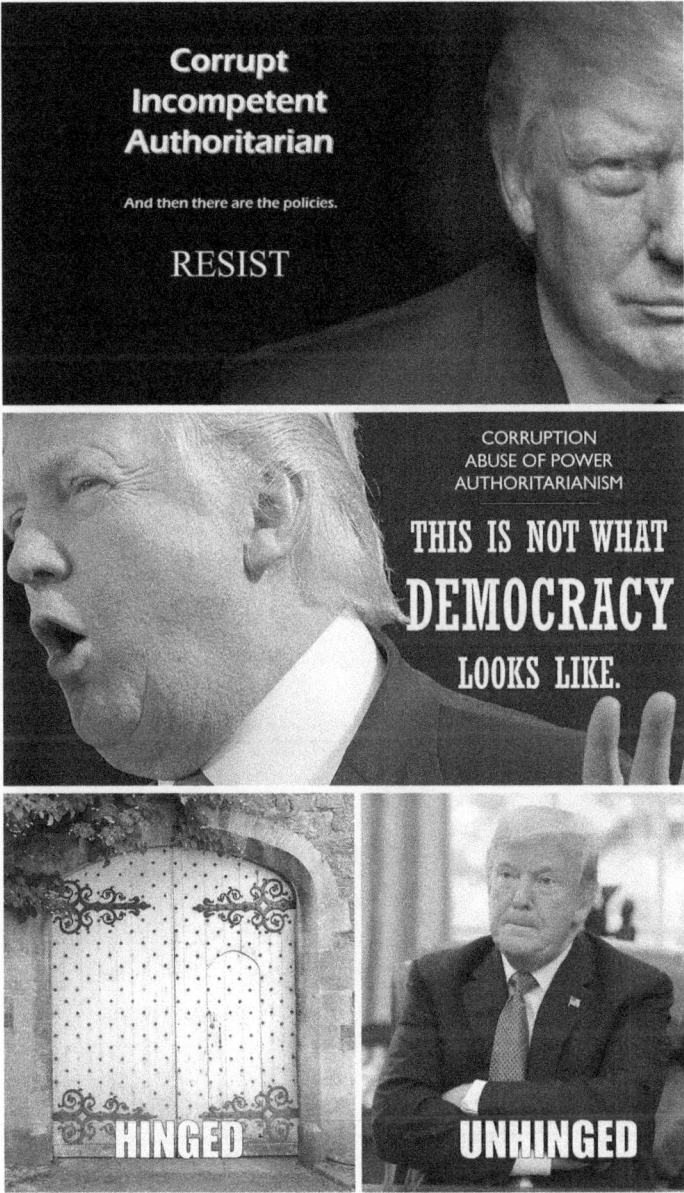

FIGURE 6.1 A sample of the memes I created for Trump's Twitter feed.

seriously, and I attempted to craft a message intended to undermine Trump's support and encourage the resistance to pull together against all he stood for. Over the next few months, I and a cadre of other anti-Trump tweeters came to believe that we played a reality-check role on the social media platform, providing aid and comfort to people who felt oppressed and overwhelmed by the online presence of his authoritarian personality and the many followers who appeared to support him. In 2017, I gained about 10,000 new followers, and my tweets garnered twenty-five million impressions.

Many of those impressions were inflicted on people who were not, apparently, impressed. We don't know how many antisemitic trolls there were on Twitter at the time, but there seemed to be a lot. My replies included "gas chamber soon," "eat a bullet, Kike!", "Cry harder, shlomo," "Ask your doctor if suicide is right for you," and "disgusting Jew rat"—and I saw more cartoons featuring antisemitic stereotypes, gas ovens, and Hitler references than I could count.

Perhaps I egged them on in the hope that more people would share my sense of outrage. Once, when some Nazi who couldn't care less about Palestinians accused me of supporting Israeli oppression—which was a common trope (I don't)—I made the mistake of sarcastically clarifying that Jews don't all think alike, tweeting: "It's hard for us to coordinate our stories sometimes, so it appears there are disagreements among us. Fortunately we all agree on the most important issues: eradicating whiteness and undermining its civilizations."

The tweet (which I deleted too late) was quickly taken out of context, with that pose of ironic, innocent obliviousness to irony that Nazis have radically perfected on social media. It became a meme of me caught in the act of admitting Jews are against white civilization that is still going around, with my face on it.

Another time, when a Nazi asked why Jews supported gun control, I joked, "armed goyim are always bad news for us, duh." This resulted in a front-page item on the white supremacist site Daily Stormer, "Kike Professor Rails Against 'Armed Goyim.'"[37] Each time, some of the social media vitriol overflowed into offline life, as various people called my office, wrote letters to my university superiors, or publicly posted my home address.

The popularity of certain anti-Trump Twitter accounts in 2017 came to the attention of Trump's social media director, Dan Scavino, who apparently took it upon himself to block some of us on Twitter. Maybe Trump was mad that our tweets were gaining attention, or maybe Scavino was just trying to keep Trump from flying off the handle and throwing ketchup plates. Whatever the reason, we were blocked right around the time that the Knight First Amendment Institute at Columbia University began to develop a program of litigation "to ensure the inclusivity and integrity of digital spaces that are increasingly important to our democracy," especially in the face of government repression.[38] The institute's lawyers were looking for cases involving state-sponsored threats to free speech online, and Trump blocking citizens on Twitter attracted their attention.

The lawyers, led by Executive Director Jameel Jaffer and attorneys Katie Fallow and Alex Abdo, brought together a group of plaintiffs to sue Trump and several aides for violating our First Amendment rights. The argument was, basically, that Trump created a "designated public forum" by performing his duties on an interactive platform, so that excluding (blocking) people based on their political expression—practicing "viewpoint discrimination," in First Amendment parlance—violated Supreme Court precedents protecting against government suppression of speech.

It was a novel argument, partly because Twitter was a privately owned platform and the interpretation of technical tools like

blocking had not yet been litigated. But leading First Amendment scholars agreed with us (filing a brief on our side[39]), and
the argument was successful. After filing a federal suit in July
2017, we won in the Southern District of New York in May 2018,
after which Trump lifted the blocks on us. Then we defeated the
government's appeal (with the Department of Justice representing the president) in the Second Circuit Court of Appeals in
July 2019 and an appeal for a rehearing in March 2020. The government appealed Trump's loss to the Supreme Court, but the
justices stalled until Trump's term ended and then declared the
case moot. Our undefeated streak thus ended in a draw (without
setting a legal precedent). However, the Knight folks were successful with several similar cases, and the practice of public officials blocking their constituents for no other reason than their
political views is now hard to defend.[40]

All credit for managing the case goes to the attorneys. However, my practice of conducting Twitter-based activism "as a
sociologist" played a role. By speaking with intellectual authority and claiming legitimacy based on my academic status (as
much as a sociologist can), I created a character that was legally
defensible and politically viable. Humorous posts aside, I had
maintained a certain decorum, refrained from profanity and *ad
hominem* attacks, made no threats, documented my claims, and
put my name over my words. In the *Gilligan's Island*–style group
of plaintiffs, I was The Professor. The others were Eugene Gu
(a doctor), Holly Figueroa (a folksinger), Nicholas Pappas (a
comedian), Joseph Papp (a bike racer), Rebecca Buckwalter-
Poza (a lawyer and journalist), and Brandon Neely (a former
Guantanamo Bay detention guard).

Here's how I put it in a *Daily Beast* op-ed:

> My anti-Trump tweets got, for me, a lot of attention. . . . Hun-
> dreds of thousands of people viewed them, thousands offered

likes and retweets, many commented. I got some death threats, heard a lot of words of encouragement, and even had a few real debates. And that's all from a tiny fraction of the people who read them. I know I risk ridicule when I say this was very valuable to me personally. I'm white (although Jewish never felt so much like a minority status as in the last year) and relatively rich even for an American, and I have a great job with health insurance. So in the grand scheme I have little to complain about. And it's not that I don't know the lengths to which the powerful have historically gone to repress those who oppose them. I'm a sociologist who studies inequality in the United States. But having my First Amendment right to free expression curtailed—in so personal a way—stung me. I am excluded from what is probably the most effective form of political speech I've ever had.[41]

We got a lot of attention in the U.S. and international media, helping to expose Trump as an enemy of democratic values and practices. I also heard good things from some higher ups on campus and in the higher education press. Opposing Trump was pretty popular in my circles, of course, but suing him for Constitutional violations went beyond protesting, it elevated the opposition to a matter of legal principle, in the courtroom, where reality (we hoped) still had a privileged status. Practically, the unblocking we achieved mattered, too. By the time of the 2020 presidential election, the Twitter app informed me, I was running at seven million impressions per month, mostly from tweets criticizing Trump. For an academic, those are big numbers.

I didn't claim that my peer-reviewed scholarly works directly justified my tweets; they weren't referenced in the "policy implications" of my papers on divorce or gender inequality. But I was the same person—publicly as well as personally, online and off—and I did my best to use my scholarly stature as support for my activist practice. Some academics hate this kind of thing, where someone poses before the public as an expert in a field other than their own (like lots of people with medical degrees shilling for fake COVID-19 treatments or against vaccines). And some people just loathe self-righteous leftist academics. Indeed, having degrees doesn't make you right about everything. But my scholarly role wasn't the basis of my practice as an opponent of Trump; it deepened it. I could have done the same thing as a chemist or physicist, but social science is more relevant. Having a substantial publication record and a legitimate job at a public university made me less of an obvious crank, at least, and helped reinforce the understanding that opposition to Trump and Trumpism was deep as well as wide, rational as well as emotional. That's why Trump followers tried to get me fired, after all.

DEDICHOTOMIZE

Conceptual dichotomies can be useful analytical tools, but imposing rigid dichotomies in the actual spaces of action within a single life is not realistic or helpful. In table 6.1, I summarize my suggested approach by comparing some traditional, or stereotypical, dichotomies between the social roles of activist and scholar, with a proposed resolution for citizen scholars. My objective is to make these two overlapping kinds of work and life more fruitful and satisfying.

There are other ways, and they offer their own trade-offs. You still might choose to strictly abstain from activism, politics, or partisanship in any public way. I find that an unacceptable compromise of my role as a citizen. You could fully merge the activist and scholarly roles, as a "scholar activist." I find that often threatens the truthiness of the activism or puts the

TABLE 6.1 STEREOTYPICAL DICHOTOMIES BETWEEN ACTIVIST AND SCHOLAR, WITH PROPOSED RESOLUTIONS

| | Stereotypical opposition | | |
	Activist	Scholar	Citizen scholar
Goals	Social change and advocacy	Knowledge and understanding	Social change and the creation and dissemination of knowledge are interdependent. They don't always happen in the same piece of work, but their paths are intertwined in spaces of interaction and over the duration of a career.
Audience	The public, activists, policymakers	Academics, students	Audiences overlap. If you write for one group, another can read it. Members of different audiences will judge all aspects of your work.
Standard of evidence	Flexible and pragmatic	Rigorous and uncompromising	Embrace the tension between the dynamic, ever-changing nature of activism and the discipline of research. Try to make it productive.
Positionality	Particularist, partial	Universalist, impartial	Both extremes are bad. Activists should ultimately care about (almost) everyone, and scholars should bend over backward to take into account the perspectives of the weak and vulnerable.
Personal objective	Improve society	Have a successful career, discover truth	In a single, actual life, these are not so separable; you are one person. You may be able to evaluate your progress on these objectives distinctly, but if your efforts and successes are too lopsided, it won't make you happy or proud.

scholar in a role where they have to compromise their scholar-ship too much. You could perform both roles, but insist on a rigid separation, so that each speech act is clearly labeled as either political or scholarly. I think it is unrealistic to assume either audience will play along with that once they find out about your other side. So, the citizen scholar model is my pro-posed compromise.

7

MAKE IT HAPPEN

"In every period, the Craft would have to be written differ-
ently. Epistemological propositions are generated by reflecting
on scientific practice—a reflection that is always governed by
the dangers that are uppermost at the moment in question."

–Pierre Bourdieu, *The Craft of Sociology*[1]

Here's a story about failure, success, dissemination, and engagement in the citizen scholar life course. It goes back to the divorce research I described in chapter 2.[2] In 2009 (as an associate professor), I was teaching an undergraduate family sociology course at the University of North Carolina at Chapel Hill. Naturally, this included a section on divorce. I was also developing a proposal for my own textbook, which framed family structures and events, including divorce, as consequences and causes of inequality. For these reasons, I was reading research about divorce along with many other family issues that were outside of my formal training and experience (in grad school, the closest I came to a family demography or family sociology course was a seminar on gender, work, and family, which I now teach).

This is how I came to be irritated by something bad the sociologist Brad Wilcox had written about divorce—and wrote about it on my new blog. Wilcox was claiming that the 2008 recession was lowering divorce rates because hard times pulled people together. It was just standard "pro-family" nonsense. We didn't yet know that divorce rates actually would fall in the years that followed, almost certainly not for the reasons he said (for instance, recessions appear to cause divorce to drop because it's difficult and expensive). I'd write about Wilcox a number of times in the following years.

By 2011—prompted by the combination of my reading, debates around my blog, and news coverage around families and the recession—I was working on a paper on divorce. The American Community Survey had recently included a new question about divorce, so the findings in this paper were new. I presented it at a demography meeting in the summer of 2011, and then revised and presented it again the following spring. Throughout, I blogged, adding data on state variation and Google search patterns, each time getting feedback from readers. A version of the paper was rejected by *Demography* in the summer of 2011 (with useful reviews). Although now discredited as "not peer reviewed" (a fact not known to the public), my commentary on divorce and the recession was nevertheless featured in an NPR story by Shankar Vedantam. Further inspired, I sent a new version (with new data) to *Demographic Research*, which also rejected the paper. I presented on the work a couple of times in 2012, getting feedback each time. By August 2012, with the paper still not "published," I was quoted describing my "divorce/recession lull-rebound hypothesis" in *New York* magazine.

The news media pieces were not simply my work appearing in the news in a one-directional manner or me commenting on other people's research, but rather me bringing data and informed commentary to stories reporters were already working on. Their work influenced my work. And all along, that news coverage was generating on- and offline conversations, as I found and shared research by other people working on these topics (like the National Center for Marriage and Family Research and the Pew Research Center). I tweeted about divorce and its association with religion, disabilities, economics, and race/ethnic inequality. I discussed my research on Facebook, in a smaller, semi-private circle.

By 2014, I finally got the paper—now with even newer data—published in a peer-reviewed journal, *Population Research and Policy Review*. This involved writing the dreaded phrase, "Thank you very much for the opportunity to revise this paper again." (Submitted October 2012, revised August 2013, revised January 2014, accepted and published February 2024.) The paper, eventually titled, "Recession and Divorce in the United States, 2008–2011," did improve over this time: new data provided better leverage on the question, and the reviewers made good suggestions. And its final version showed the lull-rebound in divorce rates, reported as "Divorces rise as economy recovers, study finds" in the *Los Angeles Times*.

Meanwhile, I used the descriptive analysis from this research in my textbook and teaching. I wrote a more general essay on family-recession issues (including birth rates and family violence) in *The Conversation*. To deepen my own understanding, I developed a method of projecting lifetime divorce probabilities (for which I shared the data and code), which also generated some news, and I did some work on occupations and divorce. When I posted the technical notes and data, I got interesting responses from scholars I didn't know, and I tried new things. Lots of people chatted on Twitter and Facebook. I wrote another paper using the same dataset.[3]

At some point, I became a legitimate expert on divorce.

At one level, this is a story about how I started working in a new area, failed to break into the top journals, and, years later, published a pair of papers in minor journals. In my academic career, it was a lot of work for two papers (my friends were busy getting better jobs and big research grants!). But who wants to live in that story?

I prefer the *engagement* story: Breaking into a new area of inquiry involved my teaching, an interactive blog, social media, news media, some peer-reviewed publishing and conference presentations, and colloquium talks. I conducted research, I argued about other people's research, I brought in politics and inequality, and I learned many things. I *love* my career.

This is not a story of how I used social media, or the news media, to *get the word out* about my research, although that happened, too. The work product, not just the "publications," was all public to varying degrees, and the discussions included all manner of students, sociologists, reporters, and interested online readers, most of whom I didn't know or wouldn't have met any other way. (Sadly, it did not involve preprints, which I hadn't yet discovered.) One clear lesson is that there is no fixed dividing line between "research" and "engagement" or "public sociology." Another is its vindication of (or capitulation to) Mark Zuckerberg's demand that we encounter the world on many platforms as one identity. And a third is that I used the experience to generate the Pentagulation model I describe in this, my closing chapter.

THE SYSTEM'S TOOLS

Like many leftists whose formative years were dominated by the American victory in the Cold War and the rise of Third Way neoliberalism, I am permanently inclined toward the pessimistic.

I also know that—despite what editors may tell you—this book might be more popular were it darker, with less breezy how-to advice and more cynical gloominess. But, wary of passing a tipping point of irreversible naysaying, I have looked for a way to have a positive influence.

Consider the intellectual fate of the prominent Italian philosopher Giorgio Agamben. During the War on Terror after 9/11, Agamben wrote *State of Exception* (which could have been translated *State of Emergency*), about how the modern state reaches new heights of repression when it suspends normal democratic privileges to mount warlike defenses of the nation. His criticism was uncompromising and totalizing. When the pandemic came and lockdowns hit Italy in 2020, Agamben rigidly applied his existing formula, going beyond critique of emergency powers to reject empirical reality, declare the pandemic a hoax, and warn of possible extinction resulting from mass vaccination.[4] As the Italian death rate fell after the first wave of COVID-19 deaths in the summer of 2020—in the lull before a much larger fall pandemic surge—his publisher even put out a book of his cantankerous essays.[5]

I take Agamben's as a cautionary tale. If you're not careful, your narrative about slippery slopes *becomes* a slippery slope, and you may miss the opportunity to grasp the handrail of reality. For a while during the pandemic, some people were using the Facebook profile frame to declare, "I have a healthy distrust of authority, and I'm vaccinated." That's my take on our information ecosystem—and social science in general. Our systems of publishing are dominated by monopolistic powers (such as Elsevier) and outright authoritarians (such as Elon Musk). Our institutions are under extreme economic pressure, as well as political assault from reactionary politicians intent on banning everything from drag queen performances to African American studies.[6] In a scene straight out of Kurt Vonnegut's *Player Piano*, in the last decade, I have watched the ratio of computer science majors to sociology majors at my liberal, blue-state public university increase from three-to-one to seventeen-to-one. *The student cannot hear the sociologist; things fall apart; the center cannot hold.* Still, although I have a justifiable pessimism about the future, I remain determined to resist the pernicious effects of that pessimism on my scholarly and civic conduct. As the sloganized saying of another radical Italian philosopher, Antonio Gramsci, goes, "Pessimism of the intellect, optimism of the will."[7]

Making a plan helps. In the maelstrom of social crises, things change in unpredictable ways. The 2020 antiracism protests revealed fissures between types of power and authority. The anti-police protestors wore masks, by and large, trusting the legitimacy of "the science" while contesting the exercise of police power. In 2019, I would not have predicted this: "To its supporters, mask-wearing is a visual expression of civic duty, an affirmation of scientific authority and a show of respect. . . . As protesters poured into the streets to protest the killing of George Floyd, the mask has taken on a new association. Wearing a mask to a protest used to signal that you were an anti-fascist or a cop suited up in anti-riot armor. But at these demonstrations, masks are ubiquitous, symbolizing civic action in more ways than one: Even as they protect the community from the virus, they protest the surveillance of the police."[8]

The behavior of the mask-wearing crowds revealed nuances of public understanding. As the quote from Bourdieu opening this chapter suggests, our choices are "governed by the dangers that are uppermost at the moment in question."

I never fully went for Audre Lorde's dictum that "the master's tools will never dismantle the master's house,"[9] because the master's tools are usually a large part of your arsenal. You have no choice but to use them. It's in the post-dismantling rebuild that we have the opportunity to introduce new tools based on a truly different logic. I may have left Twitter and boycotted Elsevier, because you have to draw the line somewhere, but I haven't forsaken all the tools and platforms of the existing information system, because we don't have replacements available just yet.

PENTAGULATE YOURSELF

So, with the caveat that using the tools of the day doesn't imply an everlasting endorsement of their systems or logic, I want to conclude this book by devoting myself to advice on working in the (extremely flawed) world today.

Specifically, I recommend an active presentation of your intellectual self. Doing citizen scholarship requires a forward stance of initiating intervention. You and your work have to be there when they're needed, and no one is going to get it there except you.

If you don't care enough to promote your research, how can you expect others to? "Self-promotion" has a bad name, but as a scholar, it's literally your job to promote your work, which is inevitably intertwined with yourself. You don't have to be a fulltime self-promoter to improve your reach and impact, but it's in everything you do. Of course, there are norms, and stepping over them makes you feel dirty. You do have to convince every reader (or reviewer or editor) there is something new and important in every book or paper you write, for instance, but if you brag without shame in the introduction, some readers will never get to your lit review. Still, there is no use pretending, or assuming, or even hoping that you're not in the business of promoting your work. Even if your social media post is just a self-effacing, "Here, I wrote this . . .," you're promoting it. And in the digital space, whether you're the one putting your work on social media or you're hoping others will—in a publisher's marketing email, a professional association newsletter, or a conference program—the work will rise or fall on its clicks.

Fortunately, even a relatively small effort, well directed, can help a lot. Don't let the perfect be the enemy of the good. It's fine to do some things pretty well even if you can't do everything to your ideal standard. It's all about making your scholarship better and your citizenship more effective—a project that includes better quality and better impact. You want more people to read and appreciate your work, not just because you want fame and fortune, but because that's what the work is for.

A little organization and effort with the big picture in mind go a long way. The key to my strategy is that the different components of your public self reference each other to work together, helping provide context for the miniaturized bits of information from and about you floating around. I call it Pentagulation, because I see five elements as key anchor points (figure 7.1).

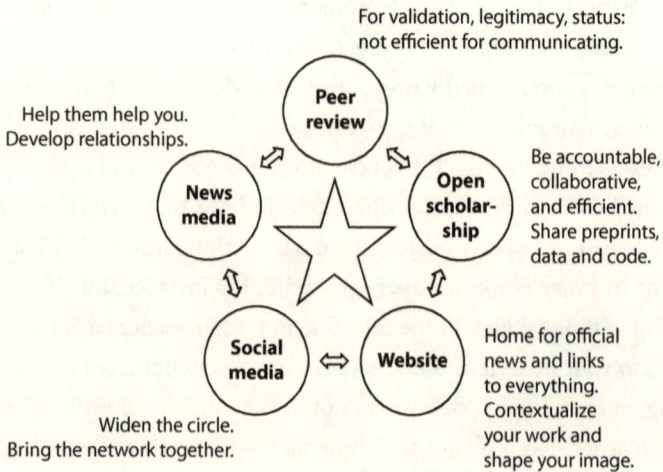

For validation, legitimacy, status: not efficient for communicating.

Help them help you. Develop relationships.

Peer review

Open scholar-ship

Be accountable, collaborative, and efficient. Share preprints, data and code.

News media

Social media

Website

Home for official news and links to everything. Contextualize your work and shape your image.

Widen the circle. Bring the network together.

FIGURE 7.1 Pentagulation.

You don't want to make your whole life transactional and strategic, where everything you do has to be meticulously aligned with your preconceived goals and intended to reach exactly the right people. And you don't need to devote equal time or resources to each component in the system. You want to focus on doing what you think is interesting and important, learning new things, working with people that inspire you, and exposing yourself to new opportunities. The citizen scholar Pentagulation lifehack is about developing great workflow and tools without the effort coming between you and your heart's destination.

Website

Your personal website is often the second thing people see about you—after they come across a piece of your work, or a mention of it, somewhere else. This discerning reader may want to know more about you before they share your work further, report on it, cite it, or offer you a job. Has this person published other work in this area? Taught related courses? Gotten grants? These are things people look for. It's not vain or obnoxious to carefully and comprehensively present this information; it's your job.

Make a comprehensive personal website and keep it up to date with information about your research, including links to freely available copies of your research and writing in categories by type (books, academic articles, essays, datasets, and so on). It's a running joke that academics are sitting behind ancient, out-of-date websites with ludicrously old photos. But contrary to popular belief, this is not the sign of a serious scholar. Include clear information about how to contact you, an actual person, that doesn't require social media apps.

Your website doesn't have to be fancy, although paying a professional to build it is often money well spent. If you are interested in being contacted by reporters, it's a good idea to have a list of previous media mentions, both so they come up in searches and so that people can see your record of playing well with others. I also recommend securing the internet domains for your name.

Listing publications without convenient links to openly accessible versions is an exclusive and off-putting practice unfortunately endemic among academics (know that, if you ask people to copy a piece of text and paste it into a browser or search engine, few will). Let people read the actual research, and let them know you *want* them to read it. If you have work that is not yet published in a journal or book, but it's ready to tell people about, post a preprint in a scholarly repository, either at your institution or in a disciplinary repository like SocArXiv, and link to it. As discussed in chapter 3, this establishes the precedence of your work and opens an avenue for feedback and collaboration months or years earlier than waiting for peer review and publication by someone else. Listing work as "in progress" or "under review" with just a title both excludes people and undermines your credibility. If it's not ready to share, it's not ready to announce. Good repositories (like SocArXiv) allow you to post revised versions at the same location as the work progresses, so people who bookmarked or cited your first draft will find the latest when they're ready to cite it.

Your website is also the place where people can find your more accessible works, such as op-eds and essays for nonacademic outlets. These can showcase your ability to translate between audiences and offer interpretations of your work in the context of the social situation of the day. Some established organizations such as Scholars Strategy Network, The Society Pages, The Conversation, and (in my kind of work) the Council on Contemporary Families, as well as academic societies, publish or help to place essays related to current scholarship. Having a lot of readers the day your essay is published is great, but that essay also serves an important function in perpetuity on your website, offering context for the range of your work and interests.

Peer Review

As discussed in chapter 4, peer review is an important component of your legitimacy and a signal of the veracity of your work. It's not everything, but it is a widely recognized foundation for credibility. And that credibility transfers between different parts of your work. For better or worse, if you have published peer-reviewed scholarship on *anything*, you're more qualified to comment on *everything*.

When you do publish in journals, use open-access journals, because it's the right thing to do and more people can read your work. Second best, if your work ends up paywalled, is to share a preprint or postprint version. This is better than paying an open-access fee to a "hybrid" journal that mixes open and closed papers, and you can almost always do it without violating your author agreement (which you should definitely read before signing). If the journal you want to publish in does not allow sharing at least the final submitted version online (without an embargo period), it is not working in the public interest and you should consider alternative outlets. (Bonus move: If your institution has a rights retention policy, as described in chapter 3, take advantage of it to share your accepted manuscripts.)

Peer review fits into your online profile through the links you provide between parts of your output. To play that role effectively, your website and social media feeds must not link to pay-walled versions of your papers. That's the click of death for someone just browsing around—plus it's elitist and antisocial. Imagine walking into a social situation and announcing, "Here is a copy of my paper for anyone wearing a blue badge."

Open Scholarship

I'm not an open-access purist, believe it or not. (If you got public money to develop a cure for cancer, that's different; then I am a purist.) Not everything we write has to be open access (books, for example, or publications that employ people and add value to your work), but the more it is the better, especially when it comes to original research. Again, this is partly an equity issue for readers and partly a way to establish trust and accountability in all of our work. As discussed in chapter 2, readers should be able to see our work product—our instruments, our code, our data—to evaluate its truthiness (and to benefit their own work). And for the vast majority of readers who don't want to get into those materials, the fact they are available still increases our individual and collective accountability and trustworthiness. I recommend using a free, nonprofit platform, such as the Open Science Framework, for research sharing and collaboration, but there are a variety of options.

Social Media

In the old days, we used to pay extra to journals for hard copy reprints of papers we published and *literally* mail them to the famous and important people we hoped would read and cite them. Nowadays, it is still appropriate (and may be considered flattering) to email them a PDF or link with a short note that says, "I thought you might be interested in this paper I wrote," as long as you don't follow up with repeated emails asking if they've read it yet. You can get some of this done using at least a basic social media presence.

Social media need not require a massive time commitment and doesn't mean you have to spend all day doomscrolling—you can always log out. But setting up a public profile on the major platforms gives people who *do* use them regularly a way to link to you and share your profile. If someone wants to show their friends one of my papers on Mastodon, X (formerly Twitter), Facebook, LinkedIn, or Bluesky (etc.), this doesn't require any effort on my part. They post, "Look at this new paper from Philip!" If I'm tagged, people click on the link and go to my profile, which tells them who I am and links to my website. I do not have to spend time on the platform for this to work as part of my Pentagulation strategy.

Of course, as discussed in chapter 5, an active social media presence does help draw people into your work, which leads to exchanging information and perspectives, getting and giving feedback, supporting and learning from others, and so on. Ideally. But even low-level attention will help attract readers: posting or tweeting links to new papers, conference presentations, other writing, and so on. (While you're there, share the work of a junior scholar or two.)

News Media

Working with news media is a big subject, and my pertinent advice is relatively narrow. Pentagulation is essential for journalists to find you and your work and decide if they want to call on you to help with a story. They jump onto your Pentagulation map by happenstance when they're working fast on a deadline or digging around an area for potential contacts, and they need to be able to move between components with minimal friction. Sometimes, in the words of one person who reviewed this chapter, this leads to "a pretty abusive relationship in which the scholar is the victim." Journalists know what they want and will only take yes for an answer. But I prefer to look on the bright side, and I've had many better outcomes. Here are a few suggestions:

- Treat reporters (and other journalists) as professionals doing an important job. Respect their work like you want them to respect yours. That is, if they deserve it. At the low end of integrity, someone asks you for a quote to validate the clickbait trend piece they have already written and contacts you an hour before their deadline. Just delete these emails. Slightly better outcomes may result when they already know the thesis and basic facts, and they need an authoritative voice to reassure their editors. You may not be able to shape the story—or stop it if they're wrong—but if it's good, your voice can help. On the high-integrity end, if they ask you serious questions with adequate time to respond and they're willing to listen to your perspective, consider giving them your attention.

- Know that journalists' important jobs do not include promoting you and your work. Many, maybe most, interviews or email exchanges will not result in your name or a mention of your publications appearing in their finished story. If their work is good, and the use of your time is reasonable, this is nonetheless a good outcome. Editors often strip a source's identifying details from the final story because they want their news publication to look original instead of derivative— and because they rightly understand that most readers don't really care about the name of a professor or their book. Your next story with the journalist, their editor, or their publication may be different.

- Decide what you want to say and say it over and over. If possible, choose one or two points to make *before* the interview, then find a way to politely say them repeatedly. The off-the-cuff, unsubstantiated sentence you drop in without thinking might well be the most interesting to the reporter, and you don't want it being the only quote that makes it in. Interviews by email are good for this—keep your answers short to limit the chance your words will be taken out of context.

- Develop relationships. Invite (good) reporters to contact you again, and drop them a short note once in a while if you see something interesting. Answer their emails, even if it's just to say you aren't the right one for a story. Suggest other people for them to talk to, even if it means you don't get quoted. Be friendly (you can even be friends).

DO I GET PAID FOR THIS?

If you've made it this far, and you are an employed scholar or in training to be one—getting paid to read this book, more or less—congratulations are due. We need you and jobs like yours if we're going to have, you know, a society. So let's hope (and work) for a future in which we keep getting paid for intellectual work in the public interest.

But the question of whether we specifically get paid for the public, engaging, civic aspects of our work is harder to answer. I love getting paid, but I don't want to get paid by my university employer for doing my duty as an engaged human citizen. And I definitely don't want them evaluating the content of my citizenship and rewarding me according to that assessment. I would just rather they didn't ask. The official position of my own discipline of sociology—according to a slew of our national association's elected presidents and other dignitaries—is that public engagement is a core ambition of our work. But the actual authorities to whom we answer are unsure how or whether to reward—or punish—scholars who succeed in bringing attention to their institutions by joining the public fray. And we have no consensus on shared goals regarding such efforts.

In most academic departments, faculty promotion is based on "research, teaching, and service," which does not principally include writing outside of academia, appearing on TV, or having a lot of followers on social media. The professional schools are different—especially in disciplines like business and journalism—with professors being amply rewarded for popular TED Talks, trade books, newspaper columns, and the like. But those academics are hired for the content (popularity) of their views as well as for the quality of their scholarship. The business of professional education, wherein popular professors sell high-price tickets to professional opportunities, has its own dynamics. In that, professional schools are more like think tanks, which have different metrics for reward.

In the traditional scholarly disciplines, what is the basis for demanding a wider remit? We probably all agree we should be protected from having the political content or implications of our politically dissenting work used *against* us—one of the benefits of the legacy tenure system and "academic freedom." But can we do that while demanding rewards when we say things the provost likes? No one is formally peer reviewing our social media posts or op-eds, so who judges whether they deserve reward? If they are in the *New York Times*, we get a raise, but if they are in *Jacobin* we get a reprimand—or vice versa? On the other hand, if we are invited to testify before Congress, doesn't that mean our work is important and worthy of reward? What about other forms of public service, like donating our time to civic groups? Can we be rewarded for the quantity or quality of our "engagement" without regard to its political content—to its very substance? Does it serve the public good, or the interests of our institutions, if we use our platforms to express our own (minority) views? If we are to be rewarded for bringing positive attention to our institutions, helping them to enhance their public image, will that just promote the most milquetoast engagement (such as extolling the tolerance of diversity)?[10]

There is a larger question embedded here, about the relationship between different kinds of power and legitimacy—different kinds of capital. If you publish an article in the *American Sociological Review* or *Science*, should the *New York Times* publish your op-ed? Then, if the *Times* publishes your op-ed, does the article count more for tenure? In other words, what is the exchange rate between the forms of capital accumulated in these different fields, the "public" and the "academic"? I have suggested working across fields in a coordinated way within a single career, but I don't have the means to definitively address this question. I think the *Times* paid me $250 for my Sunday op-ed there, which boosted my status more than a lot of the things for which I get paid more. And my undergraduate textbook—explicitly dismissed as worse than unimportant by many of my academic colleagues and discounted in all formal evaluations—now generates a substantial share of my earnings.

In Bourdieu's terms, to have influence in a field, you have to be in its game, which means having a relation of *illusio* to that field.[11] If you want to win acclaim in public, and you demand that the university include your public work in its counting of beans, then you subject yourself to its mode of bean counting, which means being judged according to the values and the imperatives of both fields. To be rewarded in both fields for doing the same work may not be possible without fatally compromising the meaning of the work in its proper context.

Put differently, demanding compensation for the public side of our citizen scholarship work may end up as a neoliberal trap, a demand in fact for our own bureaucratic disciplining. The danger is that when the rubber hits the road of bean counting, the ostensible neutrality of the process will quickly fall away, and we will be back to a set of biases from which tenure only marginally protects a shrinking minority of us.

I prefer to recognize the rewards from engagement that show up in assessments of our scholarship. Some aspects of our work that reach the public are reasonably measured as qualities of our scholarship, such as sharing data and other research materials and publishing in open-access venues. But more generally, as citizen scholars, we do better quality work that is more important and reaches more people (including people who cite it academically). In that reach, there are many sources of interaction that lead to improvements in our work. (For example, feedback related to my textbook improves my family sociology research.) So even if all we count is academic publications and citations, grants and awards, we can hope to reap professional rewards for our public engagement—and have better, more interesting, and more rewarding jobs and careers in the process.

To be a public intellectual today requires being both public in one's intellectual life and intellectual in one's public life. Being public in our academic work is increasingly recognized as a prerequisite for scholarly integrity; that's a professional responsibility. Similarly, having a public life means participating in civil society, building a network of interaction in the public sphere, and committing ourselves to the public good; that's a civic responsibility. And our intellectual skills and knowledge are valuable assets in that effort. Some people are lucky enough to get paid for doing both, but to insist that we do, to make civic intervention definitional to our professional work, is probably a dead end.

As citizen scholars, we should use scholarship in our public speech and public engagement in our scholarly research to be good citizens, because it's the right thing to do, and we should use our scholarly abilities for that because it's part of what we have to offer. Doing so is likely to improve our citizenship and our scholarship, too.

NOTES

INTRODUCTION

1. Gil Eyal, *The Crisis of Expertise* (Cambridge: John Wiley & Sons, 2019). Eyal traces the history of this attitude back to Richard Hofstadter, *Anti-Intellectualism in American Life* (New York: Vintage, 1966).

2. Neil Hall, "The Kardashian Index: A Measure of Discrepant Social Media Profile for Scientists," *Genome Biology* 15, no. 7 (July 2014): 424, https://doi.org/10.1186/s13059-014-0424-0.

3. John P. Ioannidis, "Citation Impact and Social Media Visibility of Great Barrington and John Snow Signatories for COVID-19 Strategy," *BMJ Open* 12, no. 2 (February 2022): e052891, https://doi.org/10.1136/bmjopen-2021-052891.

4. NPR, *NPR Ethics Handbook*, 2021, https://www.npr.org/about-npr/688413430/impartiality.

5. Susan Greenhalgh, "Making Demography Astonishing: Lessons in the Politics of Population Science," *Demography* 55, no. 2 (April 2018): 730, https://doi.org/10.1007/s13524-018-0660-0.

6. "Citizen, n. and Adj.," in *OED Online* (Oxford University Press), accessed January 14, 2021, http://www.oed.com/view/Entry/33513.

7. Max Weber and David S. Owen, *The Vocation Lectures*, ebook (Indianapolis, IN: Hackett, 2004), "Science as a Vocation."

8. Michiko Kakutani, *The Death of Truth: Notes on Falsehood in the Age of Trump* (New York: Tim Duggan, 2018).

9. Jason Stanley, *How Fascism Works: The Politics of Us and Them* (New York: Random House, 2018).

10. Timothy Snyder, *On Tyranny: Twenty Lessons from the Twentieth Century* (New York: Tim Duggan, 2017).

11. Francis Fukuyama, *Liberalism and Its Discontents* (New York: Farrar, Straus and Giroux, 2022).

12. Anthony Giddens, *The Consequences of Modernity* (Redwood City, CA: Stanford University Press, 1990), 34.

13. Weber and Owen, *The Vocation Lectures*, "Science as a Vocation."

14. Stephen Jay Gould, *Rocks of Ages: Science and Religion in the Fullness of Life* (New York: Ballantine, 2002).

15. Chris Buckley, "Chinese Doctor, Silenced After Warning of Outbreak, Dies from Coronavirus," *New York Times*, February 6, 2020, https://www.nytimes.com/2020/02/06/world/asia/chinese-doctor-Li-Wenliang-coronavirus.html.

16. George Packer, "The Legacy of Donald Trump," *The Atlantic*, January/February 2021, https://www.theatlantic.com/magazine/archive/2021/01/the-legacy-of-donald-trump/617255/.

17. Anthony Giddens, *The Consequences of Modernity* (Stanford, CA: Stanford University Press, 1990), 21.

18. Dylan Riley, Rebecca Jean Emigh, and Patricia Ahmed, "The Social Foundations of Positivism: The Case of Late-Nineteenth-Century Italy," *Social Science History* 45, no. 4 (November 2021): 813–42, https://doi.org/10.1017/ssh.2021.22.

19. Arthur Lupia and Colin Elman, "Openness in Political Science: Data Access and Research Transparency: Introduction," *PS: Political Science & Politics* 47, no. 1 (January 2014): 19–42, https://doi.org/10.1017/S1049096513001716.

20. Kathleen Fitzpatrick, *Generous Thinking: A Radical Approach to Saving the University* (Baltimore, MD: Johns Hopkins University Press, 2019).

21. Jesse Fox, Katy E. Pearce, Adrienne L. Massanari, Julius Matthew Riles, Łukasz Szulc, Yerina S. Ranjit, Filippo Trevisan, et al., "Open Science, Closed Doors? Countering Marginalization Through an Agenda for Ethical, Inclusive Research in Communication," *Journal of Communication* 71, no. 5 (October 2021): 764–84, https://doi.org/10.1093/joc/jqab029.

22. Donna Haraway, "Situated Knowledges: The Science Question in Feminism and the Privilege of Partial Perspective," *Feminist Studies* 14, no. 3 (1988): 590, https://doi.org/10.2307/3178066.

23. Pierre Bourdieu, *Practical Reason: On the Theory of Action* (Redwood City, CA: Stanford University Press, 1998).

24. Ralph Waldo Emerson, *The Conduct of Life* (Boston: Ticknor and Fields, 1860), 16. Unfortunately, the "odious facts" he had in mind were about the divergent fates of the human races, about which he was factually wrong.

25. Weber and Owen, *The Vocation Lectures*, "Science as a Vocation."

1. RIDE THE WAVE

1. Michael Levenson, "Scale of China's Wuhan Shutdown Is Believed to Be Without Precedent," *New York Times*, January 23, 2020, https://www.nytimes.com/2020/01/22/world/asia/coronavirus-quarantines-history.html.

2. Guobin Yang, *The Wuhan Lockdown* (New York: Columbia University Press, 2022).

3. Hubei Government, "Wuhan, Different Everyday!," September 16, 2014, http://en.hubei.gov.cn/news/newslist/201409/t20140916_526479.shtml.

4. Philip N Cohen (@familyunequal), "I Was in Wuhan in 2005 and 2009. To Me It's Massive and Overwhelming and Made Me Think How Big Humanity Is and How Fast It Changes. Sad for All the People Who Can't Be with Their Families This Year.," Twitter, January 23, 2020, https://twitter.com/familyunequal/status/1220348879264239624.

5. Andrew Noymer (@AndrewNoymer), "Duck Tape Your Underpants. 2020 Is Going to Be a Wild Ride. #coronavirus #CoronavirusOutbreak.," Twitter, February 1, 2020, https://twitter.com/AndrewNoymer/status/1223490472473059328.

6. Archived here: https://web.archive.org/web/20200714114947/https://www.faculty.uci.edu/profile.cfm?faculty_id=5373

7. Philip N Cohen (@familyunequal), "Catastrophe Crowd Gut Check. What Percentage of Americans Do You Think Will End Up Getting COVID-19?," Twitter, March 2, 2020, https://twitter.com/familyunequal/status/1234273724943290369.

8. Kristie E. N. Clarke, "Seroprevalence of Infection-Induced SARS-CoV-2 Antibodies—United States, September 2021–February 2022," *Morbidity and Mortality Weekly Report* 71, no. 17 (2022): 606–8, https://doi.org/10.15585/mmwr.mm7117e3.

9. Joel Achenbach, Katie Mettler, Lena H. Sun, and Ben Guarino, "Coronavirus May Have Spread Undetected for Weeks in Washington State, Which Reported First Two Deaths in U.S.," *Washington Post*, March 1, 2020, https://www.washingtonpost.com/health/coronavirus -may-have-spread-undetected-for-weeks-in-washington-state/2020 /03/01/of292336-5bcc-11ea-9055-5fa12981bbbf_story.html.

10. Philip N Cohen (@familyunequal), "Evidence for Undetected Spread in Washington for Weeks, per @washingtonpost. Also Here's the West Coast Plane Traffic Right Now.," Twitter, March 2, 2020, https:// twitter.com/familyunequal/status/1234343557722443776.

11. Andrew T. Levin, William P. Hanage, Nana Owusu-Boaitey, Kensington B. Cochran, Seamus P. Walsh, and Gideon Meyerowitz-Katz, "Assessing the Age Specificity of Infection Fatality Rates for COVID-19: Systematic Review, Meta-Analysis, and Public Policy Implications," *European Journal of Epidemiology* 35, no. 12 (December 2020): 1123–38, https://doi .org/10.1007/s10654-020-00698-1.

12. Philip N Cohen (@familyunequal), "Today in My Social Problems Class, with About 50 Students, I Opened the Floor to Questions About Coronavirus. As a Scientifically-Literate Person Who Reads the News, I Felt Responsible Answering Some of Their Many Questions. (If I'm Wrong Feel Free to Tell Me and I'll Tell Them).," Twitter, March 3, 2020, https://twitter.com/familyunequal/status/1234652183888617477.

13. Ed Yong, "How Science Beat the Virus," *The Atlantic*, January/February 2021, https://www.theatlantic.com/magazine/archive/2021/01/science -covid-19-manhattan-project/617262/.

14. Walter Isaacson, *The Code Breaker: Jennifer Doudna, Gene Editing, and the Future of the Human Race* (New York: Simon & Schuster, 2021).

15. Philip N. Cohen, "Disrupted Family Plans and Exacerbated Inequalities Associated With COVID-19 Pandemic," *JAMA Network Open* 4, no. 9 (September 15, 2021): e2124399, https://doi.org/10.1001/jamanetworkopen .2021.24399.

16. Philip N. Cohen, *The Family: Diversity, Inequality, and Social Change*, 3rd ed. (New York: Norton, 2021).

17. Micah Altman, Philip N. Cohen, and Jessica Polka, "Interventions in Scholarly Communication: Design Lessons from Public Health," *First Monday*, August 2023, https://doi.org/10.5210/fm.v28i8.12941.

18. Donald Sull, Charles Sull, and Ben Zweig, "Toxic Culture Is Driving the Great Resignation," *MIT Sloan Management Review*, January 2022, https://sloanreview.mit.edu/article/toxic-culture-is-driving-the -great-resignation/.

19. Alisa Tang, "An Inspector Ordered a Free-Food Pantry Removed. This Woman Sounded the Alarm," *Washington Post*, February 26, 2022, https://www.washingtonpost.com/dc-md-va/2022/02/26/takoma-park -purple-community-bins/.

20. Sascha Friesike, Leonhard Dobusch, and Maximilian Heimstädt, "Striving for Societal Impact as an Early-Career Researcher: Reflections on Five Common Concerns," in *Organizing for Societal Grand Challenges: Research in the Sociology of Organizations*, vol. 79, ed. Ali Aslan Gümüsay, Emilio Marti, Hannah Trittin-Ulbrich, and Christopher Wickert (Leeds, United Kingdom: Emerald Publishing, 2022), 239–55, https:// doi.org/10.1108/S0733-558X20220000079022.

21. Nicholas Fraser, Liam Brierley, Gautam Dey, Jessica K. Polka, Máté Pálfy, Federico Nanni, and Jonathon Alexis Coates, "The Evolving Role of Preprints in the Dissemination of COVID-19 Research and Their Impact on the Science Communication Landscape," *PLOS Biology* 19, no. 4 (April 2021): e3000959, https://doi.org/10.1371/journal.pbio.3000959.

22. Nate Breznau, "The Welfare State and Risk Perceptions: The Novel Coronavirus Pandemic and Public Concern in 70 Countries," *European Societies* 23, no. 1 (February 2021): S33–46, https://doi.org/10.1080 /14616696.2020.1793215.

23. Philip N. Cohen, "The COVID-19 Epidemic in Rural U.S. Counties," *European Journal of Environment and Public Health* 4, no. 2 (June 2020): em0050, https://doi.org/10.29333/ejeph/8331.

24. James Walker, Chris Brewster, Rita Fontinha, Washika Haak-Saheem, Stefano Benigni, Fabio Lamperti, and Dalila Ribaudo, "The Unintended Consequences of the Pandemic on Non-Pandemic Research Activities," *Research Policy* 51, no. 1 (January 2022): 104369, https://doi .org/10.1016/j.respol.2021.104369.

25. "Ed Yong @edyong209," archived at: https://web.archive.org/web /20200528011501/https://mobile.twitter.com/edyong209.

26. Ed Yong, *An Immense World: How Animal Senses Reveal the Hidden Realms Around Us* (New York: Random House, 2022).

27. Michael Barthel, Katerina Eva Matsa, and Kirsten Worden, "Coronavirus-Driven Downturn Hits Newspapers Hard as TV News Thrives," Pew Research Center's Journalism Project (blog), October 29, 2020, https://www.journalism.org/2020/10/29/coronavirus-driven-downturn -hits-newspapers-hard-as-tv-news-thrives/.

28. Lauren Harris, "Five Big Findings from the Journalism Crisis Project," Columbia Journalism Review (blog), March 3, 2021, https://www.cjr .org/business_of_news/five-findings.php.

29. Isaac Chotiner, "Noam Chomsky Believes Trump Is 'the Worst Criminal in Human History,'" New Yorker, October 30, 2020, https://www .newyorker.com/news/q-and-a/noam-chomsky-believes-trump-is-the -worst-criminal-in-human-history.

30. Interview with Bertrand Russell, McMaster University Digital Archive, http://digitalarchive.mcmaster.ca/islandora/object/macrepo%3A78002.

31. Leslie Root (@les_ja), "How Come When You Do It It's 'Being a Generalist' but When We Do It It's 'Having Hot Takes.,'" Twitter, December 12, 2023, https://twitter.com/les_ja/status/1734438714435113321.

32. Friesike, Dobusch, and Heimstädt, "Striving for Societal Impact as an Early-Career Researcher," https://doi.org/10.1108/S0733-558X20220000079022.

33. Philip N. Cohen, "Black Men Raping White Women: BJS's Table 42 Problem," Family Inequality (blog), September 25, 2016, https:// familyinequality.wordpress.com/2016/09/25/black-men-raping-white -women-bjss-table-42-problem/.

34. Philip N. Cohen, "Overturning Roe Is an Attack on the Modern Family," New Republic, May 3, 2022, https://newrepublic.com/article/166285 /overturning-roe-attack-modern-family.

35. Philip N. Cohen, "The Divorce Fairness Issue That Jeff and MacKenzie Bezos Don't Have to Worry About," CNN (blog), January 12, 2019, https://www.cnn.com/2019/01/11/opinions/divorce-unfair-bezos -opinion-cohen/index.html.

36. Philip N. Cohen, "Ukraine's Refugee Crisis Is a Demographic Crisis, Too," Family Inequality (blog), March 9, 2022, https://familyinequality .wordpress.com/2022/03/09/ukraines-refugee-crisis-is-a-demographic -crisis-too/.

37. Liz Allen, Jo Scott, Amy Brand, Marjorie Hlava, and Micah Altman, "Publishing: Credit Where Credit Is Due," Nature 508, no. 7496 (April 2014): 312–13, https://doi.org/10.1038/508312a; Alex O. Holcombe,

"Contributorship, Not Authorship: Use CRediT to Indicate Who Did What," *Publications* 7, no. 3 (September 2019): 48, https://doi.org /10.3390/publications7030048.

38. This concept is closely related to the idea of *publication* as the unit of productivity, which is a function of how scientists communicated research findings in the old days (when scientists also were more likely to work alone). Now that we have many different ways of communicating different aspects of research, we can see the limitations of reliance on (linear, print) publications. But in the meantime, we can at least use a more accurate model to allocate credit and responsibility.

2. DOING DESCRIPTION

1. Willard Cope Brinton, *Graphic Methods for Presenting Facts* (New York: Engineering Magazine Company, 1914), 2.
2. Jevin D. West and Carl T. Bergstrom, "Misinformation in and About Science," *Proceedings of the National Academy of Sciences* 118, no. 15 (April 2021): e1912444117, https://doi.org/10.1073/pnas.1912444117.
3. John Gerring, "Mere Description," *British Journal of Political Science* 42, no. 4 (October 2012): 721–46, https://doi.org/10.1017/S0007123412000130.
4. This is beside the point, but I must note I also agree with those who believe sociology in particular spills too much ink on literature reviews. A great literature review is valuable and essential, and we should all write them; we just don't need one occupying ten pages before every small increment to the knowledge base.
5. Jordan A. Conwell and Kevin Loughran, "Quantitative Inquiry in the Early Sociology of W. E. B. Du Bois," *Du Bois Review: Social Science Research on Race* (December 2023): 1–23, https://doi.org/10.1017 /S1742058X23000206.
6. Suzanne M. Bianchi, "A Demographic Perspective on Family Change," *Journal of Family Theory & Review* 6, no. 1 (2014): 35–44, https://doi .org/10.1111/jftr.12029.
7. Kieran Healy, "Public Sociology in the Age of Social Media," *Perspectives on Politics* 15, no. 3 (September 2017): 771–80, https://doi.org /10.1017/S1537592717000950.
8. Matt L. Huffman, Philip N. Cohen, and Jessica Pearlman, "Engendering Change: Organizational Dynamics and Workplace Gender

240 • 2. DOING DESCRIPTION

Desegregation, 1975–2005," *Administrative Science Quarterly* 55, no. 2 (June 2010): 255–77, https://doi.org/10.2189/asqu.2010.55.2.255.

9. Philip N. Cohen. "Maternal Age and Infant Mortality for White, Black, and Mexican Mothers in the United States," *Sociological Science* 3 (2016): 32–38, https://doi.org/10.15195/v3.a2.

10. Arline T. Geronimus, John Bound, and Landon Hughes, "Trend Toward Older Maternal Age Contributed to Growing Racial Inequity in Very-Low-Birthweight Infants in the US," *Health Affairs* 42, no. 5 (May 2023): 674–82, https://doi.org/10.1377/hlthaff.2022.01066.

11. Jiaquan Xu, Sherry L. Murphy, Kenneth D. Kochanek, and Elizabeth Arias, *Mortality in the United States, 2021*, NCHS Data Brief (Washington, DC: National Center for Health Statistics, December 21, 2022), https://doi.org/10.15620/cdc:122516.

12. Daniel Hirschman, "Controlling for What? Movements, Measures, and Meanings in the US Gender Wage Gap Debate," *History of Political Economy* 54, no. S1 (December 1, 2022): 221–57, https://doi.org/10.1215/00182702-10085710.

13. Stephen Cole, "Why Sociology Doesn't Make Progress Like the Natural Sciences," *Sociological Forum* 9, no. 2 (1994), 148.

14. W. E. B. Du Bois, *The Philadelphia Negro: A Social Study* (Philadelphia: University of Pennsylvania, 1899), iv.

15. Jeff Gill, "The Insignificance of Null Hypothesis Significance Testing," *Political Research Quarterly* 52, no. 3 (1999): 647–74, https://doi.org/10.2307/449153.

16. Philip N. Cohen, "Multiple-Decrement Life Table Estimates of Divorce Rates," 2023, https://doi.org/10.17605/OSF.IO/ZBER3.

17. Patrick E. Shrout and Joseph L. Rodgers, "Psychology, Science, and Knowledge Construction: Broadening Perspectives from the Replication Crisis," *Annual Review of Psychology* 69, no. 1 (2018): 487–510, https://doi.org/10.1146/annurev-psych-122216-011845.

18. Norbert L. Kerr, "HARKing: Hypothesizing After the Results Are Known," *Personality and Social Psychology Review* 2, no. 3 (August 1, 1998): 196–217, https://doi.org/10.1207/s15327957pspr0203_4.

19. John Muñoz and Cristobal Young, "We Ran 9 Billion Regressions: Eliminating False Positives Through Computational Model Robustness," *Sociological Methodology* 48, no. 1 (August 1, 2018), sec 4.1.

20. Mark Rubin, "When Does HARKing Hurt? Identifying When Different Types of Undisclosed Post Hoc Hypothesizing Harm Scientific

Progress," *Review of General Psychology* 21, no. 4 (December 1, 2017): 308–20, https://doi.org/10.1037/gpr0000128.

21. There are many distinctions and qualifications to be made in the statistical theory here, including that between confirmatory and exploratory hypotheses, ante hoc and post hoc theorizing, and so on—which are not necessary to resolve here. See Mark Rubin and Chris Donkin, "Exploratory Hypothesis Tests Can Be More Compelling Than Confirmatory Hypothesis Tests," *Philosophical Psychology* (2022): 1–29, https://doi.org/10.1080/09515089.2022.2113771.

22. James W. Moody, Lisa A. Keister, and Maria C. Ramos, "Reproducibility in the Social Sciences," *Annual Review of Sociology* 48, no. 1 (2022), "Implications".

23. The null hypothesis statistical test is just one technique to help demonstrate or communicate the reliability, or generalizability, of our statistical observations. These tests, and their ubiquitous p values, are flawed, and our systemic reliance on them is flawed. See Blakeley B. McShane, David Gal, Andrew Gelman, Christian Robert, and Jennifer L. Tackett, "Abandon Statistical Significance," *American Statistician* 73, no. sup1 (March 2019): 235–45, https://doi.org/10.1080/00031305.2018.1527253. However, that's beyond the scope of this discussion, which is about the value of descriptive analysis.

24. Garret Christensen, Jeremy Freese, and Edward Miguel, *Transparent and Reproducible Social Science Research: How to Do Open Science* (Oakland: University of California Press, 2019).

25. Daniel Hirschman, "Sociology and the Technopolitical Two-Step: The Case of the Regnerus Study," A (Budding) Sociologist's Commonplace Book (blog), October 1, 2012, https://asociologist.com/2012/09/30/sociology-and-the-technopolitical-two-step-the-case-of-the-regnerus-study/.

26. It was actually much less than 1 percent, with a sample of more than six million women, but I only reported the result of a test for whether it was more or less than 1 percent. There is a voluminous debate over the proper threshold for tests such as these; see Daniel J. Benjamin, James O. Berger, Magnus Johannesson, Brian A. Nosek, E.-J. Wagenmakers, Richard Berk, Kenneth A. Bollen, et al., "Redefine Statistical Significance," *Nature Human Behaviour* 2, no. 1 (January 2018): 6–10, https://doi.org/10.1038/s41562-017-0189-z.

27. A survey of *ASQ* authors confirms that the "peer review experience was dominated by interpretive challenges: extensive criticisms, suggestions,

and subsequent revision concerning conceptual and theoretical issues but limited attention to methodological and empirical aspects of the work." David Strang and Kyle Siler, "Revising as Reframing: Original Submissions Versus Published Papers in Administrative Science Quarterly, 2005 to 2009," *Sociological Theory* 33, no. 1 (March 1, 2015): 71–96, https://doi.org/10.1177/0735275115572152.

28. Thomas S. Kuhn, *The Structure of Scientific Revolutions* (Chicago: University of Chicago Press, 1969).

29. George Ritzer, "Sociology: A Multiple Paradigm Science," *American Sociologist* 10, no. 3 (1975), 156–67.

30. Max Besbris and Shamus Khan, "Less Theory. More Description," *Sociological Theory* 35, no. 2 (June 2017): 147–53, "Recommendations."

31. Kieran Healy, "Fuck Nuance," *Sociological Theory* 35, no. 2 (June 2017): 118–27, https://doi.org/10.1177/0735275117709046.

32. Besbris and Khan, "Less Theory. More Description," https://doi.org/10.1177/0735275117709776.

33. Talking Heads, "Crosseyed and Painless," *Remain in Light* (New York: Sire, 1980).

34. Steven H. Woolf, "The Meaning of Translational Research and Why It Matters," *JAMA* 299, no. 2 (January 2008): 211–13, https://doi.org/10.1001/jama.2007.26.

35. Pierre Bourdieu, Jean-Claude Chamboredon, and Jean-Claude Passeron, *The Craft of Sociology: Epistemological Preliminaries* (Berlin, Germany: Walter de Gruyter, 1991), 253.

36. John W. Tukey, "We Need Both Exploratory and Confirmatory," *American Statistician* 34, no. 1 (1980), 24.

37. Micah Altman, "Research Lifecycles," presented at the Center for Research on Equitable and Open Scholarship seminar series, MIT, February 3, 2022, https://docs.google.com/presentation/d/1EMaosGY-90JlFnTg6px5qomV4OVDY45znFYJBFK7Ejk.

38. Daniel Hirschman, "Rediscovering the 1 Percent: Knowledge Infrastructures and the Stylized Facts of Inequality," *American Journal of Sociology* 127, no. 3 (November 2021): 739–86, https://doi.org/10.1086/718451.

39. Phillip N. Cohen, "Fox NY Covers Divorce Trend Report, 9/25/2018," YouTube, September 28, 2018, video, https://www.youtube.com/watch?v=xEcdOJoIpRw.

40. Brinton, *Graphic Methods for Presenting Facts*, 343.

41. And it's also okay if we turn out to be wrong once in a while. Explanations that can't account for simple facts are reasonably challenged; surviving those challenges makes the good explanations stronger. There may be discrimination against boys in middle and high school, for example, which helps girls graduate and go to college at higher rates—even though there is also discrimination pushing women out of more lucrative majors and careers. Some of the low-hanging fruit of gender discrimination has already been picked.

42. The texting and driving panic was a historical redux of the 1970 famous "crying Indian" commercial (featuring Iron Eyes Cody, an Italian American actor who worked under an assumed Native American identity), which turned the viewers' attention from smokestacks and pollution to thoughtless individuals throwing fast food trash out a car window. The tag line was "People start pollution, people can stop it"—not, "Industrial capitalism and corporate deregulation are threatening life on earth."

43. David Leonhardt, "A Public-Health Crisis That We Can Fix," *New York Times*, March 7, 2017, https://www.nytimes.com/2017/03/07/opinion/a-public-health-crisis-that-we-can-fix.html.

44. Matt Richtel, *A Deadly Wandering: A Mystery, a Landmark Investigation, and the Astonishing Science of Attention in the Digital Age* (Boston: Mariner Books, 2015).

45. Environmental Protection Agency, *The 2022 EPA Automotive Trends Report* (Washington, DC: Environmental Protection Agency, 2022), https://www.epa.gov/system/files/documents/2022-12/420r22029.pdf.

46. I have written many blog posts about the issue of texting and traffic fatalities, which are all available at this link: https://familyinequality.wordpress.com/tag/texting/.

47. Stuart M. Hall, *Policing the Crisis: Mugging, the State, and Law and Order* (New York: Palgrave Macmillan, 2002).

3. OPEN SCHOLARSHIP

1. Her speaker fee was listed here: https://web.archive.org/web/20230620194740/https://www.speakerbookingagency.com/talent/francesca-gino. Her salary was disclosed on Harvard's 990 nonprofit IRS form:

https://projects.propublica.org/nonprofits/display_990/42103580/05_2021_prefixes_01-04%2F042103580_202006_990_2021052018155042.

2. Francesca Gino, "Do Bonuses Promote Cheating?" CNN, June 3, 2014, https://www.cnn.com/2014/06/03/opinion/gino-bonuses-promote-cheating/index.html.

3. Francesca Gino, Maryam Kouchaki, and Adam D. Galinsky, "The Moral Virtue of Authenticity: How Inauthenticity Produces Feelings of Immorality and Impurity," *Psychological Science* 26, no. 7 (July 2015): 983–96, https://doi.org/10.1177/0956797615575277.

4. Lisa L. Shu, Nina Mazar, Francesca Gino, Dan Ariely, and Max H. Bazerman, "Signing at the Beginning Makes Ethics Salient and Decreases Dishonest Self-Reports in Comparison to Signing at the End," *Proceedings of the National Academy of Sciences* 109, no. 38 (September 2012): 15197–200. https://doi.org/10.1073/pnas.1209746109.

5. Francesca Gino, Shahar Ayal, and Dan Ariely, "Contagion and Differentiation in Unethical Behavior: The Effect of One Bad Apple on the Barrel," *Psychological Science* 20, no. 3 (March 2009): 393–98, https://doi.org/10.1111/j.1467-9280.2009.02306.x.

6. Stephanie M. Lee, "3 of Francesca Gino's Allegedly Fraudulent Studies Will Be Retracted," *The Chronicle of Higher Education*, June 30, 2023, https://www.chronicle.com/article/3-of-francesca-ginos-allegedly-fraudulent-studies-will-be-retracted. One paper, which included fake data attributed to Ariely, as well as to Gino, was retracted by *Proceedings of the National Academy of Sciences*. Stephanie M. Lee, "A Big Study About Honesty Turns Out to Be Based on Fake Data," BuzzFeed News, August 25, 2021, https://www.buzzfeednews.com/article/stephaniemlee/dan-ariely-honesty-study-retraction; May R. Berenbaum, "Retraction for Shu et al., Signing at the Beginning Makes Ethics Salient and Decreases Dishonest Self-Reports in Comparison to Signing at the End," *Proceedings of the National Academy of Sciences* 118, no. 38 (September 2021): e2115397118, https://doi.org/10.1073/pnas.2115397118. Other retractions followed, and Gino was put on administrative leave at Harvard in 2023. Lee, "3 of Francesca Gino's Allegedly Fraudulent Studies Will Be Retracted." She denied everything and sued widely. Stephanie M. Lee, "Scholar Accused of Research Fraud Sues Harvard and Data Sleuths, Alleging a 'Smear Campaign,'" *The Chronicle of Higher Education*, August 3, 2023, https://www.chronicle.com/article

/scholar-accused-of-research-fraud-sues-harvard-and-data-sleuths
-alleging-a-smear-campaign.

7. Oliver Schilke, Martin Reimann, and Karen S. Cook, "Trust in Social Relations," *Annual Review of Sociology* 47, no. 1 (2021), "Two Approaches to Trust?"

8. Stephanie M. Lee and Nell Gluckman, "A Dishonesty Expert Stands Accused of Fraud. Scholars Who Worked with Her Are Scrambling," *The Chronicle of Higher Education*, June 22, 2023, https://www.chronicle
.com/article/a-dishonesty-expert-stands-accused-of-fraud-scholars
-who-worked-with-her-are-scrambling.

9. The procedures and standards used in the investigation, and the results of the Levelt Commission, make for fascinating reading. They are available at Tilburg University, here in Dutch and English: https://
www.tilburguniversity.edu/nl/over/gedrag-integriteit/commissie
-levelt.

10. Tom Bartlett, "The Unraveling of Michael LaCour," *The Chronicle of Higher Education*, June 2, 2015, https://www.chronicle.com/article
/the-unraveling-of-michael-lacour/.

11. Gowri Gopalakrishna, Gerben ter Riet, Gerko Vink, Ineke Stoop, Jelte M. Wicherts, and Lex M. Bouter, "Prevalence of Questionable Research Practices, Research Misconduct and Their Potential Explanatory Factors: A Survey Among Academic Researchers in The Netherlands," *PLOS ONE* 17, no. 2 (February 2022): e0263023, https://doi.org
/10.1371/journal.pone.0263023.

12. Nate Breznau, "Does Sociology Need Open Science?" *Societies* 11, no. 1 (March 2021): 9, https://doi.org/10.3390/soc11010009.

13. ACRL Scholarly Communications Committee, "Principles and Strategies for the Reform of Scholarly Communication," American Library Association, 2003, https://www.ala.org/acrl/publications/whitepapers
/principlesstrategies.

14. The details of this story, including some of the reviews, are in Philip N. Cohen, "Our Broken Peer Review System, in One Saga," Family Inequality (blog), October 5, 2015, https://familyinequality.wordpress
.com/2015/10/05/our-broken-peer-review-system-in-one-saga/.

15. Micah Altman, Philip N. Cohen, and Jessica Polka, "Interventions in Scholarly Communication: Design Lessons from Public Health," *First Monday*, August 2023, https://doi.org/10.5210/fm.v28i8.12941.

16. The tweets are archived at https://web.archive.org/web/20201129092735/https://twitter.com/AshleyAFrawley/status/1332979259711873024 and https://web.archive.org/web/20201129185659/https://twitter.com/jennaburrell/status/1333120260824678400.

17. Anthony Giddens, *The Consequences of Modernity* (Redwood City, CA: Stanford University Press, 1990), 89.

18. Gil Eyal, *The Crisis of Expertise* (Cambridge: Wiley, 2019).

19. Pierre Bourdieu, *The Logic of Practice* (Redwood City, CA: Stanford University Press, 1990).

20. Priya Fielding-Singh, *How the Other Half Eats: The Untold Story of Food and Inequality in America* (New York: Little, Brown, 2021).

21. Jan Mewes, Malcolm Fairbrother, Giuseppe Nicola Giordano, Cary Wu, and Rima Wilkes, "Experiences Matter: A Longitudinal Study of Individual-Level Sources of Declining Social Trust in the United States," *Social Science Research* 95 (March 1, 2021): 102537, https://doi.org/10.1016/j.ssresearch.2021.102537.

22. Károly Takács, Jörg Gross, Martina Testori, Srebrenka Letina, Adam R. Kenny, Eleanor A. Power, and Rafael P. M. Wittek, "Networks of Reliable Reputations and Cooperation: A Review," *Philosophical Transactions of the Royal Society B: Biological Sciences* 376, no. 1838 (November 2021): 20200297, https://doi.org/10.1098/rstb.2020.0297.

23. Annika S. Nieper, Bianca Beersma, Maria T. M. Dijkstra, and Gerben A. van Kleef, "When and Why Does Gossip Increase Prosocial Behavior?" *Current Opinion in Psychology* 44 (April 2022), Abstract.

24. Bruce A. Kimball and Benjamin Ashby Johnson, "The Beginning of 'Free Money' Ideology in American Universities: Charles W. Eliot at Harvard, 1869–1909," *History of Education Quarterly* 52, no. 2 (May 2012): 222–50, https://doi.org/10.1111/j.1748-5959.2011.00389.x. Gossip can be maliciously inaccurate, and powerful institutions have ways of making people trust them more than they deserve, but those problems only serve to highlight the importance of purposefully building reliable systems of trust.

25. Victor Ray, *On Critical Race Theory: Why It Matters and Why You Should Care* (New York: Random House, 2022).

26. Julie A. Ward, Elizabeth M. Stone, Paulani Mui, and Beth Resnick, "Pandemic-Related Workplace Violence and Its Impact on Public Health Officials, March 2020–January 2021," *American Journal of Public Health* 112, no. 5 (May 2022): 736–46, https://doi.org/10.2105/AJPH.2021.306649.

27. Philip N. Cohen, "The Widening Political Divide over Science," SocArXiv, 2018, https://doi.org/10.31235/osf.io/u95aw.
28. Cary Funk and Alec Tyson, "Partisan Differences over the Pandemic Response Are Growing," Pew Research Center Science and Society (blog), June 3, 2020, https://www.pewresearch.org/science/2020/06/03/partisan-differences-over-the-pandemic-response-are-growing/.
29. Stephen Cole, "Why Sociology Doesn't Make Progress Like the Natural Sciences," *Sociological Forum* 9, no. 2 (1994): 133–54.
30. One aspect of the discipline undermining public trust that Cole may not have considered is gender bias. He edited a book in 2001 titled *What's Wrong with Sociology?* (New York: Routledge, 2001), which had nineteen contributors, only four of whom were women—and two of those were married to their male co-authors. Nowadays (only two decades later), we recognize that such a gender disparity itself undermines the legitimacy of the work in the public eye.
31. Matthew Reidsma, *Masked by Trust: Bias in Library Discovery* (Sacramento, CA: Litwin, 2019).
32. Brian A. Nosek, G. Alter, G. C. Banks, D. Borsboom, S. D. Bowman, S. J. Breckler, S. Buck, et al., "Promoting an Open Research Culture," *Science* 348, no. 6242 (June 2015): 1422–25, https://doi.org/10.1126/science.aab2374.
33. Simine Vazire, "Quality Uncertainty Erodes Trust in Science," *Collabra: Psychology* 3, no. 1 (February 2017), https://doi.org/10.1525/collabra.74.
34. This may be why thousands of researchers donated to the legal defense fund for the fraud sleuths Gino sued.
35. Jeremy Freese and Molly M. King, "Institutionalizing Transparency," *Socius* 4 (January 2018), https://doi.org/10.1177/2378023117739216.
36. Erin C. McKiernan, Philip E. Bourne, C. Titus Brown, Stuart Buck, Amye Kenall, Jennifer Lin, Damon McDougall, et al., "How Open Science Helps Researchers Succeed," *eLife* 5 (July 7, 2016): e16800, https://doi.org/10.7554/eLife.16800.
37. Roundtable on Aligning Incentives for Open Science, *Developing a Toolkit for Fostering Open Science Practices: Proceedings of a Workshop* (Washington, DC: National Academies Press, 2021).
38. Marcus R. Munafò, Brian A. Nosek, Dorothy V. M. Bishop, Katherine S. Button, Christopher D. Chambers, Nathalie Percie du Sert, Uri Simonsohn, Eric-Jan Wagenmakers, Jennifer J. Ware, and John P. A. Ioannidis, "A Manifesto for Reproducible Science," *Nature*

Human Behaviour 1, no. 1 (January 2017): 1–9, https://doi.org/10.1038/s41562-016-0021.

39. Allison J. Pugh and Sarah Mosseri, "Trust-Building vs. 'Just Trust Me': Reflexivity and Resonance in Ethnography," *Frontiers in Sociology* 8 (2023), https://www.frontiersin.org/articles/10.3389/fsoc.2023.1069305.

40. Jeremy Freese and David Peterson, "Replication in Social Science," *Annual Review of Sociology* 43, no. 1 (2017), "Replication in Qualitative Social Science."

41. Michael G. Pratt, Sarah Kaplan, and Richard Whittington, "The Tumult over Transparency: Decoupling Transparency from Replication in Establishing Trustworthy Qualitative Research," *Administrative Science Quarterly* 65, no. 1 (March 1, 2020): 1–19, https://doi.org/10.1177/0001839219887663.

42. Alexandra K. Murphy, Colin Jerolmack, and DeAnna Smith, "Ethnography, Data Transparency, and the Information Age," *Annual Review of Sociology* 47, no. 1 (2021): 41–61, https://doi.org/10.1146/annurev-soc-090320-124805.

43. Douglas G. D. Russell, William J. L. Sladen, and David G. Ainley, "Dr. George Murray Levick (1876–1956): Unpublished Notes on the Sexual Habits of the Adélie Penguin," *Polar Record* 48, no. 4 (October 2012), "Introduction."

44. Penguin sexuality is serious political business, maybe because the birds look like little people. A century later, a book about a same-sex pair of Chinstrap penguins raising a chick, *And Tango Makes Three*, would be one of the most challenged books in American public schools, as conservative groups sought to prevent elementary schools from naturalizing gay sexuality. Jennifer Steele, "Challenges to Children's Picture Books with LGBTQ Themes: A 30-Year Review," *Children and Libraries* 20, no. 2 (June 17, 2022): 3–9, https://doi.org/10.5860/cal.20.2.3.

45. "Publish, v.," in OED Online (Oxford University Press, 2023).

46. Abby L. Ferber, "'Are You Willing to Die for This Work?' Public Targeted Online Harassment in Higher Education: SWS Presidential Address," *Gender & Society* 32, no. 3 (June 1, 2018): 301–20, https://doi.org/10.1177/0891243218766831.

47. Martin Lakomý, Renata Hlavová, and Hana Machackova. "Open Science and the Science-Society Relationship, *Society* 56, no. 3 (June 1, 2019): 246–55, https://doi.org/10.1007/s12115-019-00361-w.

48. This section was inspired by conversation with Tina Fetner and is partly adapted from Philip N. Cohen, "Authority, Openness, and the Soft Sciences," SocOpen: Home of SocArXiv (blog), November 17, 2017, https://socopen.org/2017/11/17/authority-openness-and-the-soft -sciences/.

49. Garret Christensen, Jeremy Freese, and Edward Miguel, *Transparent and Reproducible Social Science Research: How to Do Open Science* (Oakland: University of California Press, 2019).

50. Robert K. Merton, "Science and Technology in a Democratic Order," *Journal of Legal and Political Sociology* 1, no. 1 (1942), "Communism."

51. Sarah Sobieraj, *Credible Threat: Attacks Against Women Online and the Future of Democracy* (Oxford: Oxford University Press, 2020).

52. Eyal, *The Crisis of Expertise*.

53. Sujatha Raman and Warren Pearce, "Learning the Lessons of Climategate: A Cosmopolitan Moment in the Public Life of Climate Science," *WIREs Climate Change* 11, no. 6 (2020): e672, https://doi.org /10.1002/wcc.672.

54. Kathleen Fitzpatrick, *Generous Thinking: A Radical Approach to Saving the University* (Baltimore, MD: Johns Hopkins University Press, 2019).

55. Richard Sever, Ted Roeder, Samantha Hindle, Linda Sussman, Kevin-John Black, Janet Argentine, Wayne Manos, and John R. Inglis, "bioRxiv: The Preprint Server for Biology," bioRxiv, November 6, 2019, https:// doi.org/10.1101/833400.

56. eLife, "eLife Latest: What We Have Learned about Preprints," Inside eLife (blog), eLife Sciences Publications, July 1, 2021, https://elifesciences .org/inside-elife/e5f8f1f7/elife-latest-what-we-have-learned-about -preprints.

57. Paul Ginsparg, "ArXiv Founder Paul Ginsparg's Thoughts on Scooping," ASAPbio FAQ (blog), accessed July 4, 2023, https://asapbio.org /faq/arxiv-founder-paul-ginspargs-advice-on-scooping.

58. Lisa Janicke Hinchliffe, "The State of the Version of Record," The Scholarly Kitchen (blog), February 14, 2022, https://scholarlykitchen .sspnet.org/2022/02/14/the-state-of-the-version-of-record/.

59. Jean-Claude Guédon, "Scholarly Communication and Scholarly Publishing," Open Access Scholarly Publishing Association (blog), April 21, 2021, https://oaspa.org/guest-post-by-jean-claude-guedon-scholarly -communication-and-scholarly-publishing/.

60. Michelle N. Meyer, "Practical Tips for Ethical Data Sharing," *Advances in Methods and Practices in Psychological Science* 1, no. 1 (March 1, 2018): 131–44, https://doi.org/10.1177/2515245917747656.

61. Jesse Fox, Katy E. Pearce, Adrienne L. Massanari, Julius Matthew Riles, Łukasz Szulc, Yerina S. Ranjit, Filippo Trevisan, et al., "Open Science, Closed Doors? Countering Marginalization Through an Agenda for Ethical, Inclusive Research in Communication," *Journal of Communication* 71, no. 5 (October 2021): 764–84, https://doi.org/10.1093/joc/jqab029.

62. Margo Anderson, "The Census and the Japanese 'Internment': Apology and Policy in Statistical Practice," *Social Research: An International Quarterly* 87, no. 4 (2020): 789–812, https://doi.org/10.1353/sor.2020.0064.

63. Lynette Clemetson, "Homeland Security Given Data on Arab-Americans," *New York Times*, July 30, 2004, https://www.nytimes.com/2004/07/30/us/homeland-security-given-data-on-arab-americans.html.

64. Ummul-Kiram Kathawalla, Priya Silverstein, and Moin Syed, "Easing into Open Science: A Guide for Graduate Students and Their Advisors," *Collabra: Psychology* 7, no. 1 (January 26, 2021): 18684, https://doi.org/10.1525/collabra.18684.

65. Glenn Firebaugh, "Replication Data Sets and Favored-Hypothesis Bias: Comment on Jeremy Freese (2007) and Gary King (2007)," *Sociological Methods and Research* 36, no. 2 (November 1, 2007), 207.

66. Jeremy Freese, "Replication Standards for Quantitative Social Science: Why Not Sociology?" *Sociological Methods and Research* 36, no. 2 (November 2007): 153–72, https://doi.org/10.1177/0049124107306659.

67. Laure Perrier, Erik Blondal, and Heather MacDonald, "The Views, Perspectives, and Experiences of Academic Researchers with Data Sharing and Reuse: A Meta-Synthesis," *PLOS ONE* 15, no. 2 (February 2020): e0229182, https://doi.org/10.1371/journal.pone.0229182.

68. Oya Y. Rieger and Roger C. Schonfeld, "Common Scholarly Communication Infrastructure Landscape Review," Ithaka S+R, 2023, https://doi.org/10.18665/sr.318775.

69. Walter Isaacson, *The Code Breaker: Jennifer Doudna, Gene Editing, and the Future of the Human Race* (New York: Simon & Schuster, 2021).

70. Christensen, Freese, and Miguel, *Transparent and Reproducible Social Science Research*.

71. This was the impetus behind the rule change I proposed to the American Sociological Association in 2015, after a winning dissertation was discovered to be embargoed indefinitely, so no one could read it except the award committee. The rules now state, "To be eligible for the ASA Dissertation Award, nominees' dissertations must be publicly available." Philip N. Cohen, "Proposed Rule Change for the American Sociological Association Dissertation Award," Family Inequality (blog), June 4, 2015, https://familyinequality.wordpress.com/2015/06/04/proposal-rule -change-for-the-american-sociological-association-dissertation-award/.

72. Pugh and Mosseri, "Trust-Building vs. 'Just Trust Me.'"

73. Murphy, Jerolmack, and Smith, "Ethnography, Data Transparency, and the Information Age."

74. Matthew Desmond, *Evicted: Poverty and Profit in the American City* (New York: Crown, 2016).

75. Alice Goffman, *On the Run: Fugitive Life in an American City* (Chicago: University of Chicago Press, 2014).

76. Jerolmack and Murphy, "The Ethical Dilemmas and Social Scientific Trade-Offs of Masking in Ethnography."

77. Pugh and Mosseri, "Trust-Building vs. 'Just Trust Me.'"

78. Jeffrey Brainard and Jocelyn Kaiser, "White House Requires Immediate Public Access to All U.S.-Funded Research Papers by 2025," Science Insider (blog), August 26, 2022, https://www.science.org/content /article/white-house-requires-immediate-public-access-all-u-s--funded -research-papers-2025.

79. Samuel A. Moore, "The Politics of Rights Retention," *Publications* 11, no. 2 (2023): 28, https://doi.org/10.3390/publications11020028.

4. PEER REVIEW, UNLEASHED

1. Carl T. Bergstrom and Jevin D. West, *Calling Bullshit: The Art of Skepticism in a Data-Driven World*, ebook (New York: Random House, 2020), chapter 11. An earlier version of some of this chapter appears in the third edition of *Families as They Really Are* (New York: Norton, 2024), edited by Virginia Rutter, Kristi Williams, and Barbara Risman; it benefited from the input of Virginia Rutter.

2. Nowadays, *fidelity* also means the degree to which something is accurately—faithfully—reproduced, like a picture or a sound recording.

Fidelity is not just important to people in their romantic relationships, but also to people who like art, music, or data. If you're using *wifi* right now, incidentally, that's because the term sounded cool to people who marketed the wireless protocol in 1999—because it rhymed with "hi-fi," which was short for "high fidelity," which is what people used to call their music-playing machines when I was a kid. Like, "Whoa, that's a cool hi-fi!" Fidelity matters.

3. Larry Au and Gil Eyal, "Whose Advice Is Credible? Claiming Lay Expertise in a Covid-19 Online Community," *Qualitative Sociology* 45, no. 1 (March 1, 2022): 31–61, https://doi.org/10.1007/s11133-021-09492-1.

4. Carl Sagan, *The Demon-Haunted World: Science as a Candle in the Dark* (New York: Ballantine, 1997).

5. Anthony Giddens, *The Consequences of Modernity* (Redwood City, CA: Stanford University Press, 1990).

6. Rolf Lidskog, "In Science We Trust? On the Relation Between Scientific Knowledge, Risk Consciousness and Public Trust," *Acta Sociologica* 39, no. 1 (January 1, 1996): 31–56, https://doi.org/10.1177/000169939603900103.

7. Publons, "Global State of Peer Review," Clarivate Analytics, 2018, https://doi.org/10.14322/publons.GSPR2018.

8. Walter Isaacson, *Einstein: His Life and Universe*, ebook (New York: Simon & Schuster, 2007).

9. Jill Gordon, "John Stuart Mill and the 'Marketplace of Ideas,'" *Social Theory and Practice* 23, no. 2 (1997): 235–49.

10. Harry Collins and Robert Evans, *Rethinking Expertise* (Chicago: University of Chicago Press, 2008).

11. Andrew Abbott, *Department and Discipline: Chicago Sociology at One Hundred* (Chicago: University of Chicago Press, 2017).

12. Noah Moxham and Aileen Fyfe, "The Royal Society and the Prehistory of Peer Review, 1665–1965," *The Historical Journal* 61, no. 4 (December 2018): 863–89, https://doi.org/10.1017/S0018246X17000334; Melinda Baldwin, "Scientific Autonomy, Public Accountability, and the Rise of 'Peer Review' in the Cold War United States," *Isis* 109, no. 3 (September 2018): 538–58, https://doi.org/10.1086/700070.

13. Ben Merriman, "Peer Review as an Evolving Response to Organizational Constraint: Evidence from Sociology Journals, 1952–2018," *American Sociologist* 52, no. 2 (June 1, 2021): 341–66, https://doi.org/10.1007/s12108-020-09473-x.

14. David Pontille and Didier Torny, "From Manuscript Evaluation to Article Valuation: The Changing Technologies of Journal Peer Review," *Human Studies* 38, no. 1 (March 2015): 57–79, https://doi.org/10.1007/s10746-014-9335-z.

15. Seth Denbo, "Open Peer Review in the Humanities," The Scholarly Kitchen (blog), March 4, 2020, https://scholarlykitchen.sspnet.org/2020/03/04/guest-post-open-peer-review-in-the-humanities/.

16. Andreas Nishikawa-Pacher, "Who Are the 100 Largest Scientific Publishers by Journal Count? A Webscraping Approach," *Journal of Documentation* 78, no. 7 (January 1, 2022): 450–63, https://doi.org/10.1108/JD-04-2022-0083.

17. RELX, "RELX Annual Report and Financial Statements 2022," 2022, https://www.relx.com/~/media/Files/R/RELX-Group/documents/reports/annual-reports/relx-2022-annual-report.pdf.

18. In writing this book, I have shared drafts of chapters publicly, both so I can reach more people faster and so that I can benefit from the critiques of people interested enough to jump on a draft and give me some critical feedback—a process of informal peer review that will continue after the book's publication.

19. Kathleen Fitzpatrick, "Revising Peer Review," *Contexts* 11, no. 4 (November 1, 2012): 80, https://doi.org/10.1177/1536504212466347.

20. John Creamer, Emily A. Shrider, and Kalee Burns, "Poverty in the United States: 2021," U.S. Census Bureau, September 13, 2022, https://www.census.gov/library/publications/2022/demo/p60-277.html.

21. Philip N. Cohen, "In the Last 10 Years, the US Child Poverty Rate Has Fallen Dramatically . . . (Demographic Fact A Day),"Twitter, November 14, 2022, https://twitter.com/demfactaday/status/1592185821834379266.

22. Lydia DePillis and Jason DeParle, "Pandemic Aid Cut U.S. Poverty to New Low in 2021, Census Bureau Reports," *New York Times*, September 13, 2022, https://www.nytimes.com/2022/09/13/business/economy/income-poverty-census-bureau.html.

23. W. Bradford Wilcox, "Family Stability and the American Dream (Statement Before the Joint Economic Committee)," American Enterprise Institute, February 25, 2020, https://www.aei.org/wp-content/uploads/2020/02/Wilcox-JEC-FamilyStability-2-25.pdf.

24. Deadric T. Williams and Regina S. Baker, "Family Structure, Risks, and Racial Stratification in Poverty," *Social Problems* 68, no. 4 (November 1, 2021): 964–85, https://doi.org/10.1093/socpro/spab018.

25. Mead, Lawrence M. "Poverty and Culture." *Society*, 2020. The article was retracted but the abstract is available here: https://nyuscholars .nyu.edu/en/publications/poverty-and-culture. The retraction notice is, "A statement from Springer Nature," (July 2020), https://group .springernature.com/gp/group/media/press-releases/springer-nature -statement-society-article/18232228.

26. Philip N. Cohen, *Enduring Bonds: Inequality, Marriage, Parenting, and Everything Else That Makes Families Great and Terrible* (Oakland: University of California Press, 2018).

27. Nicholas Fraser et al., "The Evolving Role of Preprints in the Dissemination of COVID-19 Research and Their Impact on the Science Communication Landscape," *PLOS Biology* 19, no. 4 (April 2, 2021): e3000959, https://doi.org/10.1371/journal.pbio.3000959.

28. Alice Fleerackers, Kenneth Shores, Natascha Chtena, and Juan Pablo Alperin, "Unreviewed Science in the News: The Evolution of Preprint Media Coverage from 2014–2021," bioRxiv, July 15, 2023, https://doi .org/10.1101/2023.07.10.548392.

29. Apoorva Mandavilli, "People Who Accuse Science Journalists of Chasing Clicks Must Have NO IDEA about the Dozens of Bad Preprints We Pass on plus the Hundreds of Bad Press Releases We Get Pitched *every Single Day*. If What We Wanted Was Clicks, You'd Be Seeing Something Else Entirely," Twitter, February 25, 2021, https://twitter .com/apoorva_nyc/status/1364797039327010822.

30. Bergstrom and West, *Calling Bullshit*.

31. Joseph B. Bak-Coleman, Mark Alfano, Wolfram Barfuss, Carl T. Bergstrom, Miguel A. Centeno, Iain D. Couzin, Jonathan F. Donges, et al., "Stewardship of Global Collective Behavior," *Proceedings of the National Academy of Sciences* 118, no. 27 (July 2021), https://doi.org/10.1073/pnas .2025764118.

32. There is a list maintained by Retraction Watch, at https://retractionwatch .com/retracted-coronavirus-covid-19-papers/.

33. Micah Altman and Philip N. Cohen, "On Clarifying the Goals of a Peer Review Taxonomy," The Scholarly Kitchen (blog), October 1, 2020, https://scholarlykitchen.sspnet.org/2020/10/01/guest-post-on -clarifying-the-goals-of-a-peer-review-taxonomy/.

34. Micah Altman and Philip N. Cohen, "We Are in a Period of Science Policy Innovation, yet There Are Major Evidence Gaps in Evaluating

Their Effectiveness," Impact of Social Sciences (blog), July 27, 2023, https://blogs.lse.ac.uk/impactofsocialsciences/2023/07/27/we-are-in -a-period-of-science-policy-innovation-yet-there-are-major-evidence -gaps-in-evaluating-their-effectiveness/.

35. Jocelyn Kaiser, "Stanford President to Step Down Despite Probe Exonerating Him of Research Misconduct," Science Insider (blog), July 19, 2023, https://www.science.org/content/article/stanford-president-to -step-down-despite-probe-exonerating-him-of-research-misconduct.

36. Charles Piller, "Potential Fabrication in Research Images Threatens Key Theory of Alzheimer's Disease," *Science*, July 21, 2022, https://www .science.org/content/article/potential-fabrication-research-images -threatens-key-theory-alzheimers-disease.

37. Cohen, *Enduring Bonds*.

38. Christian Smith, *The Sacred Project of American Sociology* (Oxford: Oxford University Press, 2014), 166.

39. Kate Linthicum, "Amid Growing Coronavirus Threat, Mexico's President Says He's Putting Trust in Good-Luck Charms," *Los Angeles Times*, March 19, 2020, https://www.latimes.com/world-nation/story/2020-03 -19/as-mexican-peso-collapses-over-coronavirus-threat-criticism -falls-on-president-lopez-obrador.

40. Natalie Kitroeff and Paulina Villegas, "'I'd Rather Stay Home and Die,'" *New York Times*, August 10, 2020, https://www.nytimes.com/2020/08 /10/world/americas/mexico-coronavirus-hospitals.html.

41. Natalie Kitroeff, "Between the Pandemic and the President: Mexico City Mayor's Balancing Act," *New York Times*, September 5, 2020, https://www.nytimes.com/2020/09/05/world/americas/mexico-mayor -amlo-sheinbaum.html.

42. Reuters, "Fact Check-Mexico No Longer Including Ivermectin in Home COVID-19 Care Kits, Contrary to Claims on Social Media," Reuters, January 26, 2022, https://www.reuters.com/article/factcheck -imssmexico-ivermectin-idUSL1N2U626I.

43. José Merino et al., "Ivermectin and the Odds of Hospitalization due to COVID-19: Evidence from a Quasi-experimental Analysis Based on a Public Intervention in Mexico City," SocArXiv (May 4, 2021), https:// osf.io/r93g4.

44. Lex Harvey, "Mexico Went All in on Ivermectin—a Disproven COVID Cure. Now There's a Fight over 'False and Misleading,'" *Toronto Star*,

February 10, 2022, https://www.thestar.com/news/world/2022/02/10/mexico-went-all-in-on-ivermectin-a-disproven-covid-cure-now-theres-a-fight-over-false-and-misleading-science-and-claims-of-colonialist-politics.html.

45. EFE, "Gobierno Mexicano Critica 'Campaña de Ataques' por Uso de la Ivermectina," EFE, February 8, 2022, http://www.efe.com/efe/america/mexico/gobierno-mexicano-critica-campana-de-ataques-por-uso-la-ivermectina/50000545-4735550.

46. Au and Eyal, "Whose Advice Is Credible?"

47. Bergstrom and West, *Calling Bullshit*.

48. José Merino, "Es una GRAN noticia poder validar una política pública que permitió reducir impactos en salud por covid19," Twitter, May 14, 2021, https://x.com/PPmerino/status/1393263540199325699.

49. Ethan Fosse and Christopher Winship, "Analyzing Age-Period-Cohort Data: A Review and Critique," *Annual Review of Sociology* 45, no. 1 (2019): 467–92, https://doi.org/10.1146/annurev-soc-073018-022616.

50. National Academies of Sciences, Engineering, and Medicine, *Are Generational Categories Meaningful Distinctions for Workforce Management?* (Washington, DC: National Academies Press, 2020).

51. Philip N. Cohen, "Generation Labels Mean Nothing. It's Time to Retire Them," *Washington Post*, July 7, 2021, https://www.washingtonpost.com/opinions/2021/07/07/generation-labels-mean-nothing-retire-them/.

52. Andrew M. Lindner, Sophia Stelboum, and Azizul Hakim, "Embracing Generational Labels: An Analysis of Self-Identification and Sociopolitical Alignment," SocArXiv, May 8, 2023, https://doi.org/10.31235/osf.io/e2zxr.

53. Bak-Coleman et al., "Stewardship of Global Collective Behavior."

54. I know what you're thinking—yes, I have done plenty of this. I shouldn't!

5. SOCIAL MEDIA

1. Alice E. Marwick and danah boyd, "I Tweet Honestly, I Tweet Passionately: Twitter Users, Context Collapse, and the Imagined Audience," *New Media & Society* 13, no. 1 (February 2011), 116.

2. Kieran Healy, "Public Sociology in the Age of Social Media," *Perspectives on Politics* 15, no. 3 (September 2017): 771–80, https://doi.org/10.1017/S1537592717000950.

3. Rogers Brubaker, *Hyperconnectivity and Its Discontents* (Hoboken, NJ: Polity, 2022).

4. In leaving Twitter for Mastodon, and then BlueSky, to date I have cut my number of "followers" and post impressions by something like 90 percent. I have also lost touch with a lot of current discourse—a big loss that has been somewhat balanced by improved mood and mental health, as well as the fervent hope that I'm building something better for the future. At least, I tell myself, I'm not literally working for Elon Musk. I hope I haven't torpedoed my credibility to write this chapter in the process.

5. Lucio La Cava, Sergio Greco, and Andrea Tagarelli, "Understanding the Growth of the Fediverse Through the Lens of Mastodon," *Applied Network Science* 6, no. 1 (September 2021): 64, https://doi.org/10.1007/s41109-021-00392-5; Robert W. Gehl and Diana Zulli, "The Digital Covenant: Non-Centralized Platform Governance on the Mastodon Social Network," *Information, Communication & Society* (December 15, 2022): 1–17, https://doi.org/10.1080/1369118X.2022.2147400.

6. Cory Doctorow, "The 'Enshittification' of TikTok," *Wired*, January 23, 2023, https://www.wired.com/story/tiktok-platforms-cory-doctorow/.

7. A public version of the dataset and the survey materials are available at https://osf.io/wfqpj/.

8. M. F. Willson and A. Traveset, "The Ecology of Seed Dispersal," *Seeds: The Ecology of Regeneration in Plant Communities* (Boston: CABI, 2000), 85–110, https://doi.org/10.1079/9780851994321.0085.

9. Robert Dudley, "Fermenting Fruit and the Historical Ecology of Ethanol Ingestion: Is Alcoholism in Modern Humans an Evolutionary Hangover?" *Addiction* 97, no. 4 (2002), Abstract.

10. Christine Byrne, "24 Summer Cocktails That Are Perfect for Day Drinking," *BuzzFeed*, May 28, 2021, https://www.buzzfeed.com/christinebyrne/booze-and-berries-and-sunshine.

11. These and some other examples are listed, with links, at https://familyinequality.wordpress.com/2023/07/28/twitter-changed-your-brain/.

12. Brubaker, *Hyperconnectivity and Its Discontents*.

13. David Kirkpatrick, *The Facebook Effect: The Inside Story of the Company That Is Connecting the World* (New York: Simon and Schuster, 2011), 199.

14. Moran Yarchi, Christian Baden, and Neta Kligler-Vilenchik, "Political Polarization on the Digital Sphere: A Cross-Platform, Over-Time

Analysis of Interactional, Positional, and Affective Polarization on Social Media," *Political Communication* (July 14, 2020), 16.

15. One of the corrosive changes Twitter/X made after Musk took over was to stop displaying headlines and brand information in the cards of tweets that include links, which made it harder to assess credibility before clicking on a link. Siladitya Ray, "'Borderline Useless': X Removes Headlines On News Posts as Critics Say Move Changes Site's Functionality," *Forbes*, October 5, 2023, https://www.forbes.com/sites/siladityaray/2023/10/05/x-hides-headlines-from-posts-after-musk-claims-it-will-greatly-improve-the-esthetics/.

16. Brubaker, *Hyperconnectivity and Its Discontents*, 14.

17. Diana Zulli, "Capitalizing on the Look: Insights into the Glance, Attention Economy, and Instagram," *Critical Studies in Media Communication* 35, no. 2 (March 15, 2018): 137–50, https://doi.org/10.1080/15295036.2017.1394582.

18. Philip N. Cohen, *The Family: Diversity, Inequality, and Social Change*, 3rd ed. (New York: Norton, 2021).

19. Jerry Green, "Sealioning: A Case Study in Epistemic Vice," *Southwest Philosophy Review* 38, no. 1 (April 26, 2022): 123–34, https://doi.org/10.5840/swphilreview202238113.

20. This dilemma calls to mind George Ritzer's description of the "irrationality of rationality," originally written before social media existed. George Ritzer, *The McDonaldization of Society: An Investigation into the Changing Character of Contemporary Social Life* (Newbury Park, CA: Pine Forge, 1996).

21. I have discovered, incidentally, that Google Scholar sometimes counts citations on blog posts for its scoring—you never know, and Google doesn't have to tell you or anyone else how it works. They don't work for you; you work for them.

22. Yian Yin, Yuxiao Dong, Kuansan Wang, Dashun Wang, and Benjamin F. Jones, "Public Use and Public Funding of Science," *Nature Human Behaviour* 6, no. 10 (October 2022): 1344–50, https://doi.org/10.1038/s41562-022-01397-5.

23. In a 2013 *New Yorker* cartoon, the psychiatrist says to his distressed patient on the couch, "Let's try focusing on your posts that *do* receive comments." Ward Sutton, "A Shrink Consults His Patient," *New Yorker*, February 11, 2013.

24. Brubaker, *Hyperconnectivity and Its Discontents*, 18.

25. Tressie McMillan Cottom, "'Who Do You Think You Are?': When Marginality Meets Academic Microcelebrity," *Ada: A Journal of Gender, New Media, and Technology*, no. 7 (April 2015), https://scholarsbank.uoregon.edu/xmlui/handle/1794/26359.

26. Joseph B. Bak-Coleman et al.. "Stewardship of Global Collective Behavior." *Proceedings of the National Academy of Sciences* 118, no. 27 (July 6, 2021), https://doi.org/10.1073/pnas.2025764118.

27. danah boyd, "Facebook Is a Utility; Utilities Get Regulated," Apophenia (blog), May 15, 2010, https://www.zephoria.org/thoughts/archives/2010/05/15/facebook-is-a-utility-utilities-get-regulated.html.

28. Carl T. Bergstrom, "Twitter Was Influential in the Pandemic. Are We Better for It?," *New York Times*, November 19, 2022, https://www.nytimes.com/2022/11/19/opinion/pandemic-twitter.html.

29. Alice E. Marwick, "Morally Motivated Networked Harassment as Normative Reinforcement," *Social Media + Society* 7, no. 2 (April 2021), https://doi.org/10.1177/20563051211021378.

30. Dominique Brossard and Dietram A. Scheufele, "The Chronic Growing Pains of Communicating Science Online," *Science* 375, no. 6581 (February 11, 2022), 613–14.

31. Jeffrey Pomerantz, Carolyn Hank, and Cassidy R. Sugimoto, "The State of Social Media Policies in Higher Education," *PLOS ONE* 10, no. 5 (May 27, 2015): e0127485, https://doi.org/10.1371/journal.pone.0127485.

32. Talia Barnes, "Trinity Christian College Skips the Lesson on Extramural Speech, Terminates Prof's Employment for 'Unprofessional' Tweets," Foundation for Individual Rights and Expression (FIRE) (blog), February 22, 2023, https://www.thefire.org/news/trinity-christian-college-skips-lesson-extramural-speech-terminates-profs-employment.

33. Trinity Christian University, "Faculty Handbook," January 29, 2016, https://trollweb.trnty.edu/download/faculty-handbook/.

34. Lola Fadulu, "Columbia Psychiatry Chair Suspended After Tweet About Dark-Skinned Model," *New York Times*, February 23, 2022, https://www.nytimes.com/2022/02/23/nyregion/columbia-jeffrey-lieberman.html.

35. Michael Levenson, "University Must Reinstate Professor Who Tweeted About 'Black Privilege,'" *New York Times*, May 19, 2022, https://www.nytimes.com/2022/05/19/us/twitter-florida-professor-reinstated.html.

36. Robert Mackey, "Professor's Angry Tweets on Gaza Cost Him a Job," *New York Times*, September 13, 2014, https://www.nytimes.com/2014/09/13/world/middleeast/professors-angry-tweets-on-gaza-cost-him-a-job.html.

37. Lauren Ingeno, "#Penalty," *Inside Higher Ed*, August 6, 2013, https://www.insidehighered.com/news/2013/08/07/fat-shaming-professor-faces-censure-university.

6. ACTIVISM AND ACTIVE CITIZENSHIP

1. Michel Foucault, "What Is an Author?" In *Language, Counter-Memory Practice: Selected Essays and Interviews*, ed. Donald Bouchard and Sherry Simon, trans. Donald Bouchard (Ithaca, NY: Cornell University Press, 1977), 212.

2. Karl Marx, "The Class Struggles in France, 1848 to 1850, Part IV," https://www.marxists.org/archive/marx/works/1850/class-struggles-france/.

3. David S. Meyer, *How Social Movements (Sometimes) Matter* (Cambridge: Wiley, 2021).

4. Christopher Mathias, "This Man Has the Ear of Billionaires—and a White Supremacist Past He Kept a Secret," HuffPost (blog), August 4, 2023, https://www.huffpost.com/entry/richard-hanania-white-supremacist-pseudonym-richard-hoste_n_64c93928e4b021e2f295e817.

5. Jessie Daniels, "W. E. B. DuBois for the Twenty-First Century: On Being a Scholar-Activist in the Digital Era," *Sociological Forum* 33, no. 4 (2018): 1072–85, https://doi.org/10.1111/socf.12464.

6. Morris Aldon, *The Scholar Denied: W. E. B. Du Bois and the Birth of Modern Sociology* (Oakland: University of California Press, 2015).

7. Paulo Freire, *Pedagogy of the Oppressed*, trans. Myra Bergman Ramos (New York: Continuum, 2000).

8. Robin D. G. Kelley, "Black Study, Black Struggle," *Boston Review*, March 1, 2016, https://www.bostonreview.net/forum/robin-kelley-black-struggle-campus-protest/.

9. Stefano Harney and Fred Moten, *The Undercommons: Fugitive Planning and Black Study* (London: Minor Compositions, 2013), 26.

10. "Our dream, as social scientists," said Pierre Bourdieu, "might be for part of our research to be useful to the social movement, instead of being lost, as is often the case nowadays, because it is intercepted and

distorted by journalists or by hostile interpreters, etc. . . . [W]e would like to invent new forms of expression that make it possible to communicate the most advanced findings of research. But that also presupposes a change of language and outlook on the part of the researchers." Pierre Bourdieu, *Acts of Resistance: Against the New Myths of Our Time* (Bristol: Policy Press, 1998), 58.

11. Monica Prasad, "Pragmatism as Problem Solving," *Socius* 7 (January 1, 2021), https://doi.org/10.1177/2378023121993991.

12. Mark Weaver, "Weber's Critique of Advocacy in the Classroom: Critical Thinking and Civic Education," *PS: Political Science & Politics* 31, no. 4 (December 1998): 799–801, https://doi.org/10.2307/420720.

13. Philip S. Gorski, "Beyond the Fact/Value Distinction: Ethical Naturalism and the Social Sciences," *Society* 50, no. 6 (December 2013): 543–53, https://doi.org/10.1007/s12115-013-9709-2.

14. In 2023, arXiv and bioRxiv began piloting a service that produces AI-generated capsule summaries of new papers, written for audiences at three different levels of expertise. Ewen Callaway, "AI Writes Summaries of Preprints in bioRxiv Trial," *Nature* 623, no. 7988 (November 2023): 677, https://doi.org/10.1038/d41586-023-03545-x.

15. This analysis was described, with links to complete references, here: Philip N. Cohen, "Policy Implications Are Discussed (Often to Poor Effect, in Sociology Journals)," Family Inequality (blog), December 30, 2020, https://familyinequality.wordpress.com/2020/12/30/policy-implications-are-discussed-often-to-poor-effect-in-sociology-journals/.

16. Paul M. Kohn and G. W. Mercer, "Drug Use, Drug-Use Attitudes, and the Authoritarianism-Rebellion Dimension," *Journal of Health and Social Behavior* 12, no. 2 (1971): 125–31, https://doi.org/10.2307/2948519.

17. Phelan, Jo C., Bruce G. Link, and Parisa Tehranifar. "Social Conditions as Fundamental Causes of Health Inequalities: Theory, Evidence, and Policy Implications," *Journal of Health and Social Behavior* 51, no. 1_suppl (March 1, 2010), S37.

18. Michael E. Antonio, Rosalyn G. Davis, and Susan R. Shutt, "Dog Training Programs in Pennsylvania's Department of Corrections Perceived Effectiveness for Inmates and Staff," *Society & Animals* 25, no. 5 (2017): 475–89, https://doi.org/10.1163/15685306-12341457.

19. I'm not singling out specific papers here because they don't deserve negative attention for following conventions often imposed by reviewers or editors.

20. Pierre Bourdieu, *Practical Reason: On the Theory of Action* (Redwood City, CA: Stanford University Press, 1998), 88.

21. Mary Romero, "Sociology Engaged in Social Justice," *American Sociological Review* 85, no. 1 (February 2020), 1–3.

22. Mattias Ekman, "The Great Replacement: Strategic Mainstreaming of Far-Right Conspiracy Claims," *Convergence* 28, no. 4 (August 2022): 1127–43, https://doi.org/10.1177/13548565221091983.

23. United Nations Population Division, "Replacement Migration," United Nations Secretariat, 2000, https://www.un.org/development/desa/pd/sites/www.un.org.development.desa.pd/files/files/documents/2020/Jan/un_2001_replacementmigration.pdf.

24. Campbell Robertson, "The Synagogue Attack Stands Alone, but Experts Say Violent Rhetoric Is Spreading," *New York Times*, August 4, 2023, https://www.nytimes.com/2023/08/04/us/pittsburgh-synagogue-shooting-antisemitism-bowers.html; Rick Noack, "Christchurch Endures as Extremist Touchstone, as Investigators Probe Suspected El Paso Manifesto," *Washington Post*, August 7, 2019, https://www.washingtonpost.com/world/2019/08/06/christchurch-endures-extremist-touchstone-investigators-probe-suspected-el-paso-manifesto/.

25. His manifesto is archived here: https://web.archive.org/web/20120522200040/http://www.fas.org/programs/tap/_docs/2083_-_A_European_Declaration_of_Independence.pdf.

26. Douglas S. Massey, "What Critical Demography Means to Me," *Sociological Forum* 14, no. 3 (September 1999), 525.

27. Philip N. Cohen, "American Policy Fails at Reducing Child Poverty Because It Aims to Fix the Poor," *Washington Post*, April 4, 2016, https://www.washingtonpost.com/posteverything/wp/2016/04/04/american-policy-fails-at-reducing-child-poverty-because-it-aims-to-fix-the-poor/.

28. Center on Budget and Policy Priorities, "Policy Basics: The Child Tax Credit," December 7, 2022, https://www.cbpp.org/research/federal-tax/the-child-tax-credit.

29. Michael Karpman, Elaine Maag, Stephen Zuckerman, and Doug Wissoker, "Child Tax Credit Recipients Experienced a Larger Decline in Food Insecurity and a Similar Change in Employment as Nonrecipients between 2020 and 2021," Tax Policy Center, May 2022, https://www.urban.org/sites/default/files/2022-05/CTC%20Recipients%20Experienced%20Larger%20Decline%20in%20Food%20Insecurity%20

and%20Similar%20Change%20in%20Employment%20as%20Nonre-
cipients%20v2.pdf.

30. Elizabeth Ananat, Benjamin Glasner, Christal Hamilton, and Zachary Parolin, "Effects of the Expanded Child Tax Credit on Employment Outcomes: Evidence from Real-World Data from April to December 2021," Working Paper, National Bureau of Economic Research, March 2022, https://doi.org/10.3386/w29823.

31. Sarah McCammon, Lauren Hodges, and Sarah Handel, "The Child Tax Credit Was a Lifeline. Now Some Families Are Falling Back into Poverty," NPR, April 8, 2022, https://www.npr.org/2022/04/08/1091418380/child-tax-credit-return-inflation-food-gas-prices.

32. Liam Kofi Bright, "Du Bois' Democratic Defence of the Value Free Ideal," Synthese 195, no. 5 (May 1, 2018), 2230.

33. W. E. B. Du Bois, "My Evolving Program for Negro Freedom," In What the Negro Wants, ed. Rayford Whittingham Logan (Notre Dame, IN: University of Notre Dame Press, 2001), 57.

34. I wrote two columns with the progressive activist Sean McElwee, who had a regular column at Slate, focusing on the racist attitudes of voters who were supporting Trump in the Republican primaries. Sean McElwee and Philip N. Cohen, "The Secret to Trump's Success: New Research Sheds Light on the GOP Front-Runner's Stunning Staying Power," Salon, March 18, 2016, https://www.salon.com/2016/03/18/the_secret_to_trumps_success_new_research_sheds_light_on_the_gop_frontrunners_stunning_staying_power/; Sean McElwee and Philip N. Cohen, "The Vile Core of Trump's Appeal: Here's the Research That Shows How Racism Animates His Campaign," Salon, March 27, 2016, https://www.salon.com/2016/03/27/the_vile_core_of_trumps_appeal_heres_the_research_that_shows_how_racism_animates_his_campaign/.

35. The anti-Semitic practice of placing Jewish names within three parentheses, indicating an echo or spooky sound, became popular online in the Trump era.

36. Adam Gopnik, "The Music Donald Trump Can't Hear," New Yorker, January 13, 2017, https://www.newyorker.com/news/daily-comment/the-music-donald-trump-cant-hear.

37. The item is archived here: https://web.archive.org/web/20180327021923/https://dailystormer.name/kike-professor-rails-against-armed-goyim/.

38. Knight First Amendment Institute, "Free Speech and Social Media," accessed June 22, 2024, http://knightcolumbia.org/issues/free-speech-social-media.
39. Archived here: https://knightcolumbia.org/documents/a4a507b3fb.
40. The legal documents for the case are collected here: https://knightcolumbia.org/cases/knight-institute-v-trump.
41. Philip N. Cohen, "Why I'm Suing President Trump for Blocking Me on Twitter," *The Daily Beast*, July 11, 2017, https://www.thedailybeast.com/why-im-suing-president-trump-for-blocking-me-on-twitter.

7. MAKE IT HAPPEN

1. Pierre Bourdieu, *The Craft of Sociology: Epistemological Preliminaries* (Berlin: Walter de Gruyter, 1991), 252.
2. Links to the news items and essays in this anecdote are available here: https://familyinequality.wordpress.com/2018/04/01/how-i-engaged-my-way-to-excellent-research-success-and-you-can-too/.
3. Philip N. Cohen, "The Coming Divorce Decline," *Socius* 5 (January 1, 2019), https://doi.org/10.1177/2378023119873497.
4. Adam Kotsko, "What Happened to Giorgio Agamben?" *Slate*, February 21, 2022, https://slate.com/human-interest/2022/02/giorgio-agamben-covid-holocaust-comparison-right-wing-protest.html.
5. Giorgio Agamben, *Where Are We Now?: The Epidemic as Politics* (Lanham, MD: Rowman & Littlefield, 2021).
6. Special Committee, "Report of a Special Committee: Political Interference and Academic Freedom in Florida's Public Higher Education System," American Association of University Professors, November 30, 2023, https://www.aaup.org/file/AAUP_Special_Committee_Report_on_Florida_final.pdf.
7. Francesca Antonini, "Pessimism of the Intellect, Optimism of the Will: Gramsci's Political Thought in the Last Miscellaneous Notebooks," *Rethinking Marxism* 31, no. 1 (January 2, 2019): 42–57, https://doi.org/10.1080/08935696.2019.1577616.
8. Amanda Hess, "The Medical Mask Becomes a Protest Symbol," *New York Times*, June 2, 2020, https://www.nytimes.com/2020/06/02/arts/virus-mask-trump.html.

9. Audre Lorde, *Sister Outsider: Essays and Speeches* (London: Penguin, 2020), 100.

10. In my experience, public engagement criteria are only referenced positively in the tenure and promotion process, often to help cases where the academic track record is weaker, but that may just reflect the lack of formal criteria for engagement.

11. Pierre Bourdieu, *Practical Reason: On the Theory of Action* (Redwood City, CA: Stanford University Press, 1998).

ACKNOWLEDGMENTS

1. Philip N. Cohen, "Public Engagement and the Influence Imperative," *Contemporary Sociology* 48, no. 2 (March 2019): 119–23, https://doi.org /10.1177/0094306119827954; Barbara J. Risman, Kristi Williams, and Virginia E. Rutter, eds., *Families as They Really Are*, 3rd ed. (New York: Norton, 2023); Philip N. Cohen, "How Sociology Can Save Itself," *Chronicle of Higher Education*, February 7, 2024, https://www.chronicle .com/article/how-sociology-can-save-itself.

ACKNOWLEDGMENTS

This project entwined some disparate strands of work—and communities—along my meandering paths of citizen and scholar: teaching and writing for students, publicly resisting Trump and authoritarianism, contributing to the movement for open science and open scholarship in academia, and co-editing the "public-facing" journal of sociology, *Contexts*. This mashup of audiences and intellectual styles, products and processes, has made my career more interesting and more fun by widening my intellectual and social circles and diversifying the work itself. And it gave me more people to thank than I can remember.

Special thanks are due to Eric Schwartz at Columbia University Press for planting the idea that there was a book in all this and then expertly guiding it to fruition—along with the generous and helpful anonymous reviewers he mustered. The ad hoc community of sociology, library, and tech people who helped make SocArXiv happen starting in 2016 opened up a world of possibility for me, and I thank them all, including Jeff Spies and Brian Nosek and their colleagues at the Center for Open Science, Adriene Lim, Judy Ruttenberg, and the many members of the SocArXiv Steering Committee and moderation team over the years since. (As I write this, the world is more than 15,000 free, open-access papers richer for our collective efforts!) In the years after that, Chris Bourg and Micah Altman generously brought me to the Center for Research on Equitable and Open Scholarship at the MIT Libraries, making open science legitimately my day job and (with Jessica Polka) teaching me a lot about how science works.

I'm grateful to the lawyers of the Knight First Amendment Institute (also at Columbia) who put together the lawsuit against Trump: Katie Fallow, Jameel Jaffer, and Alex Abdo—whom I had the great privilege of calling "my lawyers" while it lasted. Their work is amazing. Syed Ali and Letta Page convinced me to join them in a bid to edit *Contexts* and then made it a great experience, which I appreciate hugely. Working with the Council on Contemporary Families was a great public intellectual experience, and I thank Stephanie Coontz and Virginia Rutter for their long collaboration and companionship. This project also benefited from Sasha Levitt's editing on my other book, and I thank her. I also am grateful for the fruitful, if sometimes fleeting, professional relationships with a lot of journalists and editors, and people who invited me for talks or to write for them, all of whom helped me hone my thoughts and figure out what I'm trying to say.

Some passages in this book previously partly appeared in an essay I wrote for *Contemporary Sociology*, in the third edition of *Families as They Really Are*, and in *The Chronicle of Higher Education*.[1] Some bits are adapted or updated from things I wrote on my blog, *Family Inequality*, or from other of my social media posts, in ways that are not always tracked in the footnotes (let's consider this book the version of record for those thoughts).

A lot of people gave me advice and criticism online or on my blog, many of whom I don't list here (but thanks, Bill Bielby,

Myra Marx Ferree, Andrew Gelman, Julian Hamann, Belinda Luscombe, Liana Sayer, Kim Weeden). Some commented on drafts or presentations of chapters, including Muna Adem, Orit Avishai, Shriyam Gupta, Dan Hirschman, Jelly Loblack, Jeff Lockhardt, Virginia Rutter, and Reeve Vanneman.

Letta Page edited this book for me, bringing her unparalleled sociological wordsmithing to the text (and into the comment bubbles) at all levels. She made it all (except these acknowledgements) extremely much better and more informative, effective, and fun to read. Thank you.

I describe the roles of citizen and scholar in this book, but at least for me, these identities always orbit around the family life that makes them viable. Among all the family, fictive and otherwise, whose bonds I cherish, I offer my undying gratitude to my parents, Avis and Marshall Cohen, for everything; and to my wife Judy Ruttenberg, and our daughters Charlotte and Ruby, also for everything.

REFERENCES

"Publish, v." In *OED Online*. Oxford University Press, 2023.

Abbott, Andrew. *Department and Discipline: Chicago Sociology at One Hundred*. Chicago: University of Chicago Press, 2017.

Achenbach, Joel, Katie Mettler, Lena H. Sun, and Ben Guarino. "Coronavirus May Have Spread Undetected for Weeks in Washington State, Which Reported First Two Deaths in U.S." *Washington Post*. March 1, 2020. https://www.washingtonpost.com/health/coronavirus-may-have-spread-undetected-for-weeks-in-washington-state/2020/03/01/0f292336-5bcc-11ea-9055-5fa12981bbbf_story.html.

ACRL Scholarly Communications Committee. "Principles and Strategies for the Reform of Scholarly Communication." American Library Association. 2003. https://www.ala.org/acrl/publications/whitepapers/principlesstrategies.

Agamben, Giorgio. *Where Are We Now?: The Epidemic as Politics*. Lanham, MD: Rowman & Littlefield, 2021.

Allen, Liz, Jo Scott, Amy Brand, Marjorie Hlava, and Micah Altman. "Publishing: Credit Where Credit Is Due." *Nature* 508, no. 7496 (April 2014): 312–13. https://doi.org/10.1038/508312a.

Altman, Micah. "Research Lifecycles." Presented at the Center for Research on Equitable and Open Scholarship seminar series, MIT. February 3, 2022. https://docs.google.com/presentation/d/1EMaosGY-90JlFnTg6px-5qomV4OVDY45znFYJBFK7Ejk.

Altman, Micah, and Philip N. Cohen. "On Clarifying the Goals of a Peer Review Taxonomy." The Scholarly Kitchen. October 1, 2020. https://scholarlykitchen.sspnet.org/2020/10/01/guest-post-on-clarifying-the-goals-of-a-peer-review-taxonomy/.

Altman, Micah, and Philip N. Cohen. "We Are in a Period of Science Policy Innovation, yet There Are Major Evidence Gaps in Evaluating Their Effectiveness." Impact of Social Sciences (blog). July 27, 2023. https://blogs.lse.ac.uk/impactofsocialsciences/2023/07/27/we-are-in-a-period-of-science-policy-innovation-yet-there-are-major-evidence-gaps-in-evaluating-their-effectiveness/.

Altman, Micah, Philip N. Cohen, and Jessica Polka. "Interventions in Scholarly Communication: Design Lessons from Public Health." *First Monday*. August 12, 2023. https://doi.org/10.5210/fm.v28i8.12941.

Ananat, Elizabeth, Benjamin Glasner, Christal Hamilton, and Zachary Parolin. "Effects of the Expanded Child Tax Credit on Employment Outcomes: Evidence from Real-World Data from April to December 2021." Working Paper. Working Paper Series. National Bureau of Economic Research. March 2022. https://doi.org/10.3386/w29823.

Anderson, Margo. "The Census and the Japanese 'Internment': Apology and Policy in Statistical Practice." *Social Research: An International Quarterly* 87, no. 4 (2020): 789–812. https://doi.org/10.1353/sor.2020.0064.

Antonini, Francesca. "Pessimism of the Intellect, Optimism of the Will: Gramsci's Political Thought in the Last Miscellaneous Notebooks." *Rethinking Marxism* 31, no. 1 (January 2, 2019): 42–57. https://doi.org/10.1080/08935696.2019.1577616.

Antonio, Michael E., Rosalyn G. Davis, and Susan R. Shutt. "Dog Training Programs in Pennsylvania's Department of Corrections Perceived Effectiveness for Inmates and Staff." *Society & Animals* 25, no. 5 (2017): 475–89. https://doi.org/10.1163/15685306-12341457.

Au, Larry, and Gil Eyal. "Whose Advice Is Credible? Claiming Lay Expertise in a Covid-19 Online Community." *Qualitative Sociology* 45, no. 1 (March 1, 2022): 31–61. https://doi.org/10.1007/s11133-021-09492-1.

Bak-Coleman, Joseph B., Mark Alfano, Wolfram Barfuss, Carl T. Bergstrom, Miguel A. Centeno, Iain D. Couzin, Jonathan F. Donges, et al. "Stewardship of Global Collective Behavior." *Proceedings of the National Academy of Sciences* 118, no. 27 (July 6, 2021). https://doi.org/10.1073/pnas.2025764118.

Baldwin, Melinda. "Scientific Autonomy, Public Accountability, and the Rise of 'Peer Review' in the Cold War United States." *Isis* 109, no. 3 (September 1, 2018): 538–58. https://doi.org/10.1086/700070.

Barnes, Talia. "Trinity Christian College Skips the Lesson on Extramural Speech, Terminates Prof's Employment for 'Unprofessional' Tweets | The

Foundation for Individual Rights and Expression." Foundation for Individual Rights and Expression (FIRE) (blog). February 22, 2023. https://www.thefire.org/news/trinity-christian-college-skips-lesson-extramural-speech-terminates-profs-employment.

Barthel, Michael, Katerina Eva Matsa, and Kirsten Worden. "Coronavirus-Driven Downturn Hits Newspapers Hard as TV News Thrives." Pew Research Center's Journalism Project (blog). October 29, 2020. https://www.journalism.org/2020/10/29/coronavirus-driven-downturn-hits-newspapers-hard-as-tv-news-thrives/.

Bartlett, Tom. "The Unraveling of Michael LaCour." *The Chronicle of Higher Education.* June 2, 2015. https://www.chronicle.com/article/the-unraveling-of-michael-lacour/.

Benjamin, Daniel J., James O. Berger, Magnus Johannesson, Brian A. Nosek, E.-J. Wagenmakers, Richard Berk, Kenneth A. Bollen, et al. "Redefine Statistical Significance." *Nature Human Behaviour* 2, no. 1 (January 2018): 6–10. https://doi.org/10.1038/s41562-017-0189-z.

Berenbaum, May R. "Retraction for Shu et al., Signing at the Beginning Makes Ethics Salient and Decreases Dishonest Self-Reports in Comparison to Signing at the End." *Proceedings of the National Academy of Sciences* 118, no. 38 (September 21, 2021): e2115397118. https://doi.org/10.1073/pnas.2115397118.

Bergstrom, Carl T. "Twitter Was Influential in the Pandemic. Are We Better for It?" *The New York Times.* November 19, 2022. https://www.nytimes.com/2022/11/19/opinion/pandemic-twitter.html.

Bergstrom, Carl T., and Jevin D. West. *Calling Bullshit: The Art of Skepticism in a Data-Driven World.* New York: Random House, 2020.

Besbris, Max, and Shamus Khan. "Less Theory. More Description." *Sociological Theory* 35, no. 2 (June 1, 2017): 147–53. https://doi.org/10.1177/0735275117709776.

Bianchi, Suzanne M. "A Demographic Perspective on Family Change." *Journal of Family Theory & Review* 6, no. 1 (March 1, 2014): 35–44. https://doi.org/10.1111/jftr.12029.

Bourdieu, Pierre. *Acts of Resistance: Against the New Myths of Our Time.* London: Policy Press, 1998.

Bourdieu, Pierre. *Practical Reason: On the Theory of Action.* Redwood City, CA: Stanford University Press, 1998.

Bourdieu, Pierre. *The Craft of Sociology: Epistemological Preliminaries.* Berlin: Walter de Gruyter, 1991.

Bourdieu, Pierre. *The Logic of Practice*. Redwood City, CA: Stanford University Press, 1990.

boyd, danah. "Facebook Is a Utility; Utilities Get Regulated." Apophenia (blog). May 15, 2010. https://www.zephoria.org/thoughts/archives/2010/05/15/facebook-is-a-utility-utilities-get-regulated.html.

Brainard, Jeffrey, and Jocelyn Kaiser. "White House Requires Immediate Public Access to All U.S.-Funded Research Papers by 2025." Science Insider (blog). August 26, 2022. https://www.science.org/content/article/white-house-requires-immediate-public-access-all-u-s--funded-research-papers-2025.

Breznau, Nate. "Does Sociology Need Open Science?" *Societies* 11, no. 1 (March 2021): 9. https://doi.org/10.3390/soc11010009.

Breznau, Nate. "The Welfare State and Risk Perceptions: The Novel Coronavirus Pandemic and Public Concern in 70 Countries." *European Societies* 23, suppl. 1 (February 19, 2021): S33–46. https://doi.org/10.1080/14616696.2020.1793215.

Bright, Liam Kofi. "Du Bois' Democratic Defence of the Value Free Ideal." *Synthese* 195, no. 5 (May 1, 2018): 2227–45. https://doi.org/10.1007/s11229-017-1333-z.

Brinton, Willard Cope. *Graphic Methods for Presenting Facts*. New York: The Engineering Magazine Company, 1914.

Brossard, Dominique, and Dietram A. Scheufele. "The Chronic Growing Pains of Communicating Science Online." *Science* 375, no. 6581 (February 11, 2022): 613–14. https://doi.org/10.1126/science.abo0668.

Brubaker, Rogers. *Hyperconnectivity and Its Discontents*. Hoboken, NJ: Polity, 2022.

Buckley, Chris. "Chinese Doctor, Silenced After Warning of Outbreak, Dies from Coronavirus." *New York Times*, February 6, 2020. https://www.nytimes.com/2020/02/06/world/asia/chinese-doctor-Li-Wenliang-coronavirus.html.

Byrne, Christine. "24 Summer Cocktails That Are Perfect for Day Drinking." BuzzFeed. May 28, 2021. https://www.buzzfeed.com/christinebyrne/booze-and-berries-and-sunshine.

Callaway, Ewen. "AI Writes Summaries of Preprints in bioRxiv Trial." *Nature* 623, no. 7988 (November 14, 2023): 677–677. https://doi.org/10.1038/d41586-023-03545-x.

Center on Budget and Policy Priorities. "Policy Basics: The Child Tax Credit." December 7, 2022. https://www.cbpp.org/research/federal-tax/the-child-tax-credit.

Chotiner, Isaac. "Noam Chomsky Believes Trump Is 'the Worst Criminal in Human History.'" *New Yorker.* October 30, 2020. https://www.newyorker .com/news/q-and-a/noam-chomsky-believes-trump-is-the-worst-criminal -in-human-history.

Christensen, Garret, Jeremy Freese, and Edward Miguel. *Transparent and Reproducible Social Science Research: How to Do Open Science.* Oakland: University of California Press, 2019.

Clarke, Kristie E. N. "Seroprevalence of Infection-Induced SARS-CoV-2 Antibodies—United States, September 2021–February 2022." *MMWR. Morbidity and Mortality Weekly Report* 71, no. 17 (2022): 606–8. https://doi .org/10.15585/mmwr.mm7117e3.

Clemetson, Lynette. "Homeland Security Given Data on Arab-Americans." *New York Times,* July 30, 2004. https://www.nytimes.com/2004/07/30/us /homeland-security-given-data-on-arab-americans.html.

Cohen, Philip N. "American Policy Fails at Reducing Child Poverty Because It Aims to Fix the Poor." *Washington Post.* April 4, 2016. https://www .washingtonpost.com/posteverything/wp/2016/04/04/american-policy -fails-at-reducing-child-poverty-because-it-aims-to-fix-the-poor/.

Cohen, Philip N. "Black Men Raping White Women: BJS's Table 42 Problem." Family Inequality (blog). September 25, 2016. https://familyinequality .wordpress.com/2016/09/25/black-men-raping-white-women-bjss-table -42-problem/.

Cohen, Philip N. "Disrupted Family Plans and Exacerbated Inequalities Associated with COVID-19 Pandemic." *JAMA Network Open* 4, no. 9 (September 15, 2021): e2124399. https://doi.org/10.1001/jamanetworkopen .2021.24399.

Cohen, Philip N. *Enduring Bonds: Inequality, Marriage, Parenting, and Everything Else That Makes Families Great and Terrible.* Oakland: University of California Press, 2018.

Cohen, Phillip N. "Fox NY Covers Divorce Trend Report, 9/25/2018." YouTube. September 28, 2018, video. https://www.youtube.com/watch?v=xEcdOJoIpRw.

Cohen, Philip N. "Generation Labels Mean Nothing. It's Time to Retire Them." *Washington Post,* July 7, 2021. https://www.washingtonpost.com /opinions/2021/07/07/generation-labels-mean-nothing-retire-them/.

Cohen, Philip N. "How Sociology Can Save Itself." *Chronicle of Higher Education.* February 7, 2024. https://www.chronicle.com/article/how-sociology -can-save-itself.

Cohen, Philip N. "In the Last 10 Years, the US Child Poverty Rate Has Fallen Dramatically . . . (Demographic Fact A Day)." Twitter. November 14, 2022. https://twitter.com/demfactaday/status/1592185821834379266.

Cohen, Philip N. "Maternal Age and Infant Mortality for White, Black, and Mexican Mothers in the United States." Sociological Science 3 (2016): 32–38. https://doi.org/10.15195/v3.a2.

Cohen, Philip N. "Multiple-Decrement Life Table Estimates of Divorce Rates." 2023. https://doi.org/10.17605/OSF.IO/ZBER3.

Cohen, Philip N. "Overturning Roe Is an Attack on the Modern Family." New Republic. May 3, 2022. https://newrepublic.com/article/166285/overturning -roe-attack-modern-family.

Cohen, Philip N. "Proposed Rule Change for the American Sociological Association Dissertation Award." Family Inequality (blog). June 4, 2015. https://familyinequality.wordpress.com/2015/06/04/proposal-rule-change-for -the-american-sociological-association-dissertation-award/.

Cohen, Philip N. "Public Engagement and the Influence Imperative." Contemporary Sociology 48, no. 2 (March 1, 2019): 119–23. https://doi.org/10.1177 /0094306119827954.

Cohen, Philip N. "Recession and Divorce in the United States, 2008–2011." Population Research and Policy Review 33, no. 5 (October 1, 2014): 615–28. https://doi.org/10.1007/s11113-014-9323-z.

Cohen, Philip N. "The Coming Divorce Decline." Socius 5 (January 1, 2019): 237802311973497. https://doi.org/10.1177/2378023119873497.

Cohen, Philip N. "The COVID-19 Epidemic in Rural U.S. Counties." European Journal of Environment and Public Health 4, no. 2 (June 9, 2020): em0050. https://doi.org/10.29333/ejeph/8331.

Cohen, Philip N. "The Divorce Fairness Issue That Jeff and MacKenzie Bezos Don't Have to Worry About." CNN. January 12, 2019. https://www.cnn.com/2019/01/11/opinions/divorce-unfair-bezos-opinion-cohen /index.html.

Cohen, Philip N. The Family: Diversity, Inequality, and Social Change. 3rd ed. New York: Norton, 2021.

Cohen, Philip N. "The Widening Political Divide Over Science." SocArXiv. December 15, 2018. https://doi.org/10.31235/osf.io/u95aw.

Cohen, Philip N. "Ukraine's Refugee Crisis Is a Demographic Crisis, Too." Family Inequality (blog). March 9, 2022. https://familyinequality .wordpress.com/2022/03/09/ukraines-refugee-crisis-is-a-demographic-crisis-too/.

Cohen, Philip N. "Why I'm Suing President Trump for Blocking Me on Twitter." *The Daily Beast*. July 11, 2017. https://www.thedailybeast.com /why-im-suing-president-trump-for-blocking-me-on-twitter.

Cole, Stephen. "Why Sociology Doesn't Make Progress like the Natural Sciences." *Sociological Forum* 9, no. 2 (1994): 133–54.

Collins, Harry, and Robert Evans. *Rethinking Expertise*. Chicago: University of Chicago Press, 2008.

Conwell, Jordan A., and Kevin Loughran. "Quantitative Inquiry in the Early Sociology of W. E. B. Du Bois." *Du Bois Review: Social Science Research on Race*. December 13, 2023, 1–23. https://doi.org/10.1017 /S1742058X23000206.

Cottom, Tressie McMillan. "'Who Do You Think You Are?': When Marginality Meets Academic Microcelebrity." *Ada: A Journal of Gender, New Media, and Technology*, no. 7 (April 2015). https://scholarsbank.uoregon .edu/xmlui/handle/1794/26359.

Creamer, John, Emily A. Shrider, Kalee Burns, and Frances Chen. "Poverty in the United States: 2021." Current Population Reports. Washington, DC: U.S. Census Bureau, 2022. https://www.census.gov/library/publications/2022 /demo/p60-277.html.

Daniels, Jessie. "W. E. B. DuBois for the Twenty-First Century: On Being a Scholar-Activist in the Digital Era." *Sociological Forum* 33, no. 4 (2018): 1072–85. https://doi.org/10.1111/socf.12464.

Denbo, Seth. "Open Peer Review in the Humanities." The Scholarly Kitchen (blog). March 4, 2020. https://scholarlykitchen.sspnet.org/2020/03/04 /guest-post-open-peer-review-in-the-humanities/.

DePillis, Lydia, and Jason DeParle. "Pandemic Aid Cut U.S. Poverty to New Low in 2021, Census Bureau Reports." *New York Times*. September 13, 2022. https://www.nytimes.com/2022/09/13/business/economy/income-poverty-census-bureau.html.

Desmond, Matthew. *Evicted: Poverty and Profit in the American City*. New York: Crown, 2016.

Doctorow, Cory. "The 'Enshittification' of TikTok." *Wired*. January 23, 2023. https://www.wired.com/story/tiktok-platforms-cory-doctorow/.

Du Bois, W. E. B. "My Evolving Program for Negro Freedom." In *What the Negro Wants*, ed. Rayford Whittingham Logan. Notre Dame, IN: University of Notre Dame Press, 2001.

Du Bois, W. E. B. *The Philadelphia Negro: A Social Study*. Philadelphia: University of Pennsylvania, 1899. http://archive.org/details/philadelphianegroodubo.

Dudley, Robert. "Fermenting Fruit and the Historical Ecology of Ethanol Ingestion: Is Alcoholism in Modern Humans an Evolutionary Hangover?" *Addiction* 97, no. 4 (2002): 381–88. https://doi.org/10.1046/j.1360 -0443.2002.00002.x.

EFE. "Gobierno Mexicano Critica 'Campaña de Ataques' por Uso de la Ivermectina." EFE. February 8, 2022. http://www.efe.com/efe/america /mexico/gobierno-mexicano-critica-campana-de-ataques-por-uso-la -ivermectina/50000545-4735550.

Ekman, Mattias. "The Great Replacement: Strategic Mainstreaming of Far-Right Conspiracy Claims." *Convergence* 28, no. 4 (August 1, 2022): 1127–43. https://doi.org/10.1177/13548565221091983.

eLife. "eLife Latest: What We Have Learned About Preprints." Inside eLife (blog). July 1, 2021. https://elifesciences.org/inside-elife/e5f8f1f7/elife-latest -what-we-have-learned-about-preprints.

Emerson, Ralph Waldo. *The Conduct of Life*. Boston: Ticknor and Fields, 1860. http://archive.org/details/conductlifeooemerrich.

Environmental Protection Agency. "The 2022 EPA Automotive Trends Report." Washington, DC: Environmental Protection Agency, 2022. https://www .epa.gov/system/files/documents/2022-12/420r22029.pdf.

Eyal, Gil. *The Crisis of Expertise*. Cambridge: Wiley, 2019.

Fadulu, Lola. "Columbia Psychiatry Chair Suspended After Tweet About Dark-Skinned Model." *New York Times*. February 23, 2022. https://www .nytimes.com/2022/02/23/nyregion/columbia-jeffrey-lieberman.html.

Ferber, Abby L. "'Are You Willing to Die for This Work?' Public Targeted Online Harassment in Higher Education: SWS Presidential Address." *Gender & Society* 32, no. 3 (June 1, 2018): 301–20. https://doi.org/10.1177 /0891243218766831.

Fielding-Singh, Priya. *How the Other Half Eats: The Untold Story of Food and Inequality in America*. Boston: Little, Brown, 2021.

Firebaugh, Glenn. "Replication Data Sets and Favored-Hypothesis Bias: Comment on Jeremy Freese (2007) and Gary King (2007)." *Sociological Methods & Research* 36, no. 2 (November 1, 2007): 200–209. https://doi .org/10.1177/0049124107306663.

Fitzpatrick, Kathleen. *Generous Thinking: A Radical Approach to Saving the University*. Baltimore, MD: Johns Hopkins University Press, 2019.

Fitzpatrick, Kathleen. "Revising Peer Review." *Contexts* 11, no. 4 (November 1, 2012): 80–80. https://doi.org/10.1177/1536504212466347.

Fleerackers, Alice, Kenneth Shores, Natascha Chtena, and Juan Pablo Alperin. "Unreviewed Science in the News: The Evolution of Preprint Media Coverage from 2014–2021." bioRxiv. July 15, 2023. https://doi.org /10.1101/2023.07.10.548392.

Fosse, Ethan, and Christopher Winship. "Analyzing Age-Period-Cohort Data: A Review and Critique." *Annual Review of Sociology* 45, no. 1 (2019): 467–92. https://doi.org/10.1146/annurev-soc-073018-022616.

Foucault, Michel. "What Is an Author?" In *Language, Counter-Memory Practice: Selecetd Essays and Interviews*, ed. Donald Bouchard and Sherry Simon, trans. Donald Bouchard. Ithaca, NY: Cornell University Press, 1977.

Fox, Jesse, Katy E. Pearce, Adrienne L. Massanari, Julius Matthew Riles, Łukasz Szulc, Yerina S. Ranjit, Filippo Trevisan, et al. "Open Science, Closed Doors? Countering Marginalization Through an Agenda for Ethical, Inclusive Research in Communication." *Journal of Communication* 71, no. 5 (October 1, 2021): 764–84. https://doi.org/10.1093/joc/jqab029.

Franco, Annie, Neil Malhotra, and Gabor Simonovits. "Publication Bias in the Social Sciences: Unlocking the File Drawer." *Science* 345, no. 6203 (September 19, 2014): 1502–5. https://doi.org/10.1126/science.1255484.

Fraser, Nicholas, Liam Brierley, Gautam Dey, Jessica K. Polka, Máté Pálfy, Federico Nanni, and Jonathon Alexis Coates. "The Evolving Role of Preprints in the Dissemination of COVID-19 Research and Their Impact on the Science Communication Landscape." *PLOS Biology* 19, no. 4 (April 2, 2021): e3000959. https://doi.org/10.1371/journal.pbio.3000959.

Freese, Jeremy. "Replication Standards for Quantitative Social Science: Why Not Sociology?" *Sociological Methods & Research* 36, no. 2 (November 1, 2007): 153–72. https://doi.org/10.1177/0049124107306659.

Freese, Jeremy, and Molly M. King. "Institutionalizing Transparency." *Socius* 4 (January 1, 2018): 237802311739216. https://doi.org/10.1177/237802311739216.

Freese, Jeremy, and David Peterson. "Replication in Social Science." *Annual Review of Sociology* 43, no. 1 (2017): 147–65. https://doi.org/10.1146/annurev -soc-060116-053450.

Freire, Paulo. *Pedagogy of the Oppressed*, trans. Myra Bergman Ramos. New York: Continuum, 2000.

Friesike, Sascha, Leonhard Dobusch, and Maximilian Heimstädt. "Striving for Societal Impact as an Early-Career Researcher: Reflections on Five Common Concerns." In *Organizing for Societal Grand Challenges*, ed. Ali Aslan Gümüsay, Emilio Marti, Hannah Trittin-Ulbrich, and Christopher

Wickert, 79:239–55. Research in the Sociology of Organizations. Leeds, England: Emerald Publishing Limited, 2022. https://doi.org/10.1108 /S0733-558X20220000079022.

Fukuyama, Francis. *Liberalism and Its Discontents.* New York: Farrar, Straus and Giroux, 2022.

Funk, Cary, and Alec Tyson. "Partisan Differences Over the Pandemic Response Are Growing." Pew Research Center Science & Society (blog). June 3, 2020. https://www.pewresearch.org/science/2020/06/03/partisan -differences-over-the-pandemic-response-are-growing/.

Gehl, Robert W., and Diana Zulli. "The Digital Covenant: Non-Centralized Platform Governance on the Mastodon Social Network." *Information, Communication & Society* (December 15, 2022): 1–17. https://doi.org/10.1080 /1369118X.2022.2147400.

Geronimus, Arline T., John Bound, and Landon Hughes. "Trend Toward Older Maternal Age Contributed to Growing Racial Inequity in Very-Low-Birthweight Infants in the US." *Health Affairs* 42, no. 5 (May 2023): 674–82. https://doi.org/10.1377/hlthaff.2022.01066.

Gerring, John. "Mere Description." *British Journal of Political Science* 42, no. 4 (October 2012): 721–46. https://doi.org/10.1017/S0007123412000130.

Giddens, Anthony. *The Consequences of Modernity.* Redwood City, CA: Stanford University Press, 1990.

Gill, Jeff. "The Insignificance of Null Hypothesis Significance Testing." *Political Research Quarterly* 52, no. 3 (1999): 647–74. https://doi.org/10.2307 /449153.

Gino, Francesca. "Do Bonuses Promote Cheating?" CNN. June 3, 2014. https:// www.cnn.com/2014/06/03/opinion/gino-bonuses-promote-cheating /index.html.

Gino, Francesca, Shahar Ayal, and Dan Ariely. "Contagion and Differentiation in Unethical Behavior: The Effect of One Bad Apple on the Barrel." *Psychological Science* 20, no. 3 (March 2009): 393–98. https://doi .org/10.1111/j.1467-9280.2009.02306.x.

Gino, Francesca, Maryam Kouchaki, and Adam D. Galinsky. "The Moral Virtue of Authenticity: How Inauthenticity Produces Feelings of Immorality and Impurity." *Psychological Science* 26, no. 7 (July 1, 2015): 983–96. https://doi.org/10.1177/0956797615575277.

Ginsparg, Paul. "ArXiv Founder Paul Ginsparg's Thoughts on Scooping." ASAPbio FAQ (blog). Accessed July 4, 2023. https://asapbio.org/faq /arxiv-founder-paul-ginspargs-advice-on-scooping.

Goffman, Alice. *On the Run: Fugitive Life in an American City*. Chicago: University of Chicago Press, 2014.

Gopalakrishna, Gowri, Gerben ter Riet, Gerko Vink, Ineke Stoop, Jelte M. Wicherts, and Lex M. Bouter. "Prevalence of Questionable Research Practices, Research Misconduct and Their Potential Explanatory Factors: A Survey among Academic Researchers in the Netherlands." *PLOS ONE* 17, no. 2 (February 16, 2022): e0263023. https://doi.org/10.1371/journal.pone.0263023.

Gopnik, Adam. "The Music Donald Trump Can't Hear." *New Yorker*. January 13, 2017. https://www.newyorker.com/news/daily-comment/the-music-donald-trump-cant-hear.

Gordon, Jill. "John Stuart Mill and the 'Marketplace of Ideas.'" *Social Theory and Practice* 23, no. 2 (1997): 235–49.

Gorski, Philip S. "Beyond the Fact/Value Distinction: Ethical Naturalism and the Social Sciences." *Society* 50, no. 6 (December 1, 2013): 543–53. https://doi.org/10.1007/s12115-013-9709-2.

Gould, Stephen Jay. *Rocks of Ages: Science and Religion in the Fullness of Life*. Reprint edition. New York: Ballantine, 2002.

Green, Jerry. "Sealioning: A Case Study in Epistemic Vice." *Southwest Philosophy Review* 38, no. 1 (April 26, 2022): 123–34. https://doi.org/10.5840/swphilreview20223813.

Greenhalgh, Susan. "Making Demography Astonishing: Lessons in the Politics of Population Science." *Demography* 55, no. 2 (April 1, 2018): 721–31. https://doi.org/10.1007/s13524-018-0660-0.

Guédon, Jean-Claude. "Scholarly Communication and Scholarly Publishing." Open Access Scholarly Publishing Association (blog). April 21, 2021. https://oaspa.org/guest-post-by-jean-claude-guedon-scholarly-communication-and-scholarly-publishing/.

Hall, Neil. "The Kardashian Index: A Measure of Discrepant Social Media Profile for Scientists." *Genome Biology* 15, no. 7 (July 30, 2014): 424. https://doi.org/10.1186/s13059-014-0424-0.

Hall, Stuart M. *Policing the Crisis: Mugging, the State, and Law and Order*. New York: Palgrave Macmillan, 2002.

Haraway, Donna. "Situated Knowledges: The Science Question in Feminism and the Privilege of Partial Perspective." *Feminist Studies* 14, no. 3 (1988): 575–99. https://doi.org/10.2307/3178066.

Harney, Stefano, and Fred Moten. *The Undercommons: Fugitive Planning and Black Study*. Minor Compositions, 2013.

Harris, Lauren. "Five Big Findings from the Journalism Crisis Project." *Columbia* Journalism Review (blog). March 3, 2021. https://www.cjr.org /business_of_news/five-findings.php.

Harvey, Lex. "Mexico Went All in on Ivermectin—a Disproven COVID Cure. Now There's a Fight Over 'False and Misleading." *Toronto Star*. February 10, 2022. https://www.thestar.com/news/world/2022/02/10/mexico-went -all-in-on-ivermectin-a-disproven-covid-cure-now-theres-a-fight-over -false-and-misleading-science-and-claims-of-colonialist-politics.html.

Healy, Kieran. "Fuck Nuance." *Sociological Theory* 35, no. 2 (June 1, 2017): 118–27. https://doi.org/10.1177/0735275117709046.

Healy, Kieran. "Public Sociology in the Age of Social Media." *Perspectives on Politics* 15, no. 3 (September 2017): 771–80. https://doi.org/10.1017/S1537592717000950.

Hess, Amanda. "The Medical Mask Becomes a Protest Symbol." *New York Times*. June 2, 2020. https://www.nytimes.com/2020/06/02/arts/virus-mask -trump.html.

Hinchliffe, Lisa Janicke. "The State of the Version of Record." The Scholarly Kitchen (blog). February 14, 2022. https://scholarlykitchen.sspnet.org /2022/02/14/the-state-of-the-version-of-record/.

Hirschman, Daniel. "Controlling for What? Movements, Measures, and Meanings in the US Gender Wage Gap Debate." *History of Political Economy* 54, no. S1 (December 1, 2022): 221–57. https://doi.org/10.1215/00182702-10085710.

Hirschman, Daniel. "Rediscovering the 1 Percent: Knowledge Infrastructures and the Stylized Facts of Inequality." *American Journal of Sociology* 127, no. 3 (November 2021): 739–86. https://doi.org/10.1086/718451.

Hirschman, Daniel. "Sociology and the Technopolitical Two-Step: The Case of the Regnerus Study." A (Budding) Sociologist's Commonplace Book (blog). October 1, 2012. https://asociologist.com/2012/09/30/sociology -and-the-technopolitical-two-step-the-case-of-the-regnerus-study/.

Hofstadter, Richard. *Anti-Intellectualism in American Life*. New York: Vintage, 1966.

Holcombe, Alex O. "Contributorship, Not Authorship: Use CRediT to Indicate Who Did What." *Publications* 7, no. 3 (September 2019): 48. https:// doi.org/10.3390/publications7030048.

Hubei Government. "Wuhan, Different Everyday!" September 16, 2014. http:// en.hubei.gov.cn/news/newslist/201409/t20140916_526479.shtml.

Huffman, Matt L., Philip N. Cohen, and Jessica Pearlman. "Engendering Change: Organizational Dynamics and Workplace Gender Desegregation,

1975–2005." *Administrative Science Quarterly* 55, no. 2 (June 1, 2010): 255–77. https://doi.org/10.2189/asqu.2010.55.2.255.

Ingeno, Lauren. "#Penalty." *Inside Higher Ed.* August 6, 2013. https://www .insidehighered.com/news/2013/08/07/fat-shaming-professor-faces -censure-university.

Ioannidis, John P. "Citation Impact and Social Media Visibility of Great Barrington and John Snow Signatories for COVID-19 Strategy." *BMJ Open* 12, no. 2 (February 1, 2022): e052891. https://doi.org/10.1136/bmjopen -2021-052891.

Isaacson, Walter. *Einstein: His Life and Universe.* New York: Simon & Schuster, 2007.

Isaacson, Walter. *The Code Breaker: Jennifer Doudna, Gene Editing, and the Future of the Human Race.* New York: Simon & Schuster, 2021.

Jerolmack, Colin, and Alexandra K. Murphy. "The Ethical Dilemmas and Social Scientific Trade-Offs of Masking in Ethnography." *Sociological Methods & Research* 48, no. 4 (November 1, 2019): 801–27. https://doi .org/10.1177/0049124117701483.

Kaiser, Jocelyn. "Stanford President to Step Down Despite Probe Exonerating Him of Research Misconduct." Science Insider (blog). July 19, 2023. https://www.science.org/content/article/stanford-president-to-step -down-despite-probe-exonerating-him-of-research-misconduct.

Kakutani, Michiko. *The Death of Truth: Notes on Falsehood in the Age of Trump.* New York: Tim Duggan, 2018.

Karpman, Michael, Elaine Maag, Stephen Zuckerman, and Doug Wissoker. "Child Tax Credit Recipients Experienced a Larger Decline in Food Insecurity and a Similar Change in Employment as Nonrecipients Between 2020 and 2021." Washington, DC: Tax Policy Center, May 2022. https://www .urban.org/sites/default/files/2022-05/CTC%20Recipients%20Experienced%20Larger%20Decline%20in%20Food%20Insecurity%20and%20Similar%20Change%20in%20Employment%20as%20Nonrecipients%20v2.pdf.

Kathawalla, Ummul-Kiram, Priya Silverstein, and Moin Syed. "Easing Into Open Science: A Guide for Graduate Students and Their Advisors." *Collabra: Psychology* 7, no. 1 (January 26, 2021): 18684. https://doi.org/10.1525 /collabra.18684.

Kelley, Robin D. G. "Black Study, Black Struggle." *Boston Review.* March 1, 2016. http://bostonreview.net/forum/robin-d-g-kelley-black-study-black -struggle.

Kerr, Norbert L. "HARKing: Hypothesizing After the Results Are Known." *Personality and Social Psychology Review* 2, no. 3 (August 1, 1998): 196–217. https://doi.org/10.1207/s15327957pspr0203_4.

Kimball, Bruce A., and Benjamin Ashby Johnson. "The Beginning of 'Free Money' Ideology in American Universities: Charles W. Eliot at Harvard, 1869–1909." *History of Education Quarterly* 52, no. 2 (May 2012): 222–50. https://doi.org/10.1111/j.1748-5959.2011.00389.x.

Kirkpatrick, David. *The Facebook Effect: The Inside Story of the Company That Is Connecting the World.* New York: Simon and Schuster, 2011.

Kitroeff, Natalie. "Between the Pandemic and the President: Mexico City Mayor's Balancing Act." *New York Times.* September 5, 2020. https://www.nytimes.com/2020/09/05/world/americas/mexico-mayor-amlo-sheinbaum.html.

Kitroeff, Natalie, and Paulina Villegas. "'I'd Rather Stay Home and Die.'" *New York Times.* August 10, 2020. https://www.nytimes.com/2020/08/10/world/americas/mexico-coronavirus-hospitals.html.

Kohn, Paul M., and G. W. Mercer. "Drug Use, Drug-Use Attitudes, and the Authoritarianism-Rebellion Dimension." *Journal of Health and Social Behavior* 12, no. 2 (1971): 125–31. https://doi.org/10.2307/2948519.

Kotsko, Adam. "What Happened to Giorgio Agamben?" *Slate.* February 21, 2022. https://slate.com/human-interest/2022/02/giorgio-agamben-covid-holocaust-comparison-right-wing-protest.html.

Kuhn, Thomas S. *The Structure of Scientific Revolutions.* Chicago: University of Chicago Press, 1969.

La Cava, Lucio, Sergio Greco, and Andrea Tagarelli. "Understanding the Growth of the Fediverse Through the Lens of Mastodon." *Applied Network Science* 6, no. 1 (September 1, 2021): 64. https://doi.org/10.1007/s41109-021-00392-5.

Lakomý, Martin, Renata Hlavová, and Hana Machackova. "Open Science and the Science-Society Relationship." *Society* 56, no. 3 (June 1, 2019): 246–55. https://doi.org/10.1007/s12115-019-00361-w.

Lee, Stephanie M. "3 of Francesca Gino's Allegedly Fraudulent Studies Will Be Retracted." *Chronicle of Higher Education.* June 30, 2023. https://www.chronicle.com/article/3-of-francesca-ginos-allegedly-fraudulent-studies-will-be-retracted.

Lee, Stephanie M. "A Big Study About Honesty Turns Out to Be Based on Fake Data." *BuzzFeed News.* August 25, 2021. https://www.buzzfeednews.com/article/stephaniemlee/dan-ariely-honesty-study-retraction.

Lee, Stephanie M. "Scholar Accused of Research Fraud Sues Harvard and Data Sleuths, Alleging a 'Smear Campaign.'" *Chronicle of Higher Education.* August 3, 2023. https://www.chronicle.com/article/scholar-accused-of-research-fraud-sues-harvard-and-data-sleuths-alleging-a-smear-campaign.

Lee, Stephanie M., and Nell Gluckman. "A Dishonesty Expert Stands Accused of Fraud. Scholars Who Worked with Her Are Scrambling." *Chronicle of Higher Education.* June 22, 2023. https://www.chronicle.com/article/a-dishonesty-expert-stands-accused-of-fraud-scholars-who-worked-with-her-are-scrambling.

Leonhardt, David. "A Public-Health Crisis That We Can Fix." *New York Times.* March 7, 2017. https://www.nytimes.com/2017/03/07/opinion/a-public-health-crisis-that-we-can-fix.html.

Levenson, Michael. "Scale of China's Wuhan Shutdown Is Believed to Be Without Precedent." *New York Times.* January 23, 2020. https://www.nytimes.com/2020/01/22/world/asia/coronavirus-quarantines-history.html.

Levenson, Michael. "University Must Reinstate Professor Who Tweeted About 'Black Privilege.'" *New York Times.* May 19, 2022. https://www.nytimes.com/2022/05/19/us/twitter-florida-professor-reinstated.html.

Levin, Andrew T., William P. Hanage, Nana Owusu-Boaitey, Kensington B. Cochran, Seamus P. Walsh, and Gideon Meyerowitz-Katz. "Assessing the Age Specificity of Infection Fatality Rates for COVID-19: Systematic Review, Meta-Analysis, and Public Policy Implications." *European Journal of Epidemiology* 35, no. 12 (December 1, 2020): 1123–38. https://doi.org/10.1007/s10654-020-00698-1.

Lidskog, Rolf. "In Science We Trust? On the Relation Between Scientific Knowledge, Risk Consciousness and Public Trust." *Acta Sociologica* 39, no. 1 (January 1, 1996): 31–56. https://doi.org/10.1177/000169939603900103.

Lindner, Andrew M., Sophia Stelboum, and Azizul Hakim. "Embracing Generational Labels: An Analysis of Self-Identification and Sociopolitical Alignment." SocArXiv. May 8, 2023. https://doi.org/10.31235/osf.io/e2zxr.

Linthicum, Kate. "Amid Growing Coronavirus Threat, Mexico's President Says He's Putting Trust in Good-Luck Charms." *Los Angeles Times,* March 19, 2020. https://www.latimes.com/world-nation/story/2020-03-19/as-mexican-peso-collapses-over-coronavirus-threat-criticism-falls-on-president-lopez-obrador.

Loken, Eric, and Andrew Gelman. "Measurement Error and the Replication Crisis." *Science* 355, no. 6325 (February 10, 2017): 584–85. https://doi.org/10.1126/science.aal3618.

Lorde, Audre. *Sister Outsider: Essays and Speeches*. London: Penguin, 2020.

Lupia, Arthur, and Colin Elman. "Openness in Political Science: Data Access and Research Transparency: Introduction." *PS: Political Science & Politics* 47, no. 1 (January 2014): 19–42. https://doi.org/10.1017/S1049096513001716.

Mackey, Robert. "Professor's Angry Tweets on Gaza Cost Him a Job." *New York Times*. September 13, 2014. https://www.nytimes.com/2014/09/13/world/middleeast/professors-angry-tweets-on-gaza-cost-him-a-job.html.

Mandavilli, Apoorva. "People Who Accuse Science Journalists of Chasing Clicks Must Have NO IDEA About the Dozens of Bad Preprints We Pass on Plus the Hundreds of Bad Press Releases We Get Pitched *every Single Day*. If What We Wanted Was Clicks, You'd Be Seeing Something Else Entirely." Twitter. @apoorva_nyc (blog). February 25, 2021. https://twitter.com/apoorva_nyc/status/1364797039327010822.

Marwick, Alice E. "Morally Motivated Networked Harassment as Normative Reinforcement." *Social Media + Society* 7, no. 2 (April 1, 2021): 2056305121021378. https://doi.org/10.1177/2056305121021378.

Marwick, Alice E., and danah boyd. "I Tweet Honestly, I Tweet Passionately: Twitter Users, Context Collapse, and the Imagined Audience." *New Media & Society* 13, no. 1 (February 1, 2011): 114–33. https://doi.org/10.1177/1461444810365313.

Marx, Karl. "The Class Struggles in France, 1848 to 1850, Part IV." https://www.marxists.org/archive/marx/works/1850/class-struggles-france/.

Massey, Douglas S. "What Critical Demography Means to Me." *Sociological Forum* 14, no. 3 (September 1, 1999): 525–28. https://doi.org/10.1023/A:1021455804521.

Mathias, Christopher. "This Man Has the Ear of Billionaires—and a White Supremacist Past He Kept a Secret." HuffPost (blog). August 4, 2023. https://www.huffpost.com/entry/richard-hanania-white-supremacist-pseudonym-richard-hoste_n_64c93928e4b021e2f295e817.

McCammon, Sarah, Lauren Hodges, and Sarah Handel. "The Child Tax Credit Was a Lifeline. Now Some Families Are Falling Back Into Poverty." NPR. April 8, 2022. https://www.npr.org/2022/04/08/1091418380/child-tax-credit-return-inflation-food-gas-prices.

McElwee, Sean, and Philip N. Cohen. "The Secret to Trump's Success: New Research Sheds Light on the GOP Front-Runner's Stunning Staying Power." *Salon.* March 18, 2016. https://www.salon.com/2016/03/18/the_secret_to_trumps_success_new_research_sheds_light_on_the_gop_frontrunners_stunning_staying_power/.

McElwee, Sean, and Philip N. Cohen. "The Vile Core of Trump's Appeal: Here's the Research That Shows How Racism Animates His Campaign." *Salon.* March 27, 2016. http://www.salon.com/2016/03/27/the_vile_core_of_trumps_appeal_heres_the_research_that_shows_how_racism_animates_his_campaign/.

McKiernan, Erin C., Philip E. Bourne, C. Titus Brown, Stuart Buck, Amye Kenall, Jennifer Lin, Damon McDougall, et al. "How Open Science Helps Researchers Succeed." Ed. Peter Rodgers. *eLife* 5 (July 7, 2016): e16800. https://doi.org/10.7554/eLife.16800.

McShane, Blakeley B., David Gal, Andrew Gelman, Christian Robert, and Jennifer L. Tackett. "Abandon Statistical Significance." *American Statistician* 73, no. sup1 (March 29, 2019): 235–45. https://doi.org/10.1080/00031305.2018.1527253.

Mead, Lawrence M. "Poverty and Culture." *Society*, 2020 [retracted].

Merino, José, Victor Hugo Borja, Oliva Lopez, José Alfredo Ochoa, Eduardo Clark, Lila Petersen, and Saul Caballero. "Ivermectin and the Odds of Hospitalization Due to COVID-19: Evidence from a Quasi-Experimental Analysis Based on a Public Intervention in Mexico City," SocArXiv (May 4, 2021). https://osf.io/r93g4.

Merriman, Ben. "Peer Review as an Evolving Response to Organizational Constraint: Evidence from Sociology Journals, 1952–2018." *American Sociologist* 52, no. 2 (June 1, 2021): 341–66. https://doi.org/10.1007/s12108-020-09473-x.

Merton, Robert K. "Science and Technology in a Democratic Order." *Journal of Legal and Political Sociology* 1, no. 1 (1942): 115–26.

Mewes, Jan, Malcolm Fairbrother, Giuseppe Nicola Giordano, Cary Wu, and Rima Wilkes. "Experiences Matter: A Longitudinal Study of Individual-Level Sources of Declining Social Trust in the United States." *Social Science Research* 95 (March 1, 2021): 102537. https://doi.org/10.1016/j.ssresearch.2021.102537.

Meyer, David S. *How Social Movements (Sometimes) Matter.* Hoboken, NJ: Wiley, 2021.

Meyer, Michelle N. "Practical Tips for Ethical Data Sharing." *Advances in Methods and Practices in Psychological Science* 1, no. 1 (March 1, 2018): 131–44. https://doi.org/10.1177/2515245917747656.

Moody, James W., Lisa A. Keister, and Maria C. Ramos. "Reproducibility in the Social Sciences." *Annual Review of Sociology* 48, no. 1 (2022): 65–85. https://doi.org/10.1146/annurev-soc-090221-035954.

Moore, Samuel A. "The Politics of Rights Retention." *Publications* 11, no. 2 (2023): 28. https://doi.org/10.3390/publications11020028.

Morris, Aldon. *The Scholar Denied: W. E. B. Du Bois and the Birth of Modern Sociology*. Oakland: University of California Press, 2015.

Moxham, Noah, and Aileen Fyfe. "The Royal Society and the Prehistory of Peer Review, 1665–1965." *The Historical Journal* 61, no. 4 (December 2018): 863–89. https://doi.org/10.1017/S0018246X17000334.

Munafò, Marcus R., Brian A. Nosek, Dorothy V. M. Bishop, Katherine S. Button, Christopher D. Chambers, Nathalie Percie du Sert, Uri Simonsohn, Eric-Jan Wagenmakers, Jennifer J. Ware, and John P. A. Ioannidis. "A Manifesto for Reproducible Science." *Nature Human Behaviour* 1, no. 1 (January 10, 2017): 1–9. https://doi.org/10.1038/s41562-016-0021.

Muñoz, John, and Cristobal Young. "We Ran 9 Billion Regressions: Eliminating False Positives Through Computational Model Robustness." *Sociological Methodology* 48, no. 1 (August 1, 2018): 1–33. https://doi.org/10.1177/0081175018777988.

Murphy, Alexandra K., Colin Jerolmack, and DeAnna Smith. "Ethnography, Data Transparency, and the Information Age." *Annual Review of Sociology* 47, no. 1 (2021): 41–61. https://doi.org/10.1146/annurev-soc-090320-124805.

National Academies of Sciences, Engineering, and Medicine. *Are Generational Categories Meaningful Distinctions for Workforce Management?* Washington, DC: National Academies Press, 2020. https://doi.org/10.17226/25796.

National Science Foundation. "NSF Public Access Plan 2.0: Ensuring Open, Immediate and Equitable Access to National Science Foundation Funded Research." Washington, DC. March 21, 2023. https://nsf-gov-resources.nsf.gov/2023-06/NSF23104.pdf.

Nieper, Annika S., Bianca Beersma, Maria T. M. Dijkstra, and Gerben A. van Kleef. "When and Why Does Gossip Increase Prosocial Behavior?" *Current Opinion in Psychology* 44 (April 1, 2022): 315–20. https://doi.org/10.1016/j.copsyc.2021.10.009.

Nishikawa-Pacher, Andreas. "Who Are the 100 Largest Scientific Publishers by Journal Count? A Webscraping Approach." *Journal of Documentation* 78, no. 7 (January 1, 2022): 450–63. https://doi.org/10.1108/JD-04-2022-0083.

Noack, Rick. "Christchurch Endures as Extremist Touchstone, as Investigators Probe Suspected El Paso Manifesto." *Washington Post.* August 7, 2019. https://www.washingtonpost.com/world/2019/08/06/christchurch-endures-extremist-touchstone-investigators-probe-suspected-el-paso-manifesto/.

Nosek, B. A., G. Alter, G. C. Banks, D. Borsboom, S. D. Bowman, S. J. Breckler, S. Buck, et al. "Promoting an Open Research Culture." *Science* 348, no. 6242 (June 26, 2015): 1422–25. https://doi.org/10.1126/science.aab2374.

Noymer, Andrew. "Duck Tape Your Underpants. 2020 Is Going to Be a Wild Ride. #coronavirus #CoronavirusOutbreak." Twitter. @AndrewNoymer. February 1, 2020. https://twitter.com/AndrewNoymer/status/1223490472473059328.

NPR. *NPR Ethics Handbook.* 2021. https://www.npr.org/about-npr/688413430/impartiality.

O'Grady, Cathleen. "'Overwhelmed by Hate': COVID-19 Scientists Face an Avalanche of Abuse, Survey Shows." *Science.* March 24, 2022. https://www.science.org/content/article/overwhelmed-hate-covid-19-scientists-face-avalanche-abuse-survey-shows.

Packer, George. "A Political Obituary for Donald Trump." *The Atlantic.* January/February 2021.

Perrier, Laure, Erik Blondal, and Heather MacDonald. "The Views, Perspectives, and Experiences of Academic Researchers with Data Sharing and Reuse: A Meta-Synthesis." *PLOS ONE* 15, no. 2 (February 27, 2020): e0229182. https://doi.org/10.1371/journal.pone.0229182.

Phelan, Jo C., Bruce G. Link, and Parisa Tehranifar. "Social Conditions as Fundamental Causes of Health Inequalities Theory, Evidence, and Policy Implications." *Journal of Health and Social Behavior* 51, no. 1 suppl (November 1, 2010): S28–40. https://doi.org/10.1177/0022146510383498.

Piller, Charles. "Potential Fabrication in Research Images Threatens Key Theory of Alzheimer's Disease." *Science.* July 21, 2022. https://www.science.org/content/article/potential-fabrication-research-images-threatens-key-theory-alzheimers-disease.

Pomerantz, Jeffrey, Carolyn Hank, and Cassidy R. Sugimoto. "The State of Social Media Policies in Higher Education." *PLOS ONE* 10, no. 5 (May 27, 2015): e0127485. https://doi.org/10.1371/journal.pone.0127485.

Pontille, David, and Didier Torny. "From Manuscript Evaluation to Article Valuation: The Changing Technologies of Journal Peer Review." *Human Studies* 38, no. 1 (March 1, 2015): 57–79. https://doi.org/10.1007/s10746-014 -9335-z.

Prasad, Monica. "Pragmatism as Problem Solving." *Socius* 7 (January 1, 2021). https://doi.org/10.1177/2378023121993991.

Pratt, Michael G., Sarah Kaplan, and Richard Whittington. "The Tumult Over Transparency: Decoupling Transparency from Replication in Establishing Trustworthy Qualitative Research." *Administrative Science Quarterly* 65, no. 1 (March 1, 2020): 1–19. https://doi.org/10.1177/0001839219887663.

Pugh, Allison J., and Sarah Mosseri. "Trust-Building vs. 'Just Trust Me': Reflexivity and Resonance in Ethnography." *Frontiers in Sociology* 8 (2023). https://www.frontiersin.org/articles/10.3389/fsoc.2023.1069305.

Publons. "Global State of Peer Review." Clarivate Analytics, 2018. https://doi .org/10.14322/publons.GSPR2018.

Raman, Sujatha, and Warren Pearce. "Learning the Lessons of Climategate: A Cosmopolitan Moment in the Public Life of Climate Science." *WIREs Climate Change* 11, no. 6 (2020): e672. https://doi.org/10.1002/wcc.672.

Raja, Tasneem, and Benjy Hansen-Bundy. "How Much Does Your State Fine for Texting and Driving?" *Mother Jones* (2013). https://www.motherjones .com/media/2013/10/numbers-texting-and-driving/.

Ray, Siladitya. "'Borderline Useless': X Removes Headlines on News Posts as Critics Say Move Changes Site's Functionality." *Forbes*. October 5, 2023. https:// www.forbes.com/sites/siladityaray/2023/10/05/x-hides-headlines-from -posts-after-musk-claims-it-will-greatly-improve-the-esthetics/.

Ray, Victor. *On Critical Race Theory: Why It Matters and Why You Should Care.* New York: Random House, 2022.

Reidsma, Matthew. *Masked by Trust: Bias in Library Discovery.* Sacramento, CA: Litwin, 2019.

RELX. "RELX Annual Report and Financial Statements 2022." 2022. https:// www.relx.com/~/media/Files/R/RELX-Group/documents/reports /annual-reports/relx-2022-annual-report.pdf.

Reuters. "Fact Check-Mexico No Longer Including Ivermectin in Home COVID-19 Care Kits, Contrary to Claims on Social Media." *Reuters.* January 26, 2022. https://www.reuters.com/article/factcheck-imssmexico -ivermectin-idUSL1N2U626I.

Richtel, Matt. *A Deadly Wandering: A Mystery, a Landmark Investigation, and the Astonishing Science of Attention in the Digital Age.* Boston: Mariner, 2015.

Rieger, Oya Y., and Roger Schonfeld C. "Common Scholarly Communication Infrastructure Landscape Review." *Ithaka S+R*, 2023. https://doi.org/10.18665/sr.318775.

Riley, Dylan, Rebecca Jean Emigh, and Patricia Ahmed. "The Social Foundations of Positivism: The Case of Late-Nineteenth-Century Italy." *Social Science History* 45, no. 4 (November 2021): 813–42. https://doi.org/10.1017/ssh.2021.22.

Risman, Barbara J., Kristi Williams, and Virginia E. Rutter. *Families as They Really Are.* 3rd ed. New York: Norton, 2023.

Ritzer, George. "Sociology: A Multiple Paradigm Science." *American Sociologist* 10, no. 3 (1975): 156–67.

Ritzer, George. *The McDonaldization of Society: An Investigation Into the Changing Character of Contemporary Social Life.* Newbury Park, CA: Pine Forge, 1996.

Robertson, Campbell. "The Synagogue Attack Stands Alone, but Experts Say Violent Rhetoric Is Spreading." *New York Times.* August 4, 2023. https://www.nytimes.com/2023/08/04/us/pittsburgh-synagogue-shooting-antisemitism-bowers.html.

Romero, Mary. "Sociology Engaged in Social Justice." *American Sociological Review* 85, no. 1 (February 2020): 1–30. https://doi.org/10.1177/0003122419893677.

Roundtable on Aligning Incentives for Open Science. *Developing a Toolkit for Fostering Open Science Practices: Proceedings of a Workshop.* Washington, DC: National Academies Press, 2021. https://doi.org/10.17226/26308.

Rubin, Mark. "When Does HARKing Hurt? Identifying When Different Types of Undisclosed Post Hoc Hypothesizing Harm Scientific Progress." *Review of General Psychology* 21, no. 4 (December 1, 2017): 308–20. https://doi.org/10.1037/gpr0000128.

Rubin, Mark, and Chris Donkin. "Exploratory Hypothesis Tests Can Be More Compelling Than Confirmatory Hypothesis Tests." *Philosophical Psychology* (2022): 1–29. https://doi.org/10.1080/09515089.2022.2113771.

Russell, Douglas G. D., William J. L. Sladen, and David G. Ainley. "Dr. George Murray Levick (1876–1956): Unpublished Notes on the Sexual Habits of the Adélie Penguin." *Polar Record* 48, no. 4 (October 2012): 387–93. https://doi.org/10.1017/S0032247412000216.

Sagan, Carl. *The Demon-Haunted World: Science as a Candle in the Dark.* Reprint edition. New York: Ballantine, 1997.

Schilke, Oliver, Martin Reimann, and Karen S. Cook. "Trust in Social Relations." *Annual Review of Sociology* 47, no. 1 (2021): 239–59. https://doi.org/10.1146/annurev-soc-082120-082850.

Sever, Richard, Ted Roeder, Samantha Hindle, Linda Sussman, Kevin-John Black, Janet Argentine, Wayne Manos, and John R. Inglis. "bioRxiv: The Preprint Server for Biology." bioRxiv. November 6, 2019. https://doi.org /10.1101/833400.

Shrout, Patrick E., and Joseph L. Rodgers. "Psychology, Science, and Knowledge Construction: Broadening Perspectives from the Replication Crisis." *Annual Review of Psychology* 69, no. 1 (2018): 487–510. https://doi.org /10.1146/annurev-psych-122216-011845.

Shu, Lisa L., Nina Mazar, Francesca Gino, Dan Ariely, and Max H. Bazerman. "Signing at the Beginning Makes Ethics Salient and Decreases Dishonest Self-Reports in Comparison to Signing at the End." *Proceedings of the National Academy of Sciences* 109, no. 38 (September 18, 2012): 15197–200. https://doi.org/10.1073/pnas.1209746109.

Smith, Christian. *The Sacred Project of American Sociology.* Oxford: Oxford University Press, 2014.

Snyder, Timothy. *On Tyranny: Twenty Lessons from the Twentieth Century.* New York: Tim Duggan, 2017.

Sobieraj, Sarah. *Credible Threat: Attacks Against Women Online and the Future of Democracy.* Oxford: Oxford University Press, 2020.

Special Committee. "Report of a Special Committee: Political Interference and Academic Freedom in Florida's Public Higher Education System." American Association of University Professors. November 30, 2023. https:// www.aaup.org/file/AAUP_Special_Committee_Report_on_Florida _final.pdf.

Stanley, Jason. *How Fascism Works: The Politics of Us and Them.* New York: Random House, 2018.

Steele, Jennifer. "Challenges to Children's Picture Books with LGBTQ Themes: A 30-Year Review." *Children and Libraries* 20, no. 2 (June 17, 2022): 3–9. https://doi.org/10.5860/cal.20.2.3.

Strang, David, and Kyle Siler. "Revising as Reframing: Original Submissions Versus Published Papers in Administrative Science Quarterly, 2005 to 2009." *Sociological Theory* 33, no. 1 (March 1, 2015): 71–96. https://doi .org/10.1177/0735275115572152.

Sull, Donald, Charles Sull, and Ben Zweig. "Toxic Culture Is Driving the Great Resignation." *MIT Sloan Management Review.* January 11, 2022. https:// sloanreview.mit.edu/article/toxic-culture-is-driving-the-great-resignation/.

Sutton, Ward. "A Shrink Consults His Patient." *New Yorker,* February 11, 2013.

Takács, Károly, Jörg Gross, Martina Testori, Srebrenka Letina, Adam R. Kenny, Eleanor A. Power, and Rafael P. M. Wittek. "Networks of Reliable Reputations and Cooperation: A Review." *Philosophical Transactions of the Royal Society B: Biological Sciences* 376, no. 1838 (November 22, 2021): 20200297. https://doi.org/10.1098/rstb.2020.0297.

Talking Heads. "Crosseyed and Painless." *Remain in Light*. New York: Sire, 1980.

Tang, Alisa. "An Inspector Ordered a Free-Food Pantry Removed. This Woman Sounded the Alarm." *Washington Post*. February 26, 2022. https://www.washingtonpost.com/dc-md-va/2022/02/26/takoma-park-purple-community-bins/.

Trinity Christian University. "Faculty Handbook." Trinity Christian University. January 29, 2016. https://trollweb.trnty.edu/download/faculty-handbook/.

Tukey, John W. "We Need Both Exploratory and Confirmatory." *American Statistician* 34, no. 1 (1980): 23–25. https://doi.org/10.2307/2682991.

United Nations Population Division. "Replacement Migration." United Nations Secretariat, 2000. https://www.un.org/development/desa/pd/sites/www.un.org.development.desa.pd/files/files/documents/2020/Jan/un_2001_replacementmigration.pdf.

Vazire, Simine. "Quality Uncertainty Erodes Trust in Science." *Collabra: Psychology* 3, no. 1 (February 28, 2017). https://doi.org/10.1525/collabra.74.

Walker, James, Chris Brewster, Rita Fontinha, Washika Haak-Saheem, Stefano Benigni, Fabio Lamperti, and Dalila Ribaudo. "The Unintended Consequences of the Pandemic on Non-Pandemic Research Activities." *Research Policy* 51, no. 1 (January 1, 2022): 104369. https://doi.org/10.1016/j.respol.2021.104369.

Ward, Julie A., Elizabeth M. Stone, Paulani Mui, and Beth Resnick. "Pandemic-Related Workplace Violence and Its Impact on Public Health Officials, March 2020–January 2021." *American Journal of Public Health* 112, no. 5 (May 2022): 736–46. https://doi.org/10.2105/AJPH.2021.306649.

Weaver, Mark. "Weber's Critique of Advocacy in the Classroom: Critical Thinking and Civic Education." *PS: Political Science & Politics* 31, no. 4 (December 1998): 799–801. https://doi.org/10.2307/420720.

Weber, Max. *The Vocation Lectures*. Indianapolis, IN: Hackett, 2004.

West, Jevin D., and Carl T. Bergstrom. "Misinformation in and About Science." *Proceedings of the National Academy of Sciences* 118, no. 15 (April 13, 2021): e1912444117. https://doi.org/10.1073/pnas.1912444117.

Wilcox, W. Bradford. "Family Stability and the American Dream (Statement before the Joint Economic Committee)." American Enterprise Institute. February 25, 2020. https://www.aei.org/wp-content/uploads/2020/02/Wilcox-JEC-FamilyStability-2-25.pdf.

Williams, Deadric T., and Regina S. Baker. "Family Structure, Risks, and Racial Stratification in Poverty." *Social Problems* 68, no. 4 (November 1, 2021): 964–85. https://doi.org/10.1093/socpro/spab018.

Willson, M. F., and A. Traveset. "The Ecology of Seed Dispersal." In *Seeds: The Ecology of Regeneration in Plant Communities*, 85–110. CABI, January 2000. https://doi.org/10.1079/9780851994321.0085.

Woolf, Steven H. "The Meaning of Translational Research and Why It Matters." *JAMA* 299, no. 2 (January 9, 2008): 211–13. https://doi.org/10.1001/jama.2007.26.

Xu, Jiaquan, Sherry L. Murphy, Kenneth D. Kochanek, and Arias. "Mortality in the United States, 2021." NCHS Data Brief. Washington, DC: National Center for Health Statistics, December 21, 2022. https://doi.org/10.15620/cdc:122516.

Yang, Guobin. *The Wuhan Lockdown*. New York: Columbia University Press, 2022.

Yarchi, Moran, Christian Baden, and Neta Kligler-Vilenchik. "Political Polarization on the Digital Sphere: A Cross-Platform, Over-Time Analysis of Interactional, Positional, and Affective Polarization on Social Media." *Political Communication* (July 14, 2020): 1–42. https://doi.org/10.1080/10584609.2020.1785067.

Yin, Yian, Yuxiao Dong, Kuansan Wang, Dashun Wang, and Benjamin F. Jones. "Public Use and Public Funding of Science." *Nature Human Behaviour* 6, no. 10 (October 2022): 1344–50. https://doi.org/10.1038/s41562-022-01397-5.

Yong, Ed. *An Immense World: How Animal Senses Reveal the Hidden Realms Around Us*. New York: Random House, 2022.

Yong, Ed. "How Science Beat the Virus." *The Atlantic*. 2021. https://www.theatlantic.com/magazine/archive/2021/01/science-covid-19-manhattan-project/617262/.

Zulli, Diana. "Capitalizing on the Look: Insights into the Glance, Attention Economy, and Instagram." *Critical Studies in Media Communication* 35, no. 2 (March 15, 2018): 137–50. https://doi.org/10.1080/15295036.2017.1394582.

INDEX

of, 47; in social science, 18; versus theory, 55

Desmond, Matthew, 114

Devil Wears Prada, The, 2, 122

diversity, equity, and inclusion, 92, 112

divorce, 39, 46, 50; demography of, 54, 61, 213

Doctorow, Cory, 150

Dohrn, Bernadine, 182

Doudna, Jennifer, 25

Du Bois, W. E. B., 4, 197; career of, 180; and descriptive research, 44, 49; intellectual development of, 202; *The Philadelphia Negro*, 49; as scholar activist, 181

Duke University, 81

eBird, 6

Einstein, Albert, 123

eLife, 134

Elsevier, 88, 126, 159, 217, 219

Emerson, Ralph Waldo, 17

engagement, 1; and active citizenship, 179; and advocacy organizations, 40; bureaucratic imperative of, 50, 161, 230; career goal of, 35; and debunking, 144; in demographic research, 216; with descriptive work, 59; and online harassment, 103; professional rewards for, 229, 265n10; and strategy of pentagulation, 219; and working with journalists, 226

ethnography. *See* qualitative research

European Journal of Environment and Public Health, 30

European Societies, 29

Eyal, Gil, 90, 107

Fallow, Katie, 207, 268

Family Inequality (blog), 157, 268

Fauci, Anthony, 91

feminism, 93; and divorce, 62; and science, 15

Ferree, Myra Marx, 269

fidelity, in reproduction, 25n2; sexual or marital, 10, 120;

Figueroa, Holly, 208

Firebaugh, Glen, 109

Fitzpatrick, Kathleen, 127

Floyd, George, 172, 218

Foucault, Michele, 178

Freese, Jeremy, 97, 100

Freire, Paolo, 181, 182

Friesike, Sascha, 26, 34

Gaza, 172

Gelman, Andrew, 269

Gender & Society, 85

gender segregation, 47

General Social Survey, 76, 84

generations, 141–143

Geronimus, Arline, 47

Giddens, Anthony, 13; and trust, 10

Gino, Francesca, 80, 92, 96, 137

Github, 110

Google Scholar, 95, 96, 159, 258n21

Gopnik, Adam, 203

gossip, 92, 246n24

graduate students, 13, 25; and career goals, 17; and mentoring, 35; and statistical training, 65

great replacement theory, 199

GPSR Authorized Representative: Easy Access System Europe, Mustamäe tee
50, 10621 Tallinn, Estonia, gpsr.requests@easproject.com

www.ingramcontent.com/pod-product-compliance
Lightning Source LLC
Chambersburg PA
CBHW022139020426
42334CB00015B/971